Out of Bounds

Out of Bounds

Poems and Letters from Prison
by a Conscientious Objector
to the Good War

Chuck Worley

*Edited and with an Introduction
by John Ellison*

Foreword by Kim Stafford

speak4peace.com

Seattle

Some of this material appeared earlier in *Ruminations of a Certified Groundhog,* self-published by the author in 1995.

Printed in the United States of America.
10 9 8 7 6 5 4 3 2 1

ISBN: 978-0-9828662-0-7

Published by Speak4Peace
www.Speak4Peace.com

For Betsy

who was gutsy enough
to marry me between prison sentences

Contents

Foreword

I have always thought of Chuck Worley as an existential uncle, because he was with my father on a fateful day in 1942 when they and a third man were nearly lynched in a little town in Arkansas. Their crime: refusal to kill. I was raised on stories of that day, and of the wartime "university" of Civilian Public Service Camps, where pacifists like my father and Chuck Worley were held for the duration of the war—or until they walked away. That day when someone in the Arkansas mob shouted "Get a rope!" in wartime America, the friction of patriotism on pacifism nearly erased my chance to be.

Years later, when I visited that little town, McNeil, Arkansas, in March of 2003, the week our war in Iraq began, I had felt summoned by a call I could not ignore. If I couldn't go back to the time of the near lynching, I had to go to the place, to stand where Chuck and my father had stood, by the railroad tracks on a hot afternoon. I had to try to imagine what those earlier war-scarred days had been like, and to try to sort out why we were going to war again. When I told the lynch-mob story there that day, people in McNeil were attentive, eager, friendly. They wanted to know the story from 1942. Maybe the time is right to tell such old stories in detail.

Now I have this book, and some of the gaps in my understanding of that strange time, prelude and prophecy for our own strange time, can begin to be filled. How do we decide to kill—or not to kill? Once we decide, how do we keep an open mind, giving to ongoing discovery the same loyalty they gave to original decisions? And when we meet our fellow citizens of earth, people with wide, even violent differences of belief, how do we conduct ourselves so as to keep learning, but also to witness, to be the change we want to see?

With the first letter in this book, Chuck Worley is in his tenth prison, finding the accommodations—from his already extensive experience—quite satisfactory. It's 1945, he is not on a battle line with soldiers, or a fire line with conscientious objectors. Instead, he is free to think, wonder, question. He is locked up in quarantine, reading Nehru's autobiography, and thinking by turns about justice, prejudice, aggressions, resistance—and love. Out of this isolated matrix of thought, in a world at war, he seems to be writing to his beloved wife, Betsy. But in truth, he is writing to you and me. Page by page through 1945 and 1946, Chuck Worley is fitting together his intricate observations, enigmas, manifestos, and other free-wheeling experiments of a tethered soul—for you, for me—for us now, 2010, for our life with not one war, but many. These letters are a hidden scroll, a time capsule from that time to open here and now.

Kim Stafford
Author of *Early Morning: Remembering My Father,*
   William Stafford

Introduction

When I was a boy in the 1960s, the older men in my life had been
soldiers—all had seen combat, and none liked to talk about it. The
wars they fought in had names both familiar and frightening: World
War II, comfortably turned into the "Good War"; the vague Korean
War, with its lack of an understandable victory; and this new, deadly,
jungle war called Vietnam. These men had another thing in common: they all had a blue enamel pin with a silver musket and silver
oak-leaf wreath behind it, the Combat Infantry Badge, or "CIB,"
an award given to soldiers who personally fought in the wars they
wouldn't talk about.

My father had one of these pins, which he kept hidden away
with his other military ribbons and service medals in an off-limits
bedroom dresser drawer. I can't remember now how I knew about
his CIB, I just knew he had one. Just thinking about that blue pin,
which came to me after my father's death in 1976 and which sits on
my desk now as I write this, makes me sad. For me, it is a symbol
of a terrible experience that changed my father forever, turning the
outgoing, bad-boy, always-in-trouble college kid studying business
and accounting, into the silent, distant, drinking man I called Dad.
That pin came to represent what my father lost in his war. Even after
all these years, after WW II became America's greatest achievement in
war and the measure of all we hoped to be in future wars, my father's
war was a dark thing, a poisonous shadow that covered and killed all
that he tried to do with his life and with his family.

It wasn't until a few years after his death, when I was well underway with my own unfocused college exploration for purpose and
career, that I met a few more men in my neighborhood, men of my
father's age who faced the same draft he did, the same war he did,
but they said "No" to the Good War—choosing instead to become
conscientious objectors (COs), serving out their wartime years
in labor camps, fighting forest fires, pioneering something new
called "smokejumping," fighting diseases like hookworm by building

outdoor privies in the South, working in mental hospitals, building roads and dams, and doing a thousand other stateside jobs.

The war changed these men, too, like wars change everyone and everything they touch, but the experience didn't destroy them like it destroyed my father. Being a CO seemed to give their lives *more* meaning, *more* purpose. War was real for them, too, but they felt they were helping to build something as a way of giving their wartime lives meaning, and serving their country while doing it. One of those men was my high school art teacher, William Arthur Phillips. I came to know a few of these men as neighbors, but I didn't really know them or what they did in their wars. Not then.

I went through high school and had nearly finished college before I figured out what a CO was. Bill Phillips never once talked about conscientious objection in the classroom at Woodrow Wilson High School; as far as I know, my classmates and even most of Bill's teaching colleagues knew little or nothing about that part of his past. When I returned to the high school a few years later to interview Bill about his art for my college newspaper (he was a painter, and a pretty good one), he kept the talk focused on his painting. It wasn't until many years later, when I was reading through some lists for my research, that I saw Bill's name among the COs' names. He wasn't hiding his CO past; it was just part of him, and he didn't see the need to make a big deal of it. But unlike my father, Bill would talk about war if he needed to. He frequently wrote letters to the editors of several area newspapers, criticizing America's growing military spending and war-making.

Some men can accept war, accept the enormity of it, the whirlwind of destruction it brings, and what it will call forth in them to survive it. For those men, war seems necessary sometimes, a part of human nature, temporary but inevitable. Others believe with all their hearts that that they cannot be part of any war. It's not about bravery or patriotism or duty, or any of the easy labels we've come to use to describe one choice over another. Even writing these descriptions now is a struggle because the choice to be a soldier or a conscientious objector remains a mystery and comes down to a kind of "ah ha!" moment for each of us; a moment when we must decide if we can do something or not. It's personal. Things like drafts or all-volunteer militaries, on the surface, seem to make the choices clearer, but the choices aren't easier.

Men of my father's generation, that is, men in their late teens and early twenties in the late 1930s and early 1940s, came from an America with deep scars from World War I, the Great Depression, the Dust Bowl, a boom-and-bust job market, and the continuous small sufferings of lives lived with too little money and too little work that brought family life in close and made everyone at home tense. Work usually involved the hands more than the résumé. Parents still talked about their kids getting an education to do better than they were doing, which in the 1930s wasn't that great, moneywise. There was an innocence to life, too, a thrift and tenaciousness born out of making do. People knew the times were hard, but they also knew it would get better with a little "elbow grease," one of my father's favorite expressions that seemed positively antique to me in the 1960s. Stories about precious oranges at Christmastime as the only gift, or the memory of going on a first date on horseback (a public dance with a few dozen other people all watching everything you did with your new boyfriend or girlfriend, which wasn't much beyond talking and dancing and maybe holding hands), or converting abandoned chicken coops into first homes like my folks did when they were first married and moved back to my grandmother's small farm, or even hopping freight trains to go from town to town as if that were the thing to do for public transportation. These things tell a story of life with hardship as well as adventure. Nothing was certain; life was lived on the edge, always close to collapse. Happiness was something people fit in between things, between long days of manual labor and the struggle to hold their ground. That's the soil that produced men like my father, "the greatest generation."

A few years ago I started The CO Project, an oral history project focused on collecting and preserving the history of conscientious objectors from WW II to the current wars in Iraq and Afghanistan. I decided to find some of these WW II–era men my father's age, men who did what my father couldn't do and instead became COs even as President Roosevelt made popular, patriotic radio broadcasts talking about the defense of Europe and the need for greater national security.

Today it's almost overlooked that the draft of WW II was actually implemented before the Japanese military attack on Pearl Harbor, before the United States entered the war against the Axis powers (Germany, Italy, Japan, and others). The modern draft for Americans might be said to have started with WW I in 1917, when the first Selective Service Act was passed by Congress. As a sign of America's optimism with the ambivalent victory in WW I, a heady moment if you think about it when you label a war "The War to End All Wars," it was decided that conscription needed to end, too. So the Selective Service Act, which had survived into peacetime, was discontinued in 1920. Twenty years later a new act, the Selective Training and Service Act of 1940, was passed by Congress and America's first peacetime draft was set in motion. An interesting footnote about this legislation is that it was the first legal recognition of conscientious objection status by the U.S. Government. (Being a CO in WW I was a personal statement of belief, not an officially recognized status.) Men between the ages of 21 and 35, then later 18 and 65, were required to register with the Selective Service.

The first peacetime draft in the history of the United States did not sit well with all of the citizens of this country, many who thought like Chuck Worley, the author of this collection of poems and letters. WW I taught people that war could never be good, and that some wars could be so bad that they should never be repeated under any circumstances. As they grew up in the 1920s and 1930s, they heard stories about WW I, some even had fathers who fought in that war. For young people in the late 1930s challenging some of the ideas and experiences of their parents, WW I was fertile ground for rebellion. They looked deeper into how WW I took hold of so many people and so many countries at the cost of millions of lives; a deep distrust and fear of governmental abuse sprang up with the 1940 draft legislation. Some Americans didn't like the idea of a peacetime draft in a country that had pledged to stay out of future world wars and had gone so far as to create the League of Nations after WW I to keep America out of future conflicts. That was the plan: America was at peace. Hitler had invaded Poland and the latest war in Europe was underway as the American draft system was being designed, but it wasn't universally thought that America had to get involved, nor that it should. That's where the story of these letters and poems begins in a way, even though most were written long after America entered WW II.

Charles V. "Chuck" Worley was born in 1918, at the end of WW I. As he tells the story, he was conceived in Canada and came into the world in Omaha, Nebraska. His father was a man who seriously didn't like the idea of a military draft either, disliked it so much so that he decided to leave Canada to avoid the Canadian draft for WW I. He packed up his young family and drove down to the United States to keep from being made into a soldier, and to secure one of the scarce Union Pacific Railroad jobs he'd heard about. Today Chuck jokes that his border crossing in the womb makes him part Canadian. A war resister from before birth.

Chuck arrived with plans. Even as a young boy he planned to be the first one in his family to go to college. It wasn't easy working and staying in college in those days, but he stuck to it, pausing his education when necessary to get work, but he always went back, and eventually made it through the University of Omaha (now called the University of Nebraska at Omaha), majoring in sociology. How people live and work together has always fascinated Chuck. Like many young men during the WW II years, a college deferment provided a fitful break in the rush to face what the war would mean to him, and it allowed him time to think things through. But deferments didn't keep you out of the war forever, just until graduation.

Staring at a war while working toward a deadline can focus the mind like nothing else. For Chuck, the war remained huge and not quite knowable. He stuck with his plans as best he could and kept busy. The war and the draft loomed large in all the students' thinking, so much so that to hear the stories today it seems like the war became another course of study while finishing whatever degree they were working for; every conversation swirled around how the war started and what America should or shouldn't do about it. Speakers like A.J. Muste, the socialist labor leader, pacifist, and executive director of the Fellowship of Reconciliation (FOR), came to the Omaha campus to speak out against America's need to fight in Europe.

In his college years Chuck honed his skills in thinking for himself and eventually decided he was better suited to being a conscientious objector than a soldier. Just 23 years old and idealistic, Chuck was hopeful that his emerging idealism would somehow fit with the government's new program for conscientious objectors. He read the literature about the "work of national importance" COs would be doing and thought it sounded fine. He was a man of conscience, but he could still do his part for his country. After CO camp work and at the end of the war, he thought, he could get back to his life, find a good job and raise a big family with lots of kids. A lot of WW II COs brought their religious faith as well as conscience into their decisions, and Chuck was no exception there. Then, as today, he aligned himself with the teachings of the Religious Society of Friends (the Quakers).

Chuck applied for and received his CO status in 1941, and he entered Civilian Public Service (CPS) on November 10th that year, not long before the attack on Pearl Harbor. Even today he says CPS was a system he never fully agreed with, but it was something he decided to try out, to see if he could make it work. Civilian Public Service, the World War II camp and work system for COs, was set up by the U.S. Government to oversee and direct the labor of all COs officially granted IV-E classifications by their draft boards. Even though there was Congressional definition for the system provided in the 1940 Selective Service legislation, it was the lack of funds that brought the "Peace Churches" into the daily operation of all the CPS camps. Of course, the churches were motivated to help out their own young people, so it seemed a good match, even if they were doing some of the government's war work. The "Peace Churches," which included the Church of the Brethren, the Mennonites, and the Religious Society of Friends (the Quakers), formed an association that was bundled together and called the National Service Board for Religious Objectors (NSBRO). They would pay for the authorized work and would act as liaison to the Selective Service System (SSS) in running the camps. The coming together of these churches was, in part, an outcome of the treatment of COs during WW I, which was severe and often resulted in brutal prison terms. The church leaders were realists. They hoped to make things easier for COs during this new peacetime draft, as WW II seemed to be unavoidable for the U.S.

To be a CO during WW II meant that you still had to be drafted, but then you could write an appeal to your local draft board, and sometimes appear in person, to argue your case. If the board agreed with your reasons for being a CO, the system kicked into gear and sent you off to a CPS camp and work assignment, as it did for Chuck. The camp system wasn't like being a soldier, nor was it like having paid employment; camp life meant you had to stay in camp and under the direction of the camp administration. Service was required and the pay was meager, even by 1940s standards ($2.50 a month). The work was supposed to be "work of national importance," a designation, no doubt, intended to put COs and the camp system on equal footing with what a soldier might have to do heading for boot camp and training. Like being a soldier, the "enlistment" of a CO was for an indefinite period of time.

Even with all the problems of the system, many COs participated in CPS work and "did their duty" so long as it meant they did not have to support the war effort. In this way they felt free to criticize the system while working for it, sort of like an employee might, when they felt it fell below the national standards it was designed to uphold. But there were still those individuals, Chuck included, who saw their participation in CPS as something not quite right. To them, it was forced labor and in some way or another supported the war effort because it was part of the draft. Inevitably, Chuck decided he and the system had to part company, just as his father had done in WW I. Chuck walked away from CPS and eventually landed in prison, something 6,000 other COs also did during WW II. (According to *Friends Journal,* 43,000 men served as non-combatants; 37,000 were classified as COs by the Selective Service; of those, 12,000 served in CPS and 6,000 went to jail.) The events that followed culminated in an experience that generated these remarkable poems and letters to Chuck's wife, Betsy.

The study of COs is serious business because it's also the study of war. But Chuck is one of those guys who likes to joke about what happened to him as much as he likes to relate the dispassionately rendered facts. When I first met and interviewed Chuck in 2006, his CO story seemed to me to have two chapters, divided by one memorable event. Chuck's telling of his story has light and dark moments. Like most COs, Chuck accepted the work he was told to do and knew doing so meant he was part of the "system." The stories about that early part of his CO time are convivial, almost collegial, with his fellow COs. There was no roadmap for how the war would proceed, nor was there a roadmap for what COs would go through until they became free men again.

The dividing line in Chuck's narrative came during his first CPS assignment at Camp 7, Magnolia, located in a former Civilian Conservation Corps (CCC) camp near the small town of McNeil, Arkansas. One of his fellow "campers" from Camp 7 was the poet William Stafford, who eventually settled in Oregon and became one of America's most famous WW II conscientious objectors. Stafford wrote about Magnolia in his 1947 book *Down in My Heart: Peace Witness in Wartime*. First published by the Brethren Publishing House in Elgin, Illinois, the publishing arm of the Church of the Brethren, this book is an unassuming and simple record of one man's CO experiences during WW II. It has remained in print ever since its first appearance, and generation after generation inspires new readers. It's not possible to study conscientious objection in America without discovering and exploring the writing of William Stafford. And it's in *Down in My Heart* where I first met Chuck Worley, though I didn't know it because Stafford changed Chuck's name in the book to "George" because of 1940s privacy reasons.

The event that tested Worley's beliefs and prompted him to write a poem (that today he says he wishes he could forget, a poem in which he includes a biting quote that reflects the town's racial segregation typical of 1940s America and his upset at it), took place one afternoon, on a rare day off from camp life. Stafford wrote about it in his chapter called "The Mob Scene at McNeil," and it begins with a quote by George (Chuck Worley). Stafford writes, "When the mob comes, George would say, 'I think we should try surprising them with a friendly reaction—take coffee and cookies out to them.'" That day in McNeil, Stafford, Worley, and Robert "Bob" Pope wandered into town for a change of scenery. They were young men and, like all young men, they liked time away from work to hang out, talk, and daydream about what their lives would be like when they could get back to doing what they wanted to do. There was a war on, but they still wanted the day off out from under the watchful eyes of the camp administrators. That afternoon they all tried on the role of being artists. Fate and their wandering organized their day so that they found themselves at the town's train depot, which in 1940s America represented the high-tech hub of communication, town activity, and the site of greatest military value, even if there wasn't any military value. For Worley, Stafford, and Pope it was just a good place to stop, people watch, and talk as the town went about its day. It's not hard to imagine why three young men might want to go off together and explore their small-town surroundings on a Sunday afternoon. The town, though, was uncertain about their presence.

A poet and writer all his life, Chuck was working on one of his many poems that day, a poem called "McNeil. Hmmph." The poem, which has survived and represents the only writing he saved from his CPS days, is an obvious commentary about the social problems he saw in McNeil as a young man. The poem is also a precursor of Chuck's soon-to-be awakened role as an advocate for racial integration, which he explores in his letters to Betsy. This brief poem predates all of the poems in this collection and deserves to be recognized to better understand Chuck's civil rights advocacy that would come later in prison.

McNeil. Hmmph.

Some town . . . McNeil.
Dilapidated, all run-down, no civic pride.
Why should there be?
There's nothing to be proud of here . . .
Some dirty gravel streets,
Last year's circus signs,
And weather-beaten "nigger shanties" on the hill.
Oh, true, the station's nice,
That's mostly what it is . . .
A place that folks go by.
The bus pulls up and makes the buildings shake,
And loaded freighters grumble through at night.
McNeil. Hmmph.

Bob Pope was painting a watercolor picture of the train station and a few surrounding buildings, Stafford was reading Whitman's *Leaves of Grass*, Chuck was working on drafts of his unflattering poem; all three were unaware that they might attract any sort of attention by the townspeople. However, a crowd soon gathered to confront the young men and find out who they were and what they were doing. In WW II America, young men out of uniform appearing to be idly wasting their time generated curiosity and suspicion. Finding out that all three were COs from the camp just outside of town quickly sparked hostility. Heated questions were thrown at them, Stafford's book was taken, Chuck's poem was seized and read aloud. As Stafford writes about the incident, the crowd soon came to the decision that all three were spies, documenting in words and drawings the strategic value of McNeil for the enemy, and as such the young men should all be lynched on the spot. Fortunately for everyone, cooler heads prevailed and the three young COs weren't harmed; instead they were put into the sheriff's car and driven back to camp. This might just be the only incident where COs during WW II faced a lynch mob on U.S. soil. Even though the CPS camp was well-known to the townspeople, fear overwhelmed reason. Stafford's chapter about their scrape with the town provides a window into the hidden world of America's prejudice toward COs, even as Congress legislated their right to exist, then as now. That Sunday in McNeil was an early test for Chuck, and more were to come.

Following Chuck's time at camp Magnolia, he was relocated to a camp in Santa Barbara, California, where he took up more manual labor, including building a reservoir with picks and shovels with his fellow campers. It was in Santa Barbara that Chuck seriously began to confront his acceptance of CPS and its work assignments; increasingly he came to see his work as "make work" rather than "work of national importance." He started to talk about it with other campers. There were rumors of some men refusing to be a part of the whole thing, of men walking out of camps all over the country rather than remaining in the system. As he tells the story today, his internal conflict began to weigh heavier and heavier on his mind.

For the most part Chuck liked his fellow COs and respected their diverse views. It's interesting to note that today those who talk about CPS almost universally describe the system as one more akin to college than military service. Men from diverse backgrounds and educations were forced into close quarters and, as a consequence, they shared ideas, philosophies, and religious beliefs, talking among themselves more like college students than a group of manual laborers. And like college students, young COs could try on different personas, attitudes, and ideas to see what fit. Chuck's letters here give a clue to how books, newspapers, and "bull sessions" with other COs were changing and expanding his ideas of the world. Chuck recorded a lot of detail here, including his reading lists, his reading schedule, the newspapers he wanted Betsy to track down for him, the songs he liked to sing (and sometimes needed tunes and lyrics for), the games and sports he liked to play with other COs and the other prison inmates, and strategies for taking on the Warden and the Sandstone prison administration.

America has always put some conscientious objectors in prison in times of war because inevitably there are those who refuse to accept the rules; with each war the reasons change, but the outcome is the same. Sometimes as a nation we've even done worse, like during WW I, when some COs were brutalized and died in prison. In the time I've been traveling around the U.S., Canada, and parts of Europe collecting the personal stories and history of conscientious objectors, I've come to believe that there's an unacknowledged fear of COs—maybe because they're different, but probably more because they reject the whole patriotic rush that takes hold when a nation goes to war. Simple labels don't work to explain it. Wars only work when everyone agrees to fight.

Walking out of CPS meant prison—all the men knew that. Chuck describes his "life of crime" as beginning in Wichita, Kansas, the place where he and another CO eventually ran out of luck after walking out of CPS in California. At the time he was apprehended, Chuck was trying to get back home to Omaha; he was thumbing rides across the country because he had run out of money. His folks, who knew what he had decided to do, sent him money to buy bus tickets to get home, but those funds had run out. Not being in uniform, again he was frequently asked about why he was wandering around the country without an obvious military purpose. A plain-clothes police officer soon found him and asked him what he was doing. He didn't lie—he said he was a CO who had walked away from CPS. So he was arrested.

He was first locked up in several jails before federal prison, and he found them to be cold, unfriendly places with steel bunk beds, no mattresses, few if any blankets, and lots of petty criminals, including town drunks. Another education was beginning, Chuck's introduction to the 1940s U.S. prison system. Once the legal machinery got going on his case, Chuck was escorted by U.S. Marshals back to California. As Chuck tells the story, when his case finally came to court the judge restricted his defense to a plea of no contest and he was forbidden to speak on his behalf in his own trial. There was no jury, so Chuck's conviction came down to his disobeying the Selective Training and Service Act, which he did when he walked out of the Santa Barbara CPS camp. Chuck was then sentenced to 18 months in prison and sent to Sandstone Federal Prison, in Sandstone, Minnesota, about 90 miles north of Minneapolis.

From the beginning of Chuck's prison sentence he decided he would not cooperate with the system and would use the opportunity to resist his incarceration as a political act. He was not the only conscientious objector in Sandstone. The greatest number of COs there were Jehovah's Witnesses (JWs). JWs lived outside of the rules of war and national service and were almost always sent to prison, not because they considered themselves pacifists but because they believed that all human existence would soon end and therefore they only answered to a heavenly government, not a human one with a draft and camp system. Such "crazy" beliefs in 1940s America set nearly all of them on a path to prison, though a few JWs did choose to participate in CPS. Going to prison was a way for JWs to witness for their religious freedom as they defined it. They were mostly met with curiosity by their fellow CO inmates—exotic even among the exotic world of conscientious objectors.

The journey of Chuck's prison experience makes up the bulk of this collection, both in poetry and in letters. And I think that's the most important aspect of this collection, that it is a reflection of one man's evolving personal beliefs about war and peace within the crucible of prison. Being a natural writer, Chuck's letters strove to explain the inner working of his thought processes, which at times was a rough road for him and his young wife. These letters also capture the emerging relationship he and Betsy were testing out. Unfortunately, we don't have Betsy's letters to Chuck, but it's clear that things weren't always perfect between them. Sometimes they complain at each other as they work out how to be a couple. Always, prison stands between them, making even the small arguments seem huge because they can't just talk about it. They write a letter, and then must wait, sometimes many days, for whatever comes back. Remarkably, their marriage survived and grew during the prison time, even with very few face-to-face meetings.

The letters often swing between personal declarations of undying love mixed together with political questions and explorations of a citizen's rights. Without Betsy's letters back to Chuck we can only guess about her beliefs and worries at the time. We do know that Betsy was working almost full time on behalf of Chuck and other COs to gain their release. Betsy is the character hidden in plain sight throughout this book. She becomes an important part of Chuck's resistance and perseverance.

Along with Chuck's prison sentence came his experiments with new ideas and books, prison protests, hunger strikes, and grassroots organizing. Chuck's vanished America emerges, an America in war and in peace, scarred from hardship, financial crises, and fear. But he's not all about prison and fighting the system. Chuck is also a very sentimental guy. These letters are at times funny, filled with young love and restless energy, friendship and hope for the future beyond the prison's walls. His letters chronicle an evolution of a maturing and emotional development as he openly speaks from the heart about his feelings, beliefs, and daily life behind bars. The letters form a kind of daily journal of prison life for a CO, as he explores everything on his mind from his thoughts about the roles of wives and husbands to the irony of serving a prison sentence for refusing to kill people (something other non-CO inmates saw as a novelty and necessary to gossip about).

The 37,000 WW II COs were kept busy. They moved acres of soil and built miles of roads and dams; planted entire forests of trees by hand on steep slopes burned out by forest fires; taught each other

how to jump out of low-flying airplanes and handle a parachute in
a wildfire updraft; stopped the brutalization of mental patients in
hospitals across the U.S.; and volunteered to get sick, freeze, and
starve, all for medical science. Their work changed many things, not
the least being the minds of people who thought COs shirkers.
If you look today, you can still find the changes they left behind.

History is filled with the names of people who reject war. Their
reasons are as unique as their names and individual lives. Pressure
from neighbors, friends, siblings, and parents doesn't make these
people change their minds. In fact, it often makes them more stub-
born. They're outliers; they do what's right for themselves even as
others try to force them to change their minds. They're mavericks,
freethinkers, admired even as the backbone of the individualistic,
"do-it-yourself" American mythology. But the label of "CO" often
brands them cowards, when they are, in fact, remarkably brave and
thoughtful people.

The poems and letters in this collection do not provide answers
to the big questions of war and conscience. That's not what Chuck
had in mind as he wrote them. He was simply trying to explain to
his new bride what was happening to him, to ask her to help him
stay connected outside the prison walls, to make it a little easier to
be apart by staying together on the page. I don't even think he was
trying to lock in the history he was living through. A born storyteller,
I think Chuck wrote to keep his spirits up, to talk about the things
he was missing, and to keep close to his loved ones. There's longing
in these letters for the little things newlyweds do together, like holding hands or looking into each other's eyes and talking of intimacies
shared, going for walks together, picking out apartments, sharing
picnics, visiting family, and making love.

Just as soldiers wrote home from Europe and the Pacific, Chuck
wrote these letters and poems not knowing the outcome of the war,
not knowing when parole and freedom would come. These letters
don't begin with an historical event like the attack on Pearl Harbor,
nor do they end when the war ends. By the time we get to the last
letter, there's still more time to be done. Chuck has added a brief
Afterword to bring his story out of prison. He's had a long life

outside of his time as a CO and in Sandstone, and he's stood on conscience through it all.

COs never got medals for their service to the nation. My complicated feelings about my father's CIB make me think pins or medals just get in the way, making it harder to understand what it meant to be a young man during WW II. Maybe they also make it harder to talk about things. Medals seem sometimes to embarrass their owners, for one reason or another, and must be hidden away in drawers.

Instead of medals, Chuck has left us his letters and poems to tell his story of his CO prison time. He also left it up to me to choose the title for this book. I liked the title of the poem "Out of Bounds" because it seemed to perfectly fit Chuck's life. He said "no" to the system he found himself a part of during WW II. Since before Chuck was born, he was a boundary crosser, a man who went where he felt like going. These letters and poems are about one man living his truth in a time of war. No easy labels, no easy answers, just the messy reality of a life lived out of step, out of bounds, during "the Good War."

John Ellison
The CO Project

Editor's Note

The letters in this collection were edited from electronic files of the original letters supplied by friends of the author. Every effort was made to preserve the original text. Small changes were made, however, to correct misspelled words, incorrect or confusing punctuation, incorrect book titles and author names, and typing errors. When these personal and private letters were written over 60 years ago, the idea of publication was never contemplated; therefore, crafting them into book form meant that changes had to be made for readability and clarity for readers unfamiliar with the author's life and history. The poems were drawn from several sources, the most important being Chuck's first self-published book, *Ruminations of a Certified Groundhog*, as well as from copies of poems from his personal archive. Changes to a few original versions of the poems were also made by the author during the publication process.

Whenever possible, research was done to verify the names and details mentioned in the letters and poems. Chuck's wife, Betsy, is addressed by Chuck by several different names, including several pet names he had for her. Even though the names change, she was always the intended recipient of these letters. Fellow COs' names were checked using the *Directory of Civilian Public Service, Revised 1996*, published by The National Interreligious Service Board for Conscientious Objectors (NISBCO); this directory remains the most reliable authority about COs who entered CPS during WW II. In some cases, however, it was not possible to confirm every reference or every name. Errors and oversights introduced by the editorial and publication processes are unintended.

Part 1

◘ ◘ ◘

Poems

Poems from Prison

1945–1947

Visitor at Cell 35

Bird at my window
little bird
what do you think
as you hop and peek
through the glass set deep
in ribs of steel?

What do you think
as you tilt your head
with a pert little jerk
and peer inside
do you notice how solid
and safe it is
do you see me here
on my iron bed
what do you see
as you peer inside?

What do you think
as you fly away
winging the clean air
over the wall
riding the air
to your nest in the woods
what do you think
as you fly away
what do *you* think
little bird?

Out of Bounds

You who by the grace of law go free
walk by spongy springs
and load your lungs up with the smell of things
for me.

And when dawn
yawns
and silver noises dribble from her wings
gather up such nuggets as fall free.

You who are still in luck
dig your itching fingers deep in muck
and wash your eyes with all that's fresh and green.

Summer finds me out of bounds this year . . .
but conscience clean.

Sliding Scale

Five years . . . is heavy or is light

depending how you weigh it.

To felons it's a mass of night

and bitter curses pay it.

To them its density is death,

on steel benches lay it.

But who can weigh the piece of breath

it costs the judge to say it?

Irish Elk

Did that-which-made-things smile or sigh
to see those noble creatures die
whose antlers of such great distinction
proved the cause of their extinction?

Now how does that respond again
when other creatures, known as men,
lie gasping on a bloody plain
betrayed by much too large a brain?

Reconstruction

Light a candle a wise man said.

Perish a candle, the gutters are red
and millions of people are starving for bread
and searching through ruins with sickening dread
and wandering homeless with snow for a bed
and . . .
      Light a candle the wise man said.
Darkness can be conquered only by light.

But Christ, can a candle diminish the night?
Can a candle spot hope in a forest of fright?
Can a candle burn out the fierce cancer of might?
Can a candle . . .
      be conquered only by light?

Great God I'm distraught by the stench of the dead . . .
light a candle the wise man said . . .
and I wish I were blind to this horrible sight . . .
darkness can be conquered only by light.

On the Death of FDR

He was a tested pilot they declared
and in this hour of peril couldn't be spared.
His skill and only his, they said, was great
enough to safely guide the ship of state
at this hour, on him we must depend
to heal the country's wounds and see it mend.
These facts were duly published far and wide
to every voter in the countryside.

And they in turn, as only voters can,
decided to retain the "only" man.
But wait, now what is this we hear?
Someone has gravely blundered, that is clear,
for yesterday he drew his final breath.
The silly things forgot to caution death.

Anthem of the Sandstone Recreation and
Amnesty Society (SRAS)*

I'm doin' time in prison
to pay my social debt.
I got a three-year contract
that ain't expired yet.

Chorus:
Oh, I don't want no more of prison life.
Gee, Ma, I wanta go home.

They say the guards in prison
are quite intelligent.
If that's the case when I get out
I'll be the president.

(Chorus)

The food they serve in prison
they say is mighty fine
and if you cannot eat it
they throw it to the swine.

(Chorus)

The work you do in prison
is s'posed to save your soul
and if you don't believe it
they throw you in the hole.

(Chorus)

You write home to your sweetheart
and make a funny crack
but the censor's heard that one before
and sends the letter back.

(Chorus)

On Sunday there's a preacher
who comes to sing and pray.
He says that Jesus loves you
and then he goes away.

(Chorus)

They say the warden loves you
and treats you very well
but if this is just like heaven
I'd rather go . . . away.

Final Chorus:
Oh, I don't want no more of prison life.
Gee, Ma, I wanta go,
Gosh, Ma, I wanta go,
Aw shucks, Ma, I wanta go home.

**To the tune of a popular WW II Army song*

Christmas from Sandstone
(1945)

Two-thousand years of human struggle . . . years
of rest with toil alloyed, joy with tears . . .
mark faint, receding columns of the span
that bridges time since Jesus, friend of man
and God, walked sandal-footed down a dusty path.

He, musing in a desert place apart,
found peace a flower that blossoms in the heart,
and, raising healing hands above the strife
and fears of men, showed them a way of life
that conquers hate and triumphs even over death.

But as today we celebrate his birth
unprecedented evil stalks the earth.
Mad power and crafty greed in holy guise
hold sway and rain destruction from the skies
and smother every kindly sentiment with fire.

But truth is here to stay . . . the light
He kindled still defies the darkest night.
The hope He gave for peace and freedom feeds
anew in suffering human breasts . . . like seeds
that wait in earth for snow and winter winds to pass.

The Guards

Although beyond the heavens reel

these move their quite complacent selves

within this vault of stone and steel

and stack their merchandise on shelves.

Foundation stones of justice they

assist in cooling wronged and free.

Respecting hands that sign their pay

they save the world from such as me.

Some Other Autumn

Some other autumn when the morning air
is sparkling clear
the afternoon mellow as a silver bell
when sumac torches flare
and every leaf, decked gay,
is whispering softly, as they are today,
we'll be together, Dear.

We'll vagabond together, you and I, nature's children
sauntering hand in hand, kin with everything
we'll keep no planned
routine but give free wing
to fancy. We'll stroll through fields
flush with fruit and where the wood
its spangled beauty yields.

Our wind-whipped appetites will forage fine
on autumn's sweetest gifts:
hickory nuts, crisp apples,
chilled grapes frosting on the vine.

And we'll take care
as nature's children should to harmonize the theme
of autumn color. Your hair
will go well with the gleam
of goldenrod. No need to use that threadbare
simile about your eyes
and blue October skies.
Presumably there'll be some berries bright enough
to match your lips and thus prevent
their being considered imprudent.

I'll serve for background stuff
which by contrast helps bring out
more distinct the leitmotif.
I'll rhyme with oak and sycamore.
We'll both wear woodbine scarlet in our cheeks.

And as each golden day flares bright
and slowly glows away
we'll throw our spirits open to the night
and nestle in a stillness rich in peace.
Our hearts will hold communion with the stars
and find new unity with flying geese.
Mornings we'll rise with every sense on fire
each naked nerve-end tingling like the dew
and all the hills, arrayed in crystal will inspire
us to take up our adventuring anew.

Yes, Sweetheart, there'll be other autumns just as fair
when we can be together, free from every care.
And each kiss
will be sweeter then for those we missed.

Over the Frozen Wastes

Pounding through the night . . . churning the darkness . . .
fleeing across the frozen wastes
a train roars toward the south
a Cyclops of straining steel
charging with one bright eye
seeking the cities of men.

Suddenly flung from its aching lungs
a bellow of anguish shatters the mute air.
Fragments are hurled over the river . . .
over the wall . . . past steel bars
fragments that pierce through my reverie
and lodge in my heart.

In my heart. Ah, what's the affinity there?
Why does that cry of doubt and despair
pull like a magnet . . . tug at invisible chords
in my heart?

Ours is the bond of loneliness.
Southward I too would go . . . over the frozen wastes . . .
past the long night
south to the cities of men . . . to a pair of soft eyes
as blue as the summer skies
to a smile that warms my heart
as sunbeams stir buds in the spring.

Ah, but the walls are cold and stern.
How can they know my heart's longing?
Only the train's lonesome cry
can hurtle the wall . . . can push through the bars.
Hear now how it fades in the distance . . .
vanishing southward . . . into the night . . .
over the frozen wastes . . .
seeking the cities of men.

Ends and Means

To go to heaven
we take the road to hell
then wonder why
it leads us there so well.

Selected Poems

1945–2006

The Flat Earth Society

I am sitting in the town park,
Little children laugh and scream happily
as they go up and down and around.
Sadly I reflect that in some lands
little children are dying
by the hundreds and even the thousands
because of our government,
which has a problem with their government.

And then it occurs to me
that if this happy scene
would have taken place a thousand years ago,
almost all those people passing by
would have sincerely believed
that the world was flat.

Now we know better.
Now we have science and technology.
But do we have another thousand years
to learn that, as one wise man* has said:
"There is no way to peace.
Peace *is* the way.
Peace is the way."

**A.J. Muste*

Strike Two

The nation was in trouble,
its young men and its great wealth
were being sacrificed to the god of war.
So its leaders went to the devil,
the prince of violence, and said,
"Give us the one greatest weapon of all.
We will use it to bring peace
to our suffering world,
to make war forever unthinkable,
to let evil leaders know
they may no longer poison the wells
of justice, freedom, and truth."
The devil smiled to himself and said,
"Go to your tents, the weapon is yours."

The nation used its great weapon
 in a way that all could see.
With two bombs it wiped out two cities
then it sat back and waited
for the other nations to bow down and repent.

The other nations were afraid
but they did not bow down. They said,
"This weapon is not from God, for it is evil.
It is from the evil minds of men
so let us now use those minds
to get this great weapon for ourselves.
How else can we be safe?"
And they did.

Now when the Creator of life
saw that his prize creation
was in danger of destroying itself

He cooled men's passions,
He held them apart until they could see
that there was no peace in bombs,
that only knowing
they were brothers and sisters
and that they stood or fell together
could they find peace.

Now that we have arrived at that understanding
let us move forward toward the city of God.

In-Laws

Her grandpa, God rest his soul,
was a hard-headed upright Presbyterian,
a self-made business man, he had
a horse-collar factory, only one
in town, or around. Made money.
Put folks to work. Her dad, for
instance, sold horse collars clear
across the state on his way through
college. But technology changed
all that. He became an accountant
and raised two daughters. Her uncle,
a doctor, sold his services to the
state during the great war for God
and country. Patched up the boys
over in Europe. But I don't believe
he ever liked me. Maybe he sensed,
somehow, that I would sort of liked
to have asked him, "What would he
have done if he would have been in
Hiroshima, when they set off the
Bomb?"

Ute Council Tree

Greetings old cottonwood tree
they say you are the king to this valley
time was in the exuberance of spring
when a river washed your feet
now the river has been tamed by dams
its waters run quietly within their banks
in those happy days of your youth
little brown children
laughed and tumbled in your shade
mothers prepared hides for the winter
fathers sharpened their arrows for the hunt.

Now the white man's highway
runs through the valley
his iron horses roar by
their bad breath is in the air
but there is a sign
that points to where you stand
"Ute Council Tree" it says
beneath this tree we are told
Chief Ouray with heavy heart
signed away the right of his people
to live and love, die and be buried
in the land of their ancestors
but now the strength the vitality
you so eloquently expressed is gone
now your limbs stand out gaunt and bare
like veins on an old man's arm
like a miner's cabin long forgotten
a tree stripped to its essence.

People mean to do well
they have supported your brittle old boughs
they have filled your cavities
they have tried to hide your nakedness
but now they say you are dangerous
somebody might get hurt
living things don't last forever
not even kings of a valley
but before they "put you to rest"
as they say nowadays
which interpreted means "chop you down"
I hope . . . I hope a west wind
a great wind out of the west
lays you over with one magnificent crash
so you can go out in style
with a salute fit for a king.

As Told by an Old Plumber

My partner and I used to be plumbers.
We'd go to people's houses and put in
all the "pipes, fittings, and appurtenances"
the plumbing code tells about.
We'd rod out their sewer lines,
stop the leaks, all that sort of stuff.
But in the meantime
we had a couple other jobs
we didn't tell everybody about.
Not that these jobs were especially secret
but they were a bit unusual.
We didn't get paid in money,
not even in honor.
But that's not to say they weren't important.
Fact is, they were our real jobs.
Plumbing was just what we did to make a living.

He was the Chief Rock Inspector on Grand Mesa,
that big old flat mountain out here
in Western Colorado,
and I was the Head Lightning Strike Inspector.
Nobody appointed us to these jobs,
we just took them on as a civic duty.
Somebody had to do them so we did.
Why, we even had an office
about two-thirds of the way up the mountain.
No walls, no electricity, definitely no plumbing,
just an office. And sometimes
when everybody's toilets were doing OK
we'd sneak off up there and work at our jobs.

He'd walk around and look at the rocks
to make sure they were laying alright.
It was a big job but he did it anyway.
It was probably a little harder than mine
but mine was more specialized.
(At least that's what I always thought.)
I'd sort of walk around and if
I'd happen to see a lightning strike
or where one had struck
I'd examine the situation very carefully
and draw whatever conclusions seemed necessary.

All those years we did plumbing together
we did those other jobs on the side.
And they were the best darned jobs we ever had,
lots of nice things about them . . .
nobody ever complained about our work,
or about the price,
we didn't have to keep any records,
make any reports, pay any taxes,
and the pay was just right.
It's my opinion the whole world would be better off
if everybody had some such job as those.
A person owes at least that much
to God and country.

In the Name of Security

In the name of security
People built big walls around their cities
And to some extent it worked.
Many of those walls are still standing.
But unfortunately
All the people who built them . . .
The kings, engineers, tax collectors,
Locksmiths, masons, Rotarians, etc., . . .
Have all gone to their reward.

In the name of security
Mr. Berg, a farmer
And ex-neighbor of ours,
Very cleverly fixed up a gun
In his chicken coop
To shoot the burglar who had been
Swiping his laying hens.
But unfortunately
Mr. Berg forgot about that gun
And now Mr. Berg also
Has gone out of the farming business.

In the name of security
Men have built up huge insurance companies
With billions of bucks in assets.

And the longer their
Assets on them
The more security they are
Supposed to deliver.
But unfortunately
Mr. Brown's generous policies
Designed to provide into their old age
For himself and his darling wife, Lucy,
Led to his early demise.

But Lucy, God rest her soul,
Has at last found perfect security
In the state pen at Canyon City.

In the name of security
The nations,
Especially those who could afford to do so
(Or thought they could)
Built up huge arsenals of atomic bombs
And all the engines that were needed
To deliver them to their enemies' cities.
But unfortunately
They have not yet begun to collect
The dividends
On their investments.

Diversity

Infinite diversity.
Trillions . . . maybe even zillions
of grains of sand on the beach
and yet they say
no two the same . . .
no two drops of water.
Though I did read of a guy
or maybe it was a lady
who discovered two snowflakes
which he/she claimed to be
identical.
How big the microscope
they proved it with
the story didn't say.
I hope they have those two
preserved
down at the Smithsonian,
the snowflakes, that is,
not the people.

Speaking of people
There's another case.
How many now . . . five billion?
No two the same.
Oh, sometimes you'll see one
who sure reminds you
of somebody. But if you look
close enough . . .
well, you'd better not
look that close.
Even identical twins
you mean to tell me
one of them doesn't weigh
one-thousandth of an ounce
more . . . or less.

Now, the way I've
got this figured out is
everything's made up of
such teensy little pieces
even the scrawniest little bug
you'll ever see,
and just one inconspicuous
little bump
one very slight rearrangement
of the parts
and you've got
a genuine original.

It's sort of mind-boggling really
even this poem, wow!
All I've got to say is that
whoever thought up the idea
must really like
diversity.

War

War is mankind's greatest sin against God.
Why do I say that?
Because war is the systematic, carefully planned,
deliberate destruction of God's greatest creation . . .
the one thing that, as far as we can tell,
has the ability to recognize and honor the Creator,
the only one that can sing His praises,
thank Him for what He has done and is doing,
and grow in wisdom, grace, and beauty;
the only thing in nature, we are told,
that was created in God's own likeness.

In the Christian tradition we even believe
that God sent down His own son
to show and tell people how they should live,
and this Holy One summed it up as follows:
"Love God with all your heart and soul and mind
and love your neighbor as yourself."
(In these times of modern communication and travel,
obviously the whole world is our neighbor.)

It should be apparent to anybody who thinks about it
that God doesn't love some nations and races
any more or less than He does others.
To Him they are all His children, one species . . .
black, brown, white, whatever.
And, like any right-minded human parent,
He doesn't want them to be killing each other.

This war we are now waging
against some of God's other children
Is a great sin . . . it is wrong.
So let's stop it, ask forgiveness, and try
to make restitution for what we have been doing.
If we don't, you may be sure we will be very sorry.
For God is loving, but God is also just.

(Justice is one aspect of love.)
And one can only wonder how long . . .
how long God is going to allow
this war foolishness to go on.

Dear Friends, with such wonderful growth
in our ability to kill and destroy
we have about reached the end of the idea
that good ends can be achieved by bad means.

I. The Big Bang (A Trilogy)

In the beginning was the Big Bang.
Nothing created the Big Bang.
Nothing caused it to bang.
It just banged.
And all things were created from that Big Bang.
Galaxies were hurled into space,
but even before that
space was hurled into nothingness.
(Please don't ask where the nothingness came from.)
The galaxies divided into stars and planets.
The planets divided into water and earth.
The earth divided into fish, and bugs,
and plants, and animals, and so forth.
All things came from the Big Bang
and without it, did not anything come that ever came?

This process is still going on.
It is known as the Big Bang Theory of Creation.
This theory is much more acceptable
to the people of our day and generation,
and especially to the scientists thereof.
It eliminates that unfortunate,
awkward, difficult, unscientific concept . . . God.

So sing praises to the Big Bang.
Lift up your voices and sing praises.
Great is the Big Bang and greatly to be praised.

II. The Big Bang: A Theory of Social Control

Once people
being the clever little cusses that they are
hit on the Big Bang Theory of Creation
it was only a natural and logical evolutionary process
that the same line of reasoning
came to be applied to social problems,
specifically,
how to deal with one's neighbor
when one's neighbor fails to behave
in the proper and appropriate manner
as one perceives it to be.

And so thus it was
at a time when a couple of human families
were being especially obnoxious
that another family, which was especially clever,
came up with a device
that could out-bang any other device
that had ever banged.
The idea was to see if the same theory
that had created the cosmos
could restore peace and order
to the affairs of men.

So the very clever family used their device
on one of their most obstreperous neighbors
and it worked beautifully.
Peace was restored almost instantly.
That neighbor promised to be good forever.
Those who came to know the device most intimately
became especially peaceful . . . forever.
When other neighbors saw how wonderful
this device was for making peace
they called it the "Peacemaker."
They decided that they, too,
needed this wonderful device.

Soon many of the neighboring families
possessed this wonderful device
and peace reigned throughout the cosmos.
The lion laid down with the lamb.
Little babies slept all night.
Even the dogs barked more softly.
Peace was everywhere.

III. The Big Bang: Family Reunion
or The Chickens Come Home to Roost

And then it came to be that
even though the Peacemaker
had created worldwide peace
some people were not happy.
Many complained that life was just too boring.
Some opined that if Big Bang had intended
for mankind to be so peaceful
it would have made them differently . . .
more like earthworms, for instance,
or maybe like the koala,
both of which are very peaceful.

To avoid tragic social consequences
and to build up support for peace
some of the nations
instituted a huge competition
to see who was really the most peaceful.
People polished up their Peacemakers.
Some designed bigger and better Peacemakers.
Some people got so enthusiastic
that the whole thing got a bit out of hand.
And that (to misquote another famous poet)
was how the world went out.
Not with a whimper, but with a

BIG!

BANG!

Leviathan

Step across that line
that holds us now apart.
Let your eyes look into mine;
the eyes are windows to the heart.

He stepped across the line,
sought other eyes with care,
and found a thousand restless eyes
with cold, hungry stare.

Not everything's divine,
not every creature fair.
Of eyes that see just $ signs
even angels must beware.

Matthew 5:5

Blessed are the meek:
for they shall inherit the earth.

The meek.
Not the mighty
not the rich
not the violent
not the generals
not the possessors of atom bombs
not the rulers
not the masters
not the CEOs.

But the meek.
The lowly
the mild
the forgiving

the servants
the long suffering.
Those who give no offence
who take the blame
who put others first
they shall inherit the earth.

The others shall be cast out.
Those who exercise authority
the Lord cannot use.
The Lord can't use those
who are going to be telling Him
what to do and how to do it.
The Lord wants those
who will listen to his words
and do what He asks them to do.
It is these that the Lord can use.
At least that's how I see it.

Selah.

The Snow

For a little while everything stood still.
A rabbit peeked out of his hole and pulled back.
The deer, snugly settled down beneath an old juniper,
stood up, stretched, and settled back in their dry places.
The coyotes and even the great horned owls
that normally filled the night air with their songs
were as muted as their intended prey.
It was as though they had mutually agreed
even eating was something that could wait.
Cars, trains, airplanes, and other species
that normally pass in the night were as quiet
as the ghosts of all the horses they had replaced.
And then my wife discovered that the power was off.
The clocks, freezer, and all the other
sources of nighttime activity were at rest.
It seemed to be almost a sacred moment; and maybe it was,
with the whole world deep in meditation.
I pulled on my slippers and robe, groped my way downstairs,
found a path to the old flashlight waiting patiently
in the closet, and learned the power had gone off at three.
I opened the door and looked out. The snow was two feet deep.
Back in bed I visualized all the activity
waiting to be expressed as civilization struggled
back to its feet and the wheels began to turn again.
But for right now the silence was unbroken
and for a little while everything stood still.

Time for a Change

In Altitude

When I was a young man
I used to hold the world up
with my hands.
Now I'm not young anymore
and I hold it down
with my feet.
One of these days
I'll have to use
my whole body
to hold it down.

In Attitude . . . Maybe Mine

Seems some of those guys
who like to ram around
on their all-terrain vehicles
think they have a right
to go anywhere they are
able to go. Maybe they
could learn otherwise if
the Forest Service would
put up some big signs at
the very edge of some high
cliffs saying: "Stop! No
ATVs Beyond This Point!"

In Latitude

When I visit a big city
during the rush hour and see
all those thousands of cars,
some of them going north
and some of them going south,
I often wonder why it is
that those who live up north
couldn't get a job up north
and those who live down south
couldn't get a job down south.
And then I sometimes wonder
if maybe they could if
they didn't have cars.

In Longitude

When I was a boy
I used to long to be a man
so I could do all the things
men can do.
Now that I'm a man
(a rather elderly man)
I long to do all the things
boys can do.
Maybe I need a change
in my longitude.

The Importance of Cutting Wood
or One Lion and Two Chickens

Once when Tim and I were cutting wood
up on the Mesa (it was in the Flowing
Park area) just before lunch
we heard this scream; not once,
but over . . . and over . . . and over.
What a scream. I could feel the hair
bristle up on the back of my neck.
And all while we were eating our lunch
we could hear this scream and we knew
(though cows down by the lake kept on eating)
still we knew it was a mountain lion.

Since then I've talked with Alvin . . .
he's the guy who did a study for
the Bureau about lions in the area . . .
and Alvin says he's never heard them scream,
though he had heard that a female
may do that when she's in heat.

Well, anyway, we had the idea that
it would be really neat to walk
over that way and try to get a
look at the source. I'd have
guessed it was only about a quarter,
not over half a mile away. We knew,
of course, lions don't attack people . . .
but, still, why all that screaming?
What if she was sort of crazy, didn't
know about lions not attacking people?
Well, shucks, we came up here to get wood.
Gotta get that ol' truck loaded up.
Never mind about that love-sick lady lion.
So we . . . loaded up the truck.

I Guess You'd Say

I walked up to the north end of our place,
I guess you'd say "our ranch," where by the grace
of God, the sun, and water from the hill
we have a field of hay . . . our barn to fill.
We're ranching folks I guess you'd say. At least
we have one cow, a mild mannered beast.
Between the two of us we do our best
to bolster economics in the West.
I trade her hay, a barn, and such as that
for milk and yogurt, cheese and butterfat;
and at year's end we know without a doubt
our ledgers will exactly balance out.

Well, anyway, the grass was tall and thick
and waiting to be cut. One had to pick
his way with care. I paused to look around
and up and . . . there, down on the ground . . .
just one foot more and I'd have stepped upon
a very neatly spotted little fawn.
It didn't move, it didn't even blink.
Its mom, no doubt, had gone to get a drink
and left it curled and soaking up the sun,
preprogrammed not to cry and not to run.

But I was shocked. Does this make any sense?
It surely needs a more precise defense.
Why, there are dogs and coyotes in these parts
and they respond best to the "manly arts."
But still, I'd guess, with just a little luck
he'll grow to be a handsome, healthy buck.

It's more than one can say for our own boys
in spite of all our military toys.
In fact, I guess one really ought to say
that as we plan, so go we on our way.

Woody Owl Offers a Comment
(at 2:00 A.M.)

In winter when the cold is bitter
and the wind blows, who will get up
at four and put wood in the stove?
Who, who will even remember
That's the way you used to do?

And who, who will know how to do
all the things you used to do,
that you spent many years learning:
how to do plumbing and heating,
raise a good garden, take care of goats?

Who, who will read all those books
you spent years accumulating,
many of which you have read,
some of which are important,
a clue to what went wrong . . . or right?

Who, who will send letters to the editor
the way you used to do? Mostly
good ones? Will anyone remember
that you warned them, things
can't go on this way much longer?

Who, who will live in the house
that you planned, built from the ground?
Who will sit in your place at dinner
and look that long view to the south?
Who will haul all that stuff out
of the basement, oh lord, who, who
. . . will cover up the flicker's holes?

Who, who will read the thermometer every
morning? Who will care, watch
the deer, the sunrises and sunsets,
see spring creep slowly up the mountain
and autumn slide back down again?

Who will occupy the space that you
liked to call yours, think your thoughts,
sing your songs, tell your old jokes,
and if not you, then who, who?

Nobody, that's who.
The earth will still go on.
The space you once thought yours
will pass away with you,
your minutes, your hours, your days.
All that will remain is a mystery,
a divine mystery. Who, who?

A Tonsorial Comment

We'd climbed the peak, then coming down
divided up, the fast, the slow.
Our group, the slow, had finally found
a shallow trough the way to go,
where stunted aspen seemed to say
fast moving snow had been that way.

While thus we picked our way with care,
as safety argued that we should,
a sudden crackling filled the air
and faded out beneath the wood.
One daughter, not too mountain wise,
opined we'd "caught the other guys."

But I knew well that sudden exit
wasn't made by human kind.
More likely elk had not expected
seeing us and had declined
to stick around and be inspected.
They left to keep their calves protected.

At any rate it was too good
a chance for rest to be ignored,
so rest we did. Then through the wood
a smaller crackling noise came toward
our very spot and . . . Oh, surprise!
A baby elk with wondering eyes.

He stopped just twenty feet away
and looked us over stem to stern.
We almost seemed to hear him say
he'd come to see what he could learn
about this thing description begs
that walks around on its hind legs.

High curiosity assuaged
he ran off fast to join the herd
and there his mom in talk engaged,
and this, we trust is what she heard,
"They didn't do anything to scare
me, but they sure had funny hair."

There's a Limit

The mind is an amazing piece of equipment
but there's a limit to what it can absorb.
At first it's like a sponge,
soaking up anything that gets close.
For a while it still works like it was supposed to;
you can remember several dates,
even a few telephone numbers and addresses.
You don't have to write it down
to figure out if you got cheated at the store.
A line of poetry comes to mind
just when you need it to illustrate a point.
But eventually the time comes
when it's much like putting water in a bucket,
it just keeps running out over the edge.
You've read of every injustice your countrymen
have committed among the illiterate.
It doesn't shock you any more that riches and poverty
almost always exists side by side.
The books you accumulated over the years
now sit idle, even pile up on top of the bookcase.
You still listen to the news on radio or TV
but it can't find a place to lodge.
I suppose it's expected that by this time
you will have learned what you came here to learn.
Yes, the mind is a marvelous tool
but it too has its limits, and the message
finally comes through . . . maybe it's about time
that you traded it in on something new . . .
and, hopefully, better.

A Soldier of Misfortune

They said he was a madman, a killer;
that he killed 168 people . . . civilians.
Because he was mad at the government
for what it had done at Waco and Ruby Ridge.

They said he had been trained as a soldier,
that he had served his country
with distinction in Iraq.
He had learned about bombs,
their power to destroy.
He had seen how the government
goes about its business . . . our business.

They said his was the worst act
of domestic violence in U. S. history;
but I'd have to vote for Hiroshima
where our government killed
about 100,000 people with one bomb,
mostly women, children, and old folks,
(is that domestic enough?)
while their government survived in Tokyo
and their soldiers were away at war.
It seems that's the way wars are fought now;
civilians are fair game.

They said he must die for his sins;
but in a land that claims justice and democracy,
what about our sins?
Didn't we help make him what he is?
May God have mercy.

That's What the Man Said
(a poem for Easter)

He said he came that we might have life
and have it more abundantly.
He said that what the old timers had been preaching
wasn't good enough.
He said that we should overcome evil with good;
that no one could harvest figs from thistles.
He said that we should love even our enemies.

Even his closest followers
had trouble with some of these sayings.
They suggested that he should USE HIS POWER.
But when they saw him alive
even after being killed . . . well,
here was something that spread like wildfire.

That was a long time ago.
Now there are people all over the world
who call themselves Christians.
And now the world is literally going to hell.
Hey! All you people who call yourselves Christians.
Wake up . . . Wake up . . . Wake up!
That rooster has already crowed three times.

Bill Stafford Says "So Long"

Most of us never have to live through
a hurricane, tornado, earthquake,
avalanche, not even a revolution,
Thank God!

Bill's genius was to see the excitement
of creation in little things, things
anybody can see and enjoy. As he puts it,
"On earth it is like this, a strange
gift we hold, while we look around."
And what he sees he sets down in words
that are always fresh, sparkling with surprise,
and yet so casual, nothing pretentious.

The way, for example, he anticipates
in one poem his own obituary:
"Clouds do a still-day dance called 'Disappear':
They don't move—they're gone.
And that's how I won't move, too. We'll have days,
then comes that day. So long."

But in his own quiet way he has claimed,
for all time, a little piece of the language.
So long, Bill. Or as the Spanish say,
(I like this way, too) Adios . . .

. . . a friend.

The Dance of Death

Has there ever
in the whole long history of the race
been a time like this?
It is as though the entire species
all around the globe
was engaged in a weird and wild dance.
Some seem to be getting tired,
some are still learning the step,
and the tempo is getting faster
and faster.
But it is not a dance of love
or a dance of joy.
Could it be a dance of death?
Outside of the dance hall
the night is deep;
words that once shed some light,
such words as peace, justice,
equality, brotherhood,
have lost their magic.
There was a senator on TV
yesterday, debating the federal budget.
There will be another war,
he flatly declared.
We can't afford to relax our defense.
But why, I wonder,
must there be another war?
What does he know that I don't know?
Our children are hungry,
our people are getting poorer,
and he wants billions more for defense,
star wars, everything
must now serve the big machine,
a machine of our own creation
with its own imperatives.
"Feed me, do what I say
or you will surely perish."
And the dance goes on.

The Election
(1996)

Well, the big lottery is over . . .
all the character assassination, innuendo,
wild promises, misrepresentations . . . and
the winner has been duly announced. Now
the pundits are assessing the impact it
will have on the nation, even on the next
election.

But though we have been properly
informed that ours is the greatest
democracy the world has ever known, the
fact is that only fifty percent of the
people bothered to vote.

Why is that?
Some say one thing, some another, but
few have the temerity to ask, does it
really matter? All of those points so
hotly debated are really rather minor.
The poor will continue to get poorer.
The rich will continue to get richer.
Power will continue to concentrate in
the hands of the giant corporations.
The family will continue to decline.
Community will wither.

We will continue
to try to solve all our problems by passing
laws and by putting people in jail.
But it won't work. There is no way you
can create integrity by passing laws.
The trouble lies at the root, but that's
not the place where elections are held.

As that old German mystic Jacob Boehme
said, "Babylon has already been
placed in the scales and found wanting.
She goeth to her end. Hallelujah!"

The Ballad of King George's War*

Oh, listen to the story of King George's war.
They said that George was just a wimp; that really made him sore.
So when Hussein went into Kuwait George declared he was a nut,
Vowed he'd catch that dirty stinker and he'd kick his butt.

> *Chorus:*
> That's King George kickin' up a ruckus,
> That's King George kickin' up a fuss,
> That's King George and look at where he took us,
> Took us all the way to Kuwait just to kick some butts.

King George declared that honor's what the war was all about.
Saddam was getting honor and he wasn't pulling out.
Kuwaity was a pretty girl and she was being had
Which made George get awful jealous and it made him mad.

> *(Chorus)*

The Congress voted its support for George's little war
Cause they were getting mighty tired of fighting for the poor.
They thought the time had come when they should try to help
   the rich
So they let him send the army in to fix that bitch.

> *(Chorus)*

The people thought a little war's exactly what we need
To strengthen our economy and make Iraqis bleed.
They gave the King their own support in all the latest polls,
To bomb the hell out of Iraqis just to save their souls.

    (Chorus)

That's how this country started out 200 years ago,
King George was sitting on his throne to watch the bloody show.
And now our own King George declares it's time he had his day,
To put the country out of business in the same darned way.

    (Chorus)

**To the tune of "Casey Jones"*

Little Essays for Our Times

To justify governmental assistance
to the big corporations
many quote the metaphor,
"A rising tide raises all boats."
Apparently they have forgot
the unknown thousands of boats
that lie unmoved on the ocean floor.

      Those who extol the virtues of
      an economy based on competition
      would do well to consider
      that even this system,
      great as many believe it to be,
      might serve us even better
      if it had some serious competition.

One seldom arrives at
any destination except
the one he has
been traveling toward.
Which may explain why
it is so difficult to get peace
by practicing war.

That growing group of citizens
known as the "militia"
are accused of being paranoid,
and perhaps they are.
But probably no more so
than those congressmen
who want to keep pouring
more and more money
into the military.

Anybody who supports a system
that drives the poor to desperation
must either be ignorant of history
or not too smart.

The Great Equalizer

Funny thing about dying—
when all the pieces are in place,
when the time is right,
when everything is ready
you can do it . . . yes you can.

It doesn't matter
if you don't know much about it,
don't have a degree in the subject,
don't believe you are really ready,
maybe think you are too young,
or maybe even too old, or too anything,
you, YOU can do it.
And the chances are that you will.

Further, nobody is going to die
any deader than you do,
not even the big shots
or the fat cats.

So perk up, this is one area
in which we are all equal.

Oh, some may die a bit more sheepishly,
or a bit more doggedly,
or a bit more wimpishly,
or a bit more heroically,
but nobody is going to die
any more or less dead than you.
Death is the great equalizer.
Dare I say, death is beautiful?

Now, I may be wrong about some of this.
I don't claim to be
an authority on the subject.
But if am, please forgive me.

Part 2

▫ ▫ ▫

Letters from Prison

June 25, 1945 [from the Douglas County Jail]

Dear Betsy,

It doesn't seem possible that I've been in jail a week today. When every day is so much like every other day, when there are so few events with which to measure time, it seems very short in retrospect. Fortunately, I have been relaxed both mentally and physically and have done no "hard time."

Monday was an exciting day by comparison. We started the week off right with another shower—to my pleasant surprise, we are allowed two showers a week. Then we were given clean towels, clothes, blankets, and mattress covers. Then to top it off everyone in our tank was moved into the next tank, which had just been repainted. The fresh paint makes it quite a bit lighter and makes reading easier.

Shortly before noon on the same day, the *World-Herald* reporter came up to see how I was making out. He seemed very friendly and we talked for quite a while. His article that evening started out, "Mild, bespectacled Charles Worley, clad in coveralls, is getting along fine at the county jail." Then when he left I stayed and talked to Mr. Holliday (one of the guards) until noon. He said that, though a veteran of the last war, he would have been a CO himself in this war on the basis that Negroes are denied equality of opportunity.

Yesterday General Miltonberger was also an honored guest here at the courthouse. He must have been very flustered and excited because he completely forgot to stop up and visit me. The closest we could come to seeing the parade was seeing people watch it from the windows and roof of the building across the street. We could hear some of the noise, however, and occasional strains of "The Star Spangled Banner" drifted up through our bar-dangled window. Well, the authorities certainly missed a golden opportunity. Who knows but that such a stirring spectacle may have rehabilitated me.

My Mexican friend, Francisco, has just been in trying to read this letter. We have an interesting time trying to converse. Usually when we hit an impasse, however, it is possible to circumvent it some way.

We've had several talks comparing Mexico y Los Estados Unidos, their customs, philosophies, etc.

Love,
Chuck

◙ ◙ ◙

July 3, 1945 [Sandstone, Minnesota]

Dear Betsy,

My mind is buzzing with comparing between Sandstone and Tucson, bit of description and various impressions. Where to start? We left Omaha at about 6 A.M. Sunday, with me still wearing ten days' growth of whiskers. The Deputy Marshall and guard were both very friendly, so the trip was enjoyable. At about 4 P.M. we arrived at St. Paul, where I spent the night in the town jail (number nine on my list). At 9:30 A.M. or 10 Monday morning we arrived at Sandstone. The prison is a couple miles from town, about 90 miles north of St. Paul. There is a very pretty little river (Kettle River) about a mile from camp.

The prison itself is very new, all the equipment in excellent repair. It is built in the form of a huge square enclosing an area of approximately one city block. The building is cement, two stories high. While in quarantine (first 30 days) we are confined to one wing. Each man has a small room about nine feet by six feet containing a bed, lavatory, desk, and chair.

There are about 500 inmates, sixty-five percent of whom are Jehovah's Witnesses. Unofficially (since all contact is prohibited) I have met three or four hundred spirits. In comparison to Tucson there are some advantages and some disadvantages. We are somewhat more confined here since our activities must take place in the area enclosed by the building. There is a softball diamond, volleyball court, and horseshoe court. The library appeared quite adequate. Yesterday I checked out Nehru's autobiography, *Toward Freedom,* and since we are locked in our room from 6 P.M. until morning I expect to do quite a little reading during the next 30 days. So far all the officers (they do not carry guns) have seemed quite friendly and helpful, somewhat better adjusted than those at Tucson, though, no doubt there are exceptions. Quite obviously the work project here isn't the main thing as it was at Tucson. All of the work is maintenance work and none of it seems very urgent. Frankly I doubt if I will be able to learn much from the work but I believe that the academic opportunities are pretty good.

One thing I have noticed causes me some concern—Negroes are segregated both in the dining hall and in sleeping quarters. I'm having a hard time trying to decide what my personal reaction should be about such a policy—you know how I feel about it.

The food is plain but has tasted very good so far. Of course, that is customary at first and then as time goes on and it has to take the place of sex, excitement, etc. It becomes psychologically less satisfying.

I'm afraid this is a pretty egocentric letter, Honey, but right now there isn't much else to write about. Unfortunately, I can't write about the thing I'm most interested in—you and all you are doing. I know you are having a grand time, which makes me very happy, and I know you realize how much it would mean to me to enjoy your experiences occasionally through our correspondence. You are all I have now. Whenever I think of the future plans after prison, etc., my mind quite involuntarily goes to my other half somewhere miles away. I love you, Betsy.

During quarantine I am not permitted to have any visitors or to write letters to anyone but you and Mom and Dad. I notice also that we are restricted to seven correspondents and three letters a week. I put you, Mom, Mammy, Frank, John S., Lucille, and Bill S. on my list but *may not* be permitted to write to Lucille because she is unmarried and I am married!

Sweetheart, would you please drop a card to *Fellowship* magazine and *The Christian Century* asking them to immediately change my address? And if you have lots of money, get me a year's subscription to *The Progressive,* the La Follett's paper published in Madison.

Don't let our correspondence be a burden, Honey, but I must confess a great eagerness to know what you are doing, thinking, feeling, etc.

Please have your folks send me a picture of you; the one
I have in my billfold would be OK.

Your little old husband,
Chuck

◉ ◉ ◉

July 6, 1945

Dearest Wifey,

At first I felt a little uneasy, a wee bit sorry for myself, about not
hearing from you. But now everything is OK again since I have the
feeling that you must have written but your letter is being held up
for some reason or was missent. I am doing easy time—except for
one night when I was watching the volleyball game through my
window. One of the players was quite fleshy. His breasts made me
think of you.

Since then I have been moved across the hall to the west side. It
is better. The sun shines in my window making it quite cheery and
better for reading. We men in quarantine are locked in our little
rooms from five in the evening until the next morning. From this side
of the room I watch the softball game or horseshoes instead of volleyball. Right now we are having a shower, a few huge raindrops and
scattered hailstones. Looking up from my window as straight as possible I can see nothing but blue skies and the sun is shining brightly.
This is a crazy climate. With blue skies everywhere the whole sky
seems to cloud up and rain in twenty minutes.

Not much has happened to me so far—an IQ test and one interview is at 11. Tomorrow I am scheduled for a blood test—think I
will make it? My daily job, sweeping the day-room, takes about 20
minutes to perform. Consequently, I have done quite a little reading.
Finished Nehru's autobiography yesterday. Sometime I hope you have
the leisure to read it as I did. The wonderful, selfless struggle those
people are waging against corruption and violence. So much greater
than anything we can imagine here. Makes one a bit ashamed of the
little we are willing to pay for our ideals.

I also read nearly all of *Spoon River Anthology*. You are familiar
with some of them—the Milliner; Benjamin Painter, the Lawyer; the

wealthy philanthropist; etc. There are over 250 of these little character sketches. I got a kick out of them. Right now I am reading a psychological novel, *Arrival and Departure*, by Koestler. It is fascinating. One of the other COs recommended it.

We had commissary today. There is no limit on candy bars. It is a good thing since now I will have to limit myself. Eventually I hope to cut out all extras. It is an unnecessary, selfish indulgence, not quite in keeping with my best thinking. When first arrived here I started smoking roll-your-own cigarettes. It satisfies nervousness to a certain extent. It was becoming quite easy and rather satisfying so I quit it—not wishing to tie myself to such a stupid habit.

Well, you see, Honey, my life is pretty well circumscribed in a tight little circle. I'm getting gradually acquainted with the other boys in quarantine, chiefly through our two-hour volleyball sessions from 1 to 3. I'm still somewhat surprised at the newness of all the equipment. Fitting into the routine is much easier than I expected. So far I have felt almost none of that rebellious spirit I felt so often at Tucson. I think there is less provocation here. It's really a very easy life—perhaps too easy for spiritual growth. Even the JWs are complacent.

Honey, I love you and am waiting impatiently to hear what and why and how you are doing. Won't know where to write a letter next week until I hear from you—maybe tonight—I hope. Words are too dull to express my feelings for you so I'll just close with
—*Chuck*

◘ ◘ ◘

July 8, 1945

Dearest Betsy,

I could write you a whole book tonight (if it didn't become too boring) containing nothing but the thoughts that have been running through my head all day. Not that they are interesting, worthwhile, or even leading in some general direction. As a matter of fact, the only thing that would tie them together would be that in all probability they would all indicate the feeling of uselessness and boredom that I felt all day—not just boredom, but boredom tinged with annoyance. Should I bore you with it, too, or try to periscope

my imagination over this drab enclosure and write about something
more pleasant? Sorry, Honey, I can't hear you. Well then, let me get
some of this off my chest.

I suppose the most basic cause of my boredom is that I haven't
heard a word from you for over a week now. In a way it is amusing
the way your life has become so tied up in mine. Now I know what
Mrs. Whatsername was talking about when she said the chief value
of marriage was the *feeling of belonging* it gave one. The fact that I
haven't been able to enjoy that feeling much for a week now leaves
me feeling somewhat suspended in midair. So that sometimes I'm annoyed at you, thinking, surely she should have written to me before
this; and then I get annoyed at myself for even doubting that you
have tried; and then I get annoyed at the officials here, feeling that
they are somehow responsible. (The last conviction grew mightily
yesterday when one of the other fellows here in quarantine got a letter from Chicago dated June 15, and another dated June 18.)

Yes, it surprises me to see how intertwined our lives have become
even though I have always felt that there was a gap between us—
a gap created by our difference in age and the fact that greater responsibility and hardship have forced me to learn more about myself
and life in general—a gap which I had hoped (still do) will be filled
in by our absence from each other.

Then, too, the system is beginning to wear a little more. The
pettiness I thought so contemptible at Tucson is gradually becoming
more apparent. Today, for instance, the officer in charge of us, who
is probably a good enough guy on the outside but who has spent
seventeen years in this god-awful system, gave us a little talk on
how to conduct ourselves here. The thing that got me is that he can't
speak about the regulations without an outright or implied threat of
the dire consequences of disobedience. This morning he was talking
to a couple of fat, disgusting yes-men, telling them all about the hole
(solitary confinement) in other institutions, describing in glowing
terms the effect of this or that technique (to break a man's spirit). It
was almost nauseating. I asked him if that was what he thought they
wanted to accomplish with men in prison. And then another officer,
a very surly person, cautioned us today to be sure and use the "Mr."
when addressing one of the officers. There is nothing that so goes

against my grain as the thought that we should show special defer-
ence to a person because he has physical force over us. I've been
reading Tagore and found comfort in the following line of a prayer
poem: "Give me strength never to disown the poor *or bend my knee
before insolent might.*"

Even reading hasn't been satisfying. I have before me Tagore's
poems, complete Gilbert and Sullivan, and Virginia Woolf's *To the
Lighthouse,* which is another of those introspective, psychoanalyti-
cal things that seems to do anything but satisfy me. There are some
good things in Tagore that I'd like to quote and dedicate to you but
haven't the space.

Isn't this one h--l of a letter for a man to write to his beautiful
and lovely young wife. Maybe it is this very frustration that, risen
above, can enable us to find each other richer, nobler personalities
when we meet again. But you know how it is—Sunday today, the
sun shining brightly, activity and laughter outside, and we "fish"
cooped up all day except for the brief intervals in the dining hall.

Honey, I hope you will strive to maintain our vow of absolute
honesty in your letters to me as I try to do in mine to you. Please
forgive my boredom, Sweetheart. I love you lots,
Chuck

▣ ▣ ▣

July 13, 1945

Hello, Sweetheart,
Your swell, newsy, inspiring letter came last night. It made me
feel good all over—an excellent example of what I meant by "enjoying your experiences vicariously." I would have answered immediately but the mail doesn't come around until about a half-hour before
"lights out." It's a wonderful time to get mail because it's just about
then that you come to my mind most strongly. Activities in the yard
have ceased, the sun has gone down behind E cell house, leaving
the sky a deep, soft, luminous blue with perhaps the evening star
(our star) sparkling merrily. Occasionally, a big dark cloud marching
south tears a gaping hole in the ceiling.

The routine is becoming more familiar now—get up at 6:30, breakfast at 7:15, work call at 8, lunch at 12, back to work at 1, and quit again at 4, supper at 4:30, and then the rest of the evening free. Of course, this is altered for those of us in quarantine. My job, for instance, is to sweep and dust the day room, a small room in the front of our cell block. The job takes about ten minutes twice a day. Then in the afternoon we go to the library for a few minutes and return for a couple hours of volleyball. Friday is perhaps our most strenuous day for not only do we get clean clothes and linen, but also go to the commissary. This morning about thirty seconds after the whistle blew (I had already thrown back the cover) one of the officers stuck his head in and asked if I had heard the whistle. I replied in the affirmative. His brusque rejoinder was, "That means get up!" Honestly, Honey, I really think it most unfortunate that grown men have nothing more important to do than to inject themselves into such minute details of one's personal life.

I go to the library every time I get a chance. If I already have my quota of books (around 2), I go anyway just for the walk, to browse through the books, or to watch the bees. They have a hive of bees in a glass case in the library. The entrance is through a hose projecting out of one window. It is really fascinating to watch the process of honey in the making.

Monday I was taken to the hospital for a physical exam. The exam was fairly thorough, including teeth. I passed with flying colors so I guess my scholarship is secure for two or three years. You may be interested in a card I received from the record office a few days ago. It contains a few of my vital statistics including the following: Sentence begins . . . June 20, 1945; received July 2, 1945; eligible for parole . . . July 1947; conditional release date . . . *Oct. 11, 1947;* Ex. of sentence . . . June 19, 1948.

Ha, ha. I beat you to one news flash, Honey. 1. Rev. Waltmire told me two weeks ago to say that he had a new grandson. 2. From your letter I couldn't tell whether Forest had been arrested and was out on bond or what. 3. George Roach was one of our kindred spirits at Tucson—a good boy. 4. Please have Lucille send me a sample copy of the *Pacific Center Bulletin,* if it will be permitted. I'd love to receive it. 5. Be careful how you go about getting recruits in the CPS camps. They have institutions like this for women, you know.

Well, I finally found a book that interested me, *Orchard and Small Fruit Culture*. I quite devoured it—pruning, grafting, storing fruit, soil management, spraying, etc. They have books on bee culture, poultry, cattle, and other fields relating to subsistence farming, so maybe I can pick up some practical knowledge. It's swell that you got to talk to Arthur E. I rather think we want to hit a medium somewhere between his point of view and Mil's.

Through my window I am gradually meeting some of the other COs here. I've met the 4 boys who left Mancos when I was in Tucson—Roodenko, Hutchinson, Rockwell, and White. The Supreme Court refused to rule on their case. There are a couple of fellows from Frank Lloyd Wright's group in Wisconsin. There is also one fellow who was a math prof. at Iowa U. Also there is a semanticist from Arizona—sent here before they started sending COs to Tucson. The boys who have been here some time say that the present trend is in the direction of more supervision, more regimentation on the part of the administration (which probably won't make it much easier for me here).

Goodbye, Honey. I wish you lots and lots of happiness, and growth, and success in your work this summer.

Lots and lots of love,
Chuck

◉ ◉ ◉

July 17, 1945

My Dear Little Sweetheart,

I love you! And that's no foolin'. Though the word "little" may be a slight exaggeration. I weighed only 128 at my physical exam last week—tsh, tsh, tsh, you'd better be careful, Honey.

I meant to write to you last night but felt so punk from the typhoid shot that I couldn't. But no letter came from you last night so I guess it's OK I'm still ahead of you five letters to two (counting this one) but that's alright, Honey, I haven't much else to do and here you are out saving democracy. Yo te amo.

I've been reading a very fascinating novel—*The Brothers Karamazov* by Dostoyevsky. It is a huge thing (820 pages) and a delightful mixture of psychology, philosophy, sociology, and violent emotion. When we settle on our little farm and have time to live, you must read it, Betsovna. The philosophy part especially affected me—the internal struggle I've been having between non-cooperation and active goodwill. The former can so easily become a possessive attitude at the expense of the latter. Suddenly I felt quite wrong about the attitude I had been nursing, one of pride (a grave fault of mine). I had not been making many friends because of pride, a lack of humility. I had been resenting the officers and their position of authority because of pride. How far I have been from thinking of them as brothers. I hadn't even been able to give one of them a friendly smile. Now don't worry, Honey, I've not suffered a "conversion," but I've given myself a good thinking-to and it helped. I'm already doing easier time. If I again leave prison without a genuine feeling of brotherhood towards those in authority, then I have again failed to grasp the most important lesson prison has to offer. While we're on the subject, Sweetheart, please forgive all the times I have been proud in my relations with you.

Today I still felt punk so I spent most of the afternoon in bed and then got up very refreshed, even played a little volleyball. Now, to top it off, the clouds that have been hanging on for two days suddenly cleared up, making it bright and sunshiny. Outside the boys are making lots of noise in a game of "workup." Now, if I get a letter from my wife tonight, I will lie awake for an hour or two thinking and watching the glow in the western sky, with all my body smiling at the sheets.

Mom has written three times already. Her letters are short, funny little things. I have to laugh when I read them. The things I'd like most to hear about she summarizes in a phrase. She says your folks plan to come up for a visit in August. That will be a great pleasure to me. She and Dad want to come up too before cold weather. Why don't you all get together and decide who will come when. As you know, I am permitted a one-hour visit each month as soon as I am out of quarantine. Speaking of quarantine, there is a rumor that a number of transfers are expected from Terre Haute, in which case I would be moved to a dormitory though still under quarantine restrictions. Here there are about fifty men in a dorm and they are separated according to their lineage: JWs, COs, thieves, Negroes, and men who work odd hours.

Oh, yes, while I think of it, if you have not ordered *The Progressive,* don't. They require that such subscriptions be made through the Commissary. I am not sure that I will be permitted to receive my *Fellowship* magazine and *The Christian Century* without going through them (Commissary) some way. Sweetheart, please follow the correspondence instructions carefully. It would be most distressing if one of your letters should not come through because of some insignificant little thing. Aren't you supposed to put your full name and address at the bottom?

In addition to the novel, I have a book on dairy cattle and milk production. Gee it's interesting. I've about settled on Jerseys for our subsistence farm.

I've written a couple of poems but was not greatly inspired and consequently am not too well pleased with them. Hope I get more inspired and write lots of them. If I turn out some I like, I'll send them to you.

You know, Honey, I have a confession to make. Lately I have felt a few little pangs of jealousy regarding you. It is such an amusing experience (I had always thought of myself as being quite above such a thing) that I have to smile at myself.

Did you ever read a letter with so many "I's" in it? Please forgive, Sweetheart. Have lots of fun, do a good job of opposing peacetime conscription because it is a very serious matter. Don't forget to think occasionally of what you want to do when the summer is over.

Goodbye my Darling,
Chuck

■ ■ ■

July 19, 1945

Dearest Wifey,

Last night I got three letters, one from you, one from Mammy, and one from me. The one from me was addressed to you but came back because I didn't include Drake University in the address on the ticket which is attached to the top of the page and is torn off for their records. You will probably get that letter the same day as this so maybe you'd better read it first to get the logical sequence.

Perhaps I should describe an incident which just now occurred as I was writing the above paragraph. An officer came in to inspect my cell and immediately afterward the inmate orderly came in to tell me that I had been "written up" because my desk was not in its proper position. You see, I had it turned around in the correct writing position instead of leaving it with the back side out and then straddling one hind corner to use it. I don't know just what this "writing up" means. Nothing serious I am sure. But still it is an excellent opportunity for me to explain to you my relationship to this institution. You remember, Honey, that Jesus said, "The Sabbath was made for man, not man for the Sabbath." That's the way I feel about laws and regulations—that they were made for the use and service of man, not vice versa. Now, I have determined to do everything I conscientiously can to get along with the system here, but of course I do not intend to do anything I regard as stupid or in violation of the essential worth and dignity of every man.

Unlike Tucson, they have a place here for offenders against the regulations. It is known as "the hole" or, more poetically, as "Duffy's Flats." Duffy's Flats is nothing more or less than a number of cells exactly like the one I am in now except that there is no furniture, one's bed being a mattress on the floor. The cells are upstairs here in the same wing as quarantine. For food one is given nothing but raw vegetables—carrots, cabbage, and potatoes—and bread. ONE IS NOT PERMITTED TO WRITE OR RECEIVE LETTERS THERE.

Sweetheart, I do not tell you these things to worry you but rather to set your mind at ease, for the facts are usually much easier than things our imagination may manufacture. Frankly, I never expect to make the hole. I have usually found that if one is reasonable and tolerant, the authorities will be the same.

Thank you for the swell letter last night. You needn't apologize for "preaching." We all need to be reminded of the eternal truths—especially when the sky is obscured by clouds. (Actually, I was greatly pleased at your ability to quote correctly such long phrases from our poem.) I felt a little guilty and ashamed at the effect of that one letter on you. Though in all truthfulness it was probably just the effect I had intended. I was feeling a bit lonely and sorry for myself when I wrote it and probably wanted to make you do a little hard time, too. Such an attitude is selfish and spiteful. Don't worry about my getting a warped personality, Honey. I honestly expect the net results to be just the opposite. I am only trying to be honest with you and myself, and often when we frankly analyze our true motives they are not as pure and noble as we would like to believe. (Ugh—what a key I'm harping in today. Excuse please.)

Mammy's letter (typed on Phyl's typewriter) was as welcome as the first robin. She quoted from a letter Em sent to the county jail. Em has been reading the literature and doing lots of thinking (and prejudicing Donny in my behalf). There were also quotes from Doc Phillips's and Grandma J's letters indicating their support. (Grandma had written to Marsh supporting us!) Mammy's comments were inspiring. She has decided to give more support to the FOR. She got a rise out of "Freedom Road." Her final sentence was, "Daddy is looking at the map of Minnesota—you may see the Rosses and the Worleys within the next two months."

Betsy, if you would like to do something for me, why don't you write to Frank and Marie, Beecher's City, Ill., and ask them how everything is coming along. Wasn't Marie supposed to have the baby this month? Or better yet, tell them that I will be out of quarantine on August 3 and would like to hear direct from them if they could find time to write. I'm sure Frank will be permitted on my correspondence list, though I haven't been interviewed yet, and so don't know about Lucille.

We had pork chops for lunch and I ate most of mine. It mostly made me sick. Guess I'll have to give up pork altogether. I wouldn't be surprised if I would turn out to be something of a vegetarian some day. I'm getting so I don't believe I would like to kill other animals for my food. Animal products are fine—milk, eggs, and cheese, but they don't hurt the animal any. About books, better not send any until I find out more of what it's all about. They seem to have some rule here that a person can have only two books in his possession at one time.

Your work sounds like just the thing. I'm sort of glad they're laying it on because you'll develop more that way.

G'bye, Sweetheart, I'll try to space my letters better next time.
Lots of love,
Chuck

◙ ◙ ◙

July 22, 1945

Dear Betty,

Hasn't this been a beautiful Sunday, Sweetheart? So warm and bright, and sunshiny. Though we've been pretty much cooped up all day (no exercise period on Sunday), every time we went to chow the wonderful smell of clover blossoms drifting over the walls was so keen as to be almost intoxicating. Oh, the smell of mother earth is nature's greatest enchantment here. It is particularly spicy and fresh when we get up in the morning. Today I've been thinking how wonderful it would be if you could have been here and we could have taken a long hike down the little river nearby. Honestly, Honey, it is a little beauty. I hope you can see it some time before the leaves and vegetation are gone. It ought to be especially beautiful in autumn colors. Quite unlike most Midwest rivers, this one doesn't run along at ground level but has cut out a little chasm so that the bridge to camp appears to be forty-one kilometers or fifty feet above the water.

Got another letter from my honey Friday. I can't quite imagine you making speeches to people. I hope you stick to the main point and don't fly off on a tangent or get lost in a maze of insignificant details like you used to do. ("Now isn't that nice, C.W.?" I ask myself. "Quote no." I promptly reply but still it makes one smile.) No kidding, Betsy, how do you gals make out with your speeches? Do you think some of the Quakers will be challenged? What do you say about world organizations? Frankly, I wouldn't know what to say.

I am probably at least as cynical about San Francisco and all the rest as Rayford Logan. Perhaps you remember some of the things I said about it at the Baha'i meeting that night.

I had a funny experience Thursday night and Friday. For some reason, which I was totally unable to discover (though I tried to psychoanalyze myself from every angle), I had an intense feeling of nervousness. It was as though I had some very great fear but couldn't discover the cause of it. I thought it had gone away Friday but then that night about bedtime it came back again—a very miserable feeling though all emotional, not physical.

So Saturday I went to talk to the doctor about it. The doc turned out to be a good egg. He wrote down my life history and then asked me all the questions I had been asking myself and got the same answers. He had my IQ score which he said was high. He knew also that I had studied some psychology so we had more of a discussion than an interview. We couldn't arrive at any definite conclusions. The doctor thought that I might have a repressed phobia of having epilepsy or that the time I have had to serve in prison may be the cause, even though I am not doing any hard time. Whatever it was that brought the feeling about or what it might have been are still a mystery.

But when I left the doctor's office it completely disappeared. Personally, I rather think it was a phobia of insanity, though all the psychologists agree that there is no surer sign of sanity. Besides, I don't know why I should have a fear of insanity. Now that I look back, it all seems so foolish and unreal as to be amusing, but it certainly seemed real enough at the time. I even mentioned a "feeling of nervousness" in a letter Friday to the folks. They may be a bit alarmed since the feeling hadn't been resolved then. So if they mention it to you, you may reassure them that I am again my blithe, unconscious self.

We had fried chicken for dinner today. My portion was a leg and thigh—quite delicious, and for supper, apple pie. I am still satisfied with the cooking, but of course it doesn't come up to yours. The only thing they make better here than you used to make is gravy. I could never brag much about your gravy. (For one thing, there was never enough.) I hope you realize, Sweetheart, that I'm teasing you. Some

day I will write a famous song or poem in your honor to atone for
my orneriness. 'Cause truly Betsy, I love you lots and lots.

I finished one small book on bees and am still reading the one on
dairy cattle. But I'm about due for a change in reading matter. They
have *The Reporter* (National Service Board for Religious Objectors
publication) in the library so I'm getting caught up on world affairs.
There is one book in our library entitled *Betsy Ross: Quaker Rebel.*
Don't let the Quakers hear about it or your influence will be shot.
Incidentally, I know a Quaker boy who lived on a farm near Oska-
loosa, Iowa, and went to William Penn College. His name was
Olin Byerly. He was in our gang at Fellowship Farm in Wisconsin.
Maybe you will meet him or his sister, whom I met later at an FOR
conference.

Friday I was moved upstairs in the quarantine wing. I can see a
little more of the world from here. Right now there are some brilliant
little dimpling clouds all shimmering silver just above the prison.
We have a little more peace and privacy up here so I like it better.
The past few days have been our first really warm ones, but I like it.
This is an awful lot of drivel that I'm writing, Honey, but I'll think of
something important to say one of these days.

B' bye again.
With lots of affection,
Chuck

◙ ◙ ◙

July 26, 1945

Hello, Honey!

This is me, C.V., your husband. ?Tu sabes? I love you muchismo.
Tuesday I got a double-barreled letter from my wife and I thought,
Gee, ain't it swell that Betty is getting the works like that. I'll bet you
already feel like those principles you represent are more truly yours.
Now when the summer is over you will feel justified in seeking a job
with some organization representing those principles . . . if that is
what you would like. I've been telling the other COs what my better
half is doing. They think it's swell.

Already it's getting to the point where I can't think of much to write about. After the caravan is over you may have more time so we could read the same book and discuss in letters our reactions, impressions, etc. Right now I'm reading a book which would lend itself to such a treatment. It is Wm. James's *The Varieties of Religious Experience*. Any person who wants to understand religion and his own position regarding it would find the book valuable I think. Perhaps I should say "I was reading it," for a new CO came in yesterday, transferred here from Ashland, Kentucky. He was with Bayard Rustin and seven other fellows there who refused to cooperate with the prison because of racial segregation. Apparently they plan to break up the group by distributing them around to various prisons. Bayard he expected to be transferred to Springfield. This fellow told about his experiences as a non-cooperator in three successive government-operated CPS camps—Mancos, Colorado; La Pine, Oregon; and Germfask, Michigan. I'm not sure how far I go along with such a policy. Doesn't seem quite honorable to me. I believe I'd rather accept the institution or else reject it entirely by leaving. But, of course, every person should follow his own light.

Incidentally, two of the COs here have asked for work changes out of the hospital because on the last of this month all doctors in the Public Health Service (including ours) become commissioned officers in the military setup. So far, the Warden has refused to honor their requests, so I'm not sure what will develop—probably they will end up in the hole. I'm mentally organizing a letter to the Warden expressing my concern over the matter, and also over the segregation system. Out of fairness and honesty I think it is perhaps best that they know I am concerned about these matters. The racial situation got a boost the other day in the right direction as they transferred a JW Negro into a JW dorm.

This new CO says that those who should know, judges, etc., expect COs in prison to be given amnesty when the war ends. Hope he's right but have begun to doubt it. The big problem then will be employment and if they can withstand public pressure for amnesty, I think they would just as soon not have 3,000 COs and JWs competing for jobs with the veterans. Well, we'll see. I'll bet there are many, many more COs here with over three years than with under three years. Maybe we were lucky. Tomorrow we are expecting a new CO who got five years and a $1,000 fine. And he will have to pay the fine because he has enough property to cover it. Yes, maybe we were lucky.

A few personal items: I have a new hobby—dressing my hair. Maybe I can stall off pattern baldness a few years. I've been shaving every other day here in prison where I have no sweet wife to hug and kiss. Go ahead and say it—ain't that a @#$%@#$%! (censored). Gosh, it hardly seems real that I used to hold a lovely creature like you in my arms. If it was a dream, I hope it comes back soon. I asked Mom to have Pappy send me a four inch by six inch picture of you (we are furnished frames that size). Hope one comes soon so I can show you off to the boys.

Bye, Honey. Have fun, and don't make writing a chore. I like you!

Chuck

◉ ◉ ◉

July 31, 1945

Hi Betsy Baby,

It is very flattering to have been made an honorary member of your caravan. However (for reasons which I will not mention), I would greatly prefer being an actual member of that particular caravan. Be that as it may, what can I do to advance "the kingdom" in my present capacity?

Friday I leave quarantine and recently the interviews have been coming thick and fast. Friday I talked to my Parole Officer for over an hour. Talked is the correct word—about anything and everything—prison, petty regulation, its effect on the prison, on the employee, pacifism, social work, psychiatry, religion, etc., very little about parole. He said, "I suppose you're familiar with this 8641 parole plan." I said, "Yes." A period of silence. Me: "Have there been any changes since I was at Tucson?" He: "I guess not!" Regarding pacifism he was very liberal, heartily disagreed when I said war didn't settle anything but only made matters worse. He said that if he were drafted he would probably go because he has no well-developed philosophy opposing it, but that he very largely agrees with the COs, especially on economic grounds.

The next day I was interviewed by the Associate Warden. He seemed to be a pretty good Joe. We talked about a lot of things—prison, social work, even wrestling. He said I would probably be placed in minimum custody and would more than likely work outside, probably on the farm. They all asked what work do you want to do, but as far as I can see there isn't much choice so I haven't expressed any. All of their jobs here are concerned with maintenance, raising food, or building up or maintaining the institution. As far as work goes, I prefer to be just one of the boys—the less one is tied up in a job, the freer he is to follow his conscience—if you see what I mean.

Today I was interviewed by the Educational Director. It didn't take long. He asked what my major was at school and if I wanted to take any classes here. My answer, "Yes, if they have anything I might be interested in." School starts in about five weeks so we will see.

The Parole Officer informed me that Lucille cannot be on my list since she is an unmarried female. Married men are not permitted to write to other women. I told the Parole Officer that you said the idea was ridiculous but it didn't make any difference. He also said that your folks had written for permission but the regulations didn't permit it until I had been here five months. The reason he gave for the regulations was so weak that I immediately wrote to the Warden asking for special permission for them to visit. No answer yet.

We got a new CO yesterday from Denver. I met him once before when he was visiting at our camp in Santa Barbara. His case parallels mine—eighteen months the first time (at El Reno) and three years this time. I certainly appreciated having Ike here to talk to. He is a very intelligent, very individualistic fellow. I'm going to learn bee-keeping from him. He maintains sixty hives in Portland as a hobby. He is an introverted, pessimistic, physically active guy. At La Pine, Oregon, CPS camp he once hiked 55 miles in 24 hours.

I'm still reading *The Varieties of Religious Experience*. I never realized how utterly bare my mind is of any religious conviction. It is as if my mind was a blank piece of white paper waiting to be written on, or a broad plowed field without a seed planted in it. Right now it doesn't seem like I have any ideas about life, either optimistic or pessimistic. This philosophical barrenness will probably continue as long as I am segregated from a more active life as at present.

Have surely fallen behind on the news. Didn't learn until today that England had a new prime minister. Incidentally, Honey, did you ask *The Christian Century* and *Fellowship* magazine to change my address? So far I haven't got either or a notice of their being received here.

At my interview with the Educational Director today, he decided to test my typing speed since I had stated on a questionnaire that I could probably type thirty words per minute. I did forty-two words a minute.

Hope I hear from you tonight, Betsy, and that you have gotten some of my letters. I've written two each week to you but when quarantine is over I may only write three letters to you every two weeks. Would that be satisfactory with you, ma chérie? That's French, you know.

Have fun, Honey, G'bye.
With a looong kiss
Chuck

◙ ◙ ◙

August 3, 1945

Dearest Betsy,

Hi, Honey! I am now a citizen at Sandstone. At about 10 A.M. we seven fish appeared one at a time before the Classification Committee (Warden, Associate Warden, Parole Officer, Doctor, and Education Director). My interview was short and sweet with the Warden doing the talking. He said I would be in minimum custody, that I would be entitled to all privileges "as long as I behave myself," suggested that I take some kind of advanced schooling, said I would work on Labor 1, the crew preparing the grounds for the new cow barn. He asked if I had any questions. I said, "No,"and that was all. Then we went back, got our stuff, and moved to new quarters.

Ike and I were moved into G2 with the other COs. It has been good to meet the boys, sort of like old times.

Though I was doing easy time in quarantine, getting in some good reading, etc., it does seem freer to be out wandering around in the evening. My bed is on the west side as I had hoped and gives a good view of the sunset off across the river. Tonight I watched the ball game from behind the backstop. It seemed so different from watching it from my cell where all the players looked little and inefficient and where the high bar looked so easy that I'd have sworn I could do anything the other boys did. And yet I tried today and couldn't do even the easiest things. Dormitory life is sort of a drug. The process of being a social animal somewhat excludes thinking, studying, etc., especially for an undisciplined person like me.

I wrote a letter to the Warden yesterday requesting special permission to put Lucille on my list. I quote one paragraph:

> Undoubtedly many run-of-the-mill convicts regard lightly the sacredness of the marriage vows but I trust that the COs have always demonstrated attitudes in this matter that are quite exemplary. In my own case it is quite ludicrous to imagine that my affection could be transferred from a very attractive, 22-year-old, red-headed wife [that's you, Honey] whom I love very much, to a fat, 45-year-old social worker who is almost like a mother to me. COs may be crazy but they aren't that crazy.

So we'll see what happens.

About the problem which you proposed, Betsy, I don't know what to say. Frankly, I don't believe a visit from you would make me do either harder or easier time. If it would have any such effect I can't anticipate it now. So all that I can suggest is that you make the decision. Is that unfair, Honey? From the tone of your letter I'd guess that you feel you might do harder time if you visited. Maybe it would be a good idea if you waited. After all, I may be here for a few years. There's lots of time still. (The boys are singing some of the old radical songs and I can't concentrate on this letter very well. It's in honor of one of the boys who leaves tomorrow on parole to a hospital in Chicago—who says it can't happen here?)

I read a book on the Ozarks yesterday, all about their customs, superstitions, traditions, etc. One line that particularly caught my eye was where a fellow explained a birthmark by saying that his mother had been scared by a "Betsy bug." Do you suppose our children will suffer that way?

Guess I'd better sign off, Honey. I can't concentrate on this anyway in this bedlam. I love you lots and lots, Baby. Mom's going to send me a picture of you—that will be swell.

Your lovin' husbin,
Chuck

P.S. Hope I didn't forget anything important.

◙ ◙ ◙

August 8, 1945

Dearest Betsy,

Hello, Sweetheart, Cómo estás, Querida?

I am sitting in the day room in G2, my new home. Across from me, Bill, a former math professor at Iowa University, is writing to his wife. Ike and Everett, both CPS walkouts, are playing a game of chess. Rocky and Keith, a couple more COs, are arguing about atomic force. The radio is adding its bit to the general confusion. It is just getting dark. Tonight's sunset was one of the most unusual I have ever seen. There were no bright colored clouds, but the sun itself was a most beautiful, brilliant red.

Well, I'm one of the boys now, on Labor 1, at present digging the ditch for a cow-barn foundation. From about 8 to 3:40 I am on the business end of an idiot stick (shovel). The cow barn is being built about a half-mile from the prison. We ride to and from work, about 25 men standing up in a dump truck with sides about 16 inches high. It is one of the most stupid ways of transporting men I have ever seen. At Tucson we'd have had a month's goodtime shot if we had ever taken such chances.

Before we leave the walls and after we return we are "frisked" to prevent smuggling anything in or out (I guess). Just east of our cow barn is a big flock of bronze turkeys, and to the northwest, a big bunch of Chester White hogs. Some of the boys on the job have watches, but those of us who don't can keep track of time by the train that goes through Sandstone at 10:10.

My reaction to this work is, as I feared, rather unpleasant. I can't seem to get in the mood to appreciate rendering slave labor to a system for which I have little respect. I think sometimes of *The Prophet*'s statement, that "it is better to beg alms by the wayside than to work with bitterness in one's heart." Here, of course, the alternative is not begging alms but doing time in "Duffy's Flats," the hole to you. Maybe my reaction is the natural, unpleasant feeling caused by doing hard work when one's muscles are soft from inaction. Well, we'll give it a try and see.

Lots of talk has been stirred up by this atomic bomb business. The whole idea seems so ghastly as to be impossible to me, but most of the talk centers around the idea that the war may be over soon. What's "civilization" coming to, Honey? Do you think the Ozarks are sufficiently isolated to enable people to live sensibly?

Your letter was very newsy and interesting. Regarding your question about pictures. I think it is a good idea to have them sent through you. Please send the one of my wife immediately if not quicker. I'm allowed two pictures in August and in every other month. (Mom sent two in July.)

I'm reading Aldous Huxley's *Brave New World*—just finished it, in fact, and found it quite enjoyable. But the theme could have been more convincingly presented—i.e., that pleasure alone isn't worth living for.

My goodness, I wish I shared Emma's opinion of me. It would be wonderful, especially if I honestly believed it. If you haven't sent the Round Robin on yet (for shame), include my love to all the gang. If you should ever become a lady of leisure, you could include longer quotations from such letters. I'd truly enjoy that.

Incidentally, Betsy, when your address changes, please let me know sometime in advance what it will be so our correspondence won't be interrupted.

Got a letter from the Warden tonight denying my request to have Lucille put on my correspondence list.

Hatch and I went on a five-mile hike around the compound to-night. It was a good feeling. Hope you are in good hiking trim when I get out so I won't feel that you are being drug along when we go on a long, long hike.

Tomorrow night six or eight of us are to meet to get a small chorus started. Funny thing, in quarantine we had too much solitude and here in the dorm we don't have any. However, there are a dozen or more COs here that are truly kindred spirits and it is wonderful to get acquainted with them.

I love you lots, and lots, and lots, Honey. Have fun and live fully.
Chuck

◙ ◙ ◙

August 10, 1945

Hi Betsy,

How's my gal?

Mom sent me a picture of you yesterday—an enlargement of the shot your dad took of us on the front porch. Looks real swell on my desk. With the picture were letters, one from Mom and one from my wife at Scattergood Friends School. Tsch, tsch, tsch, such a sissy, getting all sore from picking a few beans! I hadn't intended to write to you until Sunday but my list of correspondents still hasn't been approved. Guess I'll have to drop the Parole Officer a note to see what the trouble is.

Tuesday I got another memo from the Warden, this time denying the permission for Mom and Pop (Ross) to visit this month. The reason given was the same as that for refusing Lucille on my correspondence list—no exceptions can be made to the rules regardless of the situation involved. It's about like arguing that since a few persons are dangerous criminals the whole population should be locked up in prison. Though a regulation may actually apply to only one percent of the inmate population, it is "only fair" that it be applied indiscriminately to all 100%.

Today was the first time I've really enjoyed rain for a long time. It drizzled all morning but the only benefit then was that we didn't

get overheated on the job. But this afternoon the drizzle increased
to a mild rain and after sitting in a little shack for about an hour we
were finally brought back to the joint. So I checked out a couple new
books—*Dragon's Teeth* by Upton Sinclair, and *Not So Deep as a Well*
by Dorothy Parker.

Wednesday night a small group of us COs met in the auditorium
for choir practice. Bill Berg, the mathematician, is our pianist, and
is he good! For about an hour he played for us—Bach, Beethoven,
Brahms, etc. Gee, it was wonderful. I've never enjoyed music as
much—out of this world. Then we tried singing a few numbers,
"Nut Brown Maiden," "The Bulldog on the Bank," and a few others.
It was fun.

The buzz that followed the atomic bomb has turned to quite a
rumble here in camp. Nearly every day some wag rushes into the
dorm and announces that the war is all over . . . all over the Pacific.
One of the latest gags (in ridicule of Executive Order 8641 and
parole) is that all the COs are now going to be paroled on 8642. You
should have heard Hutch take on in response to President Roosevelt's
statement that the atomic bomb was a gift from God to be used for
his purposes, etc. Sometimes some of these guys get off some pretty
good ones.

My feeling of rebellion to the system here continues. Frankly,
I think I'd have greater peace if I were to discontinue any further
cooperation, but I'm not ready for that position yet and will have to
do lots more thinking about it, unless, of course, some incident pre-
cipitates things. Maybe this attitude is only a passing stage. Maybe
it is just a normal reaction when a person who loves democracy and
freedom comes up against a totalitarian regime.

Yes, I guess I'll be glad when you are settled down so we can
discuss things together, but just the same I'm very happy about
the experience you are getting now. Don't you think we'll be more
kindred spirits for the experiences you are having now? Once you
said that you'd like to be learning some skills that would be handy
in subsistence living. One thing we'll surely have to know, Honey,
is how to preserve food of various kinds. Food is one of the things
most essential to life. If necessary, a guy can sit on the floor and eat
with his fingers, but there's lots to learn about laying up food for the

winter—cold-packing meat, canning vegetables, all that sort of thing. And that is one thing I know nothing about.

Ike and I have been having a discussion on whether or not a person can be free and be married, too. His opinion is colored, I think, by an experience he had with a gal just before going to CPS. She was apparently quite exacting in her demands. I've maintained that if you agree to respect each other's personalities, to be absolutely honest with each other, to be unselfish in your relationships, that marriage and freedom are possible at the same time, and overlap considerably. Don't know whether I'll be able to sell him on the idea or not.

It's still a little hard for me to concentrate any attention to a letter with so much competition here in the dorm, so this letter may not make much sense. Will try to do better, especially when we have more to discuss.

I love you, Sweetheart.
Chuck

◙ ◙ ◙

August 15, 1945

Dear Betsy,

Well, the war is over. We have a radio in our dorm and we're always in touch with the latest developments. Last night the steam whistle in town kept up a hideous wail until late at night. Right after the lights went out, when everything was quiet, the town whistle began to moan low and mournful. It sounded exactly like an old tom cat tuning up in the alley. Suddenly one of the boys meowed back. Everyone roared.

Oh, we were in high spirits. I had intended to write to you last night but it was lovely outdoors, and the sunset was so beautiful. Several of us walked round and round the yard, talking, planning, joking. Nearly all of the fellows think we will be out soon. Whether or not we are depends, I think, on how much public pressure is brought to bear on the administration (the President). There is, of course, no logical reason for keeping Selective Service cases in prison now that the war is over, but I greatly fear that the administration's concern for unemployment may work against it. When your caravan is over, why don't you inquire of the Fellowship of Reconciliation, the War Resisters League, etc., as to the most effective way to bring pressure for our release and see what you can do. Right now I am quite strongly opposed to anything less than an unconditional release. It would irk me no end to have to make reports to a Parole Officer, be confined to one district, etc. What I'd like to do when released is take a prolonged honeymoon with my honey, not put my poor little pug nose to any grindstones.

Gee, this has been a lovely day, bright and warm with gorgeous white clouds flying over. Our crew is working right near the institution digging a ditch for a pipeline out to the cattle barn. The ditch is to be six feet wide and about ten feet deep. Quite a project. It would be a wonderful thing if my heart were in it, but the disaffection I mentioned in my last letter continues. So much so, in fact, that I can't help but feel that there will have to be a parting of the ways soon. Among the causes for this feeling are: 1) The fact that it is slave labor rendered to the same system that holds me a prisoner, 2) The fact that the work is so insignificant when one burns with a desire to really benefit humanity, and 3) I'm sure I could use my time more pleasantly and valuably in study (it's a part of the Bureau of Prisons' stupid system of applying the same treatment to every inmate—so much labor for everyone, so many letters for everyone, pacifists bound to regulations intended for murderers, murderers bound to regulations intended for pacifists, etc., ad infinitum).

If I should refuse to work, one of these days I will undoubtedly be put in the hole. If I am put in the hole my privileges will, no doubt, be suspended, in which case I'll probably go on a hunger strike until the following conditions are provided: 1) Full meals the same as everyone else, 2) Full library privileges, 3) Full correspondence privileges, 4) A bed or mattress all day, not just a few hours at night, and 5) At least an hour outside of the cell each day for exercise. Wish I could get your reaction to this matter, also to my feelings about parole, etc., but I realize how hard that is right now. Anyway, if you don't get any letters for some time you'll know the reason. But don't worry about it because I'll be okay. For some reason or other the Bureau of Prisons jealously guards the physical well-being of its charges.

The boys in our dorm got up a petition to get a Negro CO transferred in with us. Who do you think refused to sign it—one Nazi and one CO!

I'm not so sure what your chances are for a job in some liberal movement now, though the unemployment may not affect the labor market in that particular field as much as in others.

Wish we had our little farm bought now as there are possibilities of our little nest egg being greatly diminished by a general inflation. But guess there's nothing we can do about it. Especially since a decision as to where we settle is too important to be decided by one of us.

Haven't had but one letter from your folks and it came through Mom. Wonder where they are and what they are doing. My correspondence list still hasn't been approved, dad gummit! Our camp semanticist got a big kick out of your remark that Arthur Evans has trouble expressing himself.

Goodbye, lots of love,
Chuck

◘ ◘ ◘

August 30, 1945

Dear Betsy,

How are you all? Gee it must be wonderful to be home again resting up, eating, and catching up on all the gossip. How does it seem? Wish I could help you enjoy some of that cooking. I told the folks Sunday that I was putting on weight and to prove it went up Monday to get weighed. All my clothes and a full stomach couldn't put the pointer past 133. They have had pears and peaches in the commissary lately and they really taste wonderful. Would you believe it, I've squandered $7 already on commissary stuff. Isn't that awful? For a subsistence liver? Guess I'll swear off for awhile.

As you know, Mom and Pop were here Sunday. We had a good visit. I'm glad you decided to come up alone though. I was quite surprised when an officer told me I had visitors since I hadn't expected them until next Sunday. They can tell you all about the visiting conditions so there is no use of repeating that. The folks still think there is a technicality on which I might get out of this joint. I really don't think there is but I promised to write to a very capable and sympathetic lawyer in Chicago about the case. Tell the folks that I've decided to write direct rather than have them forward the letter as we had planned. The folks also said you had sent instructions to refrain from any drastic action until you came up, so naturally that's what I will do. Though I really hadn't made any specific plans yet.

Lately, a few of us have been thinking about ways to get out, and about 20 of the boys in G2, myself included, asked for one of the forms provided for the purpose of applying for a presidential pardon. We feel that every legal means should be exhausted before any direct action is taken to attract public attention to the situation. The application for pardon has a place for signatures, so as soon as I have filled it out I will send it to you for signers (provided I am permitted to do so).

I've been trying to get the JWs interested in applying for pardons, but of course they couldn't think of doing anything like that without first consulting Jehovah through his official representative in the Watch Tower Bible and Tract Society. So I hope Jehovah gets on the ball pretty soon. It's going to take pressure from both inside and outside of prison to get anything accomplished. Incidentally, anything folks do now to oppose the idea of peacetime conscription would help out in the long run, I think.

I have a book on carpentry now but can't seem to find much time to study it. I'm sure I could do a much better job of rehabilitating myself than the government is doing. Today ten of us from Slavery 1 shoveled coal. Just what good, I asked myself, does it do either society or number 2473 to have the latter shoveling coal, or digging a ditch, or digging out for the foundation for a cow barn?

Bill Berg was talking to me tonight about the idea of settling in Canada. You know Lin Brown, a peace-caravan buddy of mine, suggested the same idea. We certainly owe it to ourselves to travel around some before we ever settle down in one spot—another reason why I'm not interested in anything as restrictive as parole. I've been thinking that if the weather is agreeable, the thing I'd like to do most upon release from prison is spend about a month in a cabin up in the mountains with my wife and a few books so we could think and plan and get acquainted again. What do you think of the idea?

We've been having weekly shows lately and every one deepens my conviction that our civilization isn't worth saving. The movies provide wonderful illustrations of the sensuality, the materialism, the disintegration of our civilization. Aimlessness in Technicolor.

Nearly every time Hutch sits on my bed and sees that picture of you he remarks that he can't understand how a guy like me ever rated anything like that. So then I have to tell him about my sparkling personality, my sterling character, my good looks, etc. Bill has been worrying himself and me lately about this taxation business. You know, we'll still be paying the price of this war a long time from now. I think the solution is to make too little money to pay taxes. What do you think?

I've nearly forgotten what it's like to have a wife, but I still think it's a great idea. I love you, Honey. Give my regards to all the folks in Omaha. I'm returning herewith a hug and kisses for those you sent in your last letter.

Chuck

◘ ◘ ◘

September 13, 1945

Dear Betsy,

Yes, indubitably you are still my most favoritest wife. Your visit tended to remind me how much I miss you, what an important part of my life you are. Though I must confess that I didn't seem as near to you as I did when we parted last June. Intellectually we may be closer now, but that feeling of oneness is something that is best maintained by practice—at least so it seems to me.

One of my first impressions when I saw you through the gate was—how tall she is. It must be that I recall best your height as you went bustling about in your mukluks. And then I was surprised all over again how blue your eyes were and how golden your hair—as bright-colored as a flower. The picture I have of you is very nice, but after all, it is only black and white. To their great envy I showed the fellows that little smudge of lipstick on my handkerchief. Anyway, I'm glad you came, Honey. For a while (about two hours) I sort of floated around without touching the ground, but I haven't done any hard time, and it made me feel good to see your spirits so high. Incidentally, you literally took our sunshine away when you left. About two hours later a big, black storm blew up in the west and it has been cold and cloudy ever since.

I'm really very pleased with your intention to acquire ideas and skills for subsistence farming, community pioneering. Hope you are able to find a place that meets the requirements. After all, if you want to show poor people a way they can follow, you just about have to start from the same place they'll have to start from. Cooperation wouldn't be easily secured without others if we were living on one standard and they on another. Also, I know that I'd enjoy comfort more if it required a little effort, a little discomfort to secure it.

This week has been a busy one, the air in G2 is charged with electricity. We reprobates have been making our battle plans, drawing up a statement, etc. The statement should be ready to release Monday. I'll send you a copy, or try to, and you may relay it to one of the two parties mentioned. These days have reminded me lots of our pre-AWOL days—the same joking, planning, laughing, etc. I'm happy that our group has discovered a unanimity I hadn't expected.

Mal and I are still digging our ditch—the same one. Mal is naturally a vigorous, robust person, but his heart makes a peculiar design on a cardiograph so he was ordered to "take it easy." Of course, if he is downstairs throwing up the dirt I can't throw it away any faster than I get it. It's a dirty shame—deprives me of a part of my "privilege," as it were.

Under separate cover I am sending you today my "application for executive clemency." Only two signatures are necessary but you may get as many as you wish. Don't spend too much time on it, however, as I'd rather like to have it in the Attorney General's office before Oct. 1. Complete instructions are on the reverse side of page one and on the bottom of page seven.

Since you jilted Ike, he has gone from bad to worse. Now he has another picture on his desk—a jitterbug gal with her skirts twirled high above her knees. Poor fellow, I feel sorry for him.

A note to the Warden about magazines revealed that they have been coming but have been refused at the post office, though no one bothered to mention that fact to me. The regulation is so unreasonable that I am preparing a note to the Warden and if no results are obtained I shall write to the Director of the Bureau of Prisons.

Despite our frustrations, a little piece of heaven occasionally falls our way—a fresh peach purchased in the commissary, a wild aster sparkling with dew, a steaming ear of sweet corn smuggled into the working hours, a Brahms or Beethoven opus given during our choral practice. Yes, life has loveliness to sell. You're a part of it to me.

Lots of love, Sweetheart.

Chuck

◙ ◙ ◙

September 18, 1945

My Dear Wife,

Hello, Honey. What are you doing nowadays? My, this has been an interesting week. Sunday we five reprobates finally got together a statement which satisfied all of us—quite a job! And Monday night mailed copies to Tom C. Clark, Attorney General; the Director of the Bureau of Prisons; and Warden G.W. Humphrey.

Getting the letters off was like lifting a big weight off my shoulders. I felt about the same freedom of spirit as when I left CPS back in California. To the thousands of wise things that have been said of freedom, I have conceived the following: The way to secure freedom is to stop being a slave. Now that the die is cast it seems so silly that all this time I should have been rendering slave labor for the stupid system that unjustly imprisoned me. I think even Mom got the idea because in her last letter she said, very cleverly, "Crying out loud, how long does that cow ditch have to be? Think how much good you fellows could do if you were free. The stupid slavery gets me more every day. Looks like you fellows more or less do the work around there to keep things going." Ain't that a b---h. The letter reads as follows:

Hon. Tom C. Clark
Attorney General
Washington, DC

Dear Sir:

We, the undersigned, being held prisoners at the Federal Correctional Institution at Sandstone, Minnesota, are conscientiously opposed to working in cooperation with the Federal Prison System for the following reasons:

We believe that the government is unjustified in imprisoning conscientious objectors to war since such imprisonment is a denial of every person's right to freedom of conscience.

We believe further that the Federal Prison System is detrimental to society in that it tends to destroy the character and personality of inmates, and to develop anti-social attitudes. It does this through unnecessary restrictions, authoritarian control, and the lack of any truly rehabilitative program.

As an expression of these beliefs we are going to discontinue working for the Federal Prison System on the morning of October 1, 1945. It is our belief that we should not be penalized for taking this course of action. However, should unduly restrictive or punitive measures be resorted to by the prison authorities as a consequence of our action, we then intend immediately to commence fasting as a protest against such retributive punishment. In this we will act as a group, and as individuals we will decline to discuss the matter with prison authorities, although we will always be willing to do so as a group.

Signed,
Parker, Hutchinson, Worley, Adamowicz, Gormly

Others of the fellows are talking along lines that indicate we may have company soon. Would you make a few carbon copies of this statement and send them to the most interested persons: A.J., Evan Thomas, Bill S., Frank and Marie, Lucille, Paul, and any others you wish. Looks like this will be the only letter I'll be able to write this week as I have just been swindled out of two letter privileges. The way it happened, I think, is that my recent letters have gone further than the censor and were held over past the week they were mailed, and they were counted for the week the prison mailed them rather than for the week when I mailed them. It's a dirty deal, but what can one do about it? There are innumerable examples of such petty stinkiness, but I think our general indictment of the FPS covers them all.

Betsy, I saw a copy of the *Roadrunner* Sunday. There were lots of familiar names including a write-up of my friend John Dinning, who was expected to be released July 24. Would you please write to him for me, congratulate him on the release, and tell him the latest developments in my situation. His address is in my little black address book, same as Dick's. Mal and I have been in such high spirits thinking of October 1 (O1 day) that we spent today composing limericks about other COs (red hots that for various reasons didn't go along with us), such as:

> A federal "con" named Roodenko,
> Sent the powers that be this memento,
> Though I'm still in the clink
> I prefer that you think
> That I'm really muy mucho contento.

> A cue ball domed, gold brick named Ike
> Said, "I wouldn't even think of strike.
> My job is so fittin',
> I do it all sittin'
> Making calluses just where I like."

And we made up a really classy one about our doctor of math, Bill Berg, but a person has to be a mathematician to read it.

Mom says Pop has been writing letters to congressmen to get me out. I'm quite proud of the folks. The pacifist organizations have had one interview with Tom Clark and are hard at it.

Am eager to know what you are doing and how your plans are coming along. You are still permitted to write twice a week if you wish to.

I love you, Honey, g'night Sweetheart,
Chuck

◉ ◉ ◉

September 23, 1945 [No. 1]

Dearest Betsy,

Well, Honey, this has certainly been an interesting past week, all full of new experiences, a fact of which you may have had some inkling by this time. Maybe I should start at the beginning to give you a complete picture. Wednesday morning Malcolm and I were selected in a group of five from Labor 1 to carry coke into the homes of officers living here at the institution. Learning immediately what the job was to be, we asked the officer in charge of our crew if he would assign others to that job since we felt it wrong for prisoners of the State to perform labor for the exclusive benefit of private individuals. The officer then assigned others to the job but stated that he would have to "write us up" for disciplinary action, and we went back to work on our ditch. At noon we were given passes notifying us to report to the Associate Warden's office, where the disciplinary court meets.

In court I was charged with refusing to carry coke into the officers' homes, and we had some discussion about why it was wrong. The officers apparently feel that since the houses are a part of the institution property they are justified in using inmate labor in their maintenance. Whereas I agree that a certain amount of maintenance is justified, just as any renter of a home may expect the same, I think it wrong to use this free labor as a personal servant—to tend their lawns and gardens, fix their furnaces, carry in their coal, etc., as is done here. I was removed from court while they (Associate Warden, a captain, and the doctor) deliberated, and then I was called back and given the alternatives to hauling coke or having disciplinary action taken against me. My reply was that I still declined to do work which I felt was wrong, so I was taken up to the hole and Mal went into court.

Before entering the hole, I was given a pair of coveralls in place of pants and shirt, and a pair of cloth slippers in place of shoes. The hole is a small room, six feet by nine feet, in the quarantine cell block. There were no furnishings except a toilet, a wash bowl, a steam register, a window, and a Bible. A few minutes later Mal was brought up and put in another cell. That was about 1:30 Wednesday afternoon. Frankly, I was surprised at their action since we had not refused to work, but had quietly and courteously asked not to be assigned to that job.

That night we were given two cooked potatoes and four slices of white bread for supper. I ate most of my supper though Mal refused, and thereafter we both refused to eat until we were finally released Saturday and had our regular supper in the dining hall.

But that is only half of the story. Fourteen of our fellow COs in G2 felt that since they would also have to refuse such service, they were as morally guilty as we, and the next day at noon we saw the whole gang of them trooping into the office for interviews with the Associate Warden. Of course, Mal and I missed most of the excitement: the dormitory discussions of what to do, the interviews, etc., but the next morning (Friday), shortly after morning work call, we saw two lieutenants depart for G2 and return in a few minutes with one of the boys who had refused to go to work in protest to our continued confinement. We didn't see them come back out and a few minutes later faintly heard them shouting at us through the ventilator from upstairs cells in the quarantine section. They were allowed beds, however, and gradually received more privileges: correspondence, one hour of exercise, and full meals, though four of them fasted in sympathy with Mal and me. In the meantime, four other fellows were also fasting, marching past the chow line with empty trays. The results were quite electrifying. The whole prison seemed to be interested in the matter.

Well, Saturday afternoon Mal and I were called again before court (separately, of course). I was asked if I wished to go back to work, to which I said, "Yes," with the qualification that I'd still have to decline any job to which I was conscientiously opposed. I was released and instructed to go to work Monday. A few minutes later Mal joined me. Great indeed was the rejoicing, and from those who had interviews I've been led to believe that persons having objections to such personal service will no longer to asked to perform it. Though our buddies are still in segregation, we all agreed to call off the hunger strike and give the authorities a reasonable time to release them.

It certainly felt good to eat again; three days isn't as bad as one might suppose. I did feel a little weak in the knees, however, and could easily notice the loss of flesh on my cheeks and ribs.

Our cells were rather cool and we had nothing but the cold cement to lie on except from 10 P.M. to 5 A.M. when we were given a mattress and three blankets. I have never appreciated a Bible so much—during the day it served as both chair and pillow—I even read a few books in the New Testament. I think the cold caused me more discomfort than the lack of food, though on the last day I had even adjusted to that pretty well. The doctor came up every day to see how we were and an officer would look in on us every two hours or so. It's funny how they want to punish you but don't want to punish you too much. It's also strange how free one feels when he is detached from his bodily comfort enough so that it can't be used as a club over his head. Mal even refused mattress and blankets. Guess I'll have to discuss the October 1 deal in another letter, so hold on for a minute.

Chuck

▣ ▣ ▣

September 23, 1945 [No. 2]

Dear Wifey,

Saturday night I got four letters in one shot—two from you and one from each mom. I may not get letters to the moms sent this week because Paul's name has been added to my list and I'd like to write him. If you'll share your letters with both sets of folks maybe they won't mind too much.

Well, Betsy, I'd be much more surprised if you did completely understand our October 1 (O1) plans than I am by the fact that you don't. The situation was the same as when I left CPS; nearly all of my very dear friends failed to get the idea. Even Frank and Marie, I think, felt it was probably due to bad personal adjustment, or maybe to feelings of persecution. Bill and Scud Hollister sent word for me to not attack too many windmills. Lucille thought prison was "so nega-tive," etc. It almost shattered my own faith in the idea, though time has, for myself at least, completely vindicated the position.

Now, regarding the O1 idea. In the first place, no one who has never been to prison has anything but a very distorted or confused idea of what it is like or how it works. In the second place, it took me two years to arrive at my present position. One can hardly appreciate some idea which he hasn't arrived at himself.

I hope you have received a copy of our statement by now. It was included in my letter of last Tuesday. The statement is so simple and direct, however, that it may not satisfy those who want to understand. Even so, anything I might say would only be an enlargement on the two main ideas therein presented. The first point—that the government is unjustified in imprisoning COs because it is a denial of their right to freedom of conscience—pretty well summarizes the things we have always felt along that line: it violates our constitutional guarantees, doesn't permit religious freedom, is inconsistent with democracy, etc. The second point (i.e., that the prison system is detrimental to society in that it tends to destroy character through unnecessary restrictions, authoritarian control, and lack of a truly rehabilitative program) covers even a greater multiplicity of sins. So much so, in fact, that it is probably meaningless to persons who don't see the specific referents. A list of such referents could be made very, very long, as you probably realize from some of the incidents I've told you from my experience in Tucson. It would include such things as:

- Making your bed a certain way.
- Your desk has to be a certain way: a) no more than two books, b) pictures only of a certain size, c) standard picture frames, and d) towels placed in a particular a way.
- Walking on the sidewalk to meals, not straggling.
- Receiving magazines only through commissary; books same way.
- Walking in a column of twos in going to work.
- Taking showers at certain times.
- Every man doing so many hours of similar work regardless of his personal needs.
- Certain ways of addressing officers.

– How often you should shave.

– Etc., etc., ad infinitum.

All of which are little things in themselves but which add up
to regimentation, training for slaves, not free men. And God alone
knows how many petty regulations there are that I've never heard
of or can't think of at the moment.

Why the work becomes the object of attack is rather obvious,
I think. By the work we do we are actually helping and strengthening and perpetuating the government's "right" to imprison us, and
doing the same for a system which we regard as generally detrimental to the inmates, and thus, to society. I think anyone who knows
me personally will agree, also, that I can use my time more valuably
studying than digging dirt 42 hours a week. Not only is my shoveling of little use to the institution, but my future contribution to
society can be increased if I can study things relative to my future
plans.

One thing that confuses folks is that they think objecting to
something is just negative. But whenever we say "No" to one thing,
we say "Yes" to something else. If we O1'ers are not permitted to
use our time more constructively than we would on a work project,
it will be the administration's fault, not ours.

Don't know whether this will help you understand better or
not. First attempts at such explanation are never too good. I suppose, to an outsider, it seems more heroic for a CO in prison to
play the role of the noble martyr, to march proudly and meekly to
his fate, head high with a prayer on his lips. But I have no desire to
be a martyr. I just want to live my own life in peace, and express
my own personality, and do what seems right to me.

Not much space left for personal items is there? I enjoyed
Mammy's letter on religion, etc. We need a good bull session. The
dinner with the folks sounds like I should have been there. Roger
is apparently a true Worley from the way he likes food. Karen is
not—she thought school should be work not just a lot of play—
unheard of. Betsy, I have already read *Interlinear to Cabeza de
Vaca*. It doesn't conflict with anything I believe. Undoubtedly, great
physical cures can be wrought by psychological effects. No wonder

Phyl enjoys astronomy. She probably never noticed that there were stars when she was out with Austin.

G'bye, Honey. I love you lots. Every time I see these superficial movies ("Tonight and Every Night" today), I love you more for being so real and solid.

Life is interesting, especially if one gives his conscience a chance.
Chuck

◙ ◙ ◙

September 30, 1945

My very dear wife,

Hello, Honey. It's a typical Sunday afternoon here at Sandstone Federal Correction Institution. In the day room the amplifier renders the NBC symphony. The boys have just come back from today's movie and speak very highly of it: "A Song to Remember," based on the life of Chopin. I was scheduled to play softball with an FCI team opposing Sandstone village but the game didn't materialize. I'll see the movie tonight and spend the evening celebrating October 1 (O1) with the boys. Nestlé bars will probably be liberally consumed in the process. There is a good bunch of fellows here and I'll miss them. But unless something very definite develops from this October meeting with the Attorney General, there will undoubtedly be several of our friends joining us after that time.

This past week has been rather enjoyable with lots of joking about how "short" Mal and I were getting. On Slavery I an attitude of carefree indifference generally prevailed—there was lots of horse-play, lots of gold-bricking, and corn roasting. And the boss didn't seem greatly concerned. The officer in charge of the cell house where our seven friends (those who stopped work protesting Mal's and my punishment) are still maintained is a very friendly fellow and we have been joking with him about O1 day. He said today that it ought to be called "CO1 day."

I'm very happy that there has been so little tension and personal feeling in this matter. Think I'll try to write a suitable note to the Warden assuring him that I have no personal ill will against any of the officials here, but appreciate that they have always been gentlemen toward me. Of course we really don't know what to expect tomorrow—it could be anything. But we hopefully expect "Administrative Segregation" rather than "the hole," and living conditions reasonable enough to make a hunger strike unnecessary: full meals, adequate exercise, full reading and writing privileges. Also hope that you all will use your influence with the Warden and Director of U.S. Bureau of Prisons to secure these essentials to physical and mental health, if necessary.

Have any of you written to the Attorney General or Nebraska senators and representatives urging freedom for COs in prison? I got a reply from Sen. Kenneth Wherry Thursday, as follows:

> Just a line to acknowledge your recent letter. Have been in touch with the proper authorities but as yet have nothing definite to report. Please rest assured that I will do what I can and will keep you advised. Appreciating the opportunity of at least trying to serve you, I remain, etc.

Might pay for someone to follow up. And if a decision is due from the Attorney General in October, now seems to me like the appropriate time for letters. The application for executive clemency entails so much red tape that it won't come to the attention of the big shots for a long time yet. Incidentally, looks to me like you did a swell job on the application for E.C. Youse a good wife. I'sa fond of you. Very much so.

Just got back from "A Song to Remember." It's wonderful. Bill has played so much of the music for us that it meant more to me. This one show was more worth seeing than all the others combined. A fitting conclusion to my "movie privilege."

The boys are getting ready for a little going-away party for Mal and me. I'll miss this dorm but maybe I can recapture some of my visual images of you for company. Incidentally, Sweetheart, you'd better have *The Christian Century* and *Fellowship* magazine transferred to your address as I'll have very little power to get them admitted to me after tomorrow, and someone might as well get some good out of them. Since we may not be permitted any newspapers or magazines (as the boys are not at present), you may be my only news source. Why don't you subscribe to *The C.O.* and keep me in touch with things?

I'm more thankful every day that there is a part of me still at large. I love you, Betsy, and am very glad to know that you are with me in spirit in future developments.

Got a letter from Paul the other day. Our letters must have passed somewhere in the Rockies. Frank and Marie are still unapproved but their letter to the Warden may get results. Folks on the outside can do more than we can in here.

Do you think the *Omaha World-Herald* would be interested in our statement as a follow-up story on my case? Mammy might have some idea on the effect of such a story and whether it could be arranged. My idea is that folks should be reminded of the fact that there are some 3,500 war victims imprisoned in "the land of the free and the home of the brave." You should see my hair, Honey. I should do easy time for six months because I could never return to my wife like this—hair ½ inch long. Thought I might as well dress my role.

Made a list of books but didn't see any I thought we should read together. Part of my aim was to select big ones as we are permitted (under present rules) only two each week. My own reading will probably be very diversified—poetry, philosophy, sociology, agriculture, etc., and alternate fiction and non-fiction. Think I'll start on Tolstoy's *War and Peace.* Am getting the urge to try some writing. Hope it will be possible.

G'bye, Sweetheart. Hope I hear from you next week because if I don't, I'll probably be very hungry. Love to our folks and friends, but something more to you.

Chuck

◙ ◙ ◙

October 2, 1945

Hi Sweetie Pie!

You have no idea how happy I am to be able to write to you. Do you want the whole story? Well, yesterday morning Mal and I stayed in the dorm at work call and a few minutes later an officer came over and asked if we were not going to work. Assured that we weren't, he then said, "Then come along with me." Gathering together our personal property, we did—over to C2 where the other boys were. As you can see I was permitted to keep my newly purchased fountain pen, also sanitary facilities. Blankets, sheets, soap, towels were brought in, and shortly later, 9:30–10:30, we were reunited with the other incorrigibles in our morning exercise period.

Right after dinner Mal and I were taken to court. My case went somewhat as follows:

> Mr. Madigan (Associate Warden): "Worley, I have here a disciplinary report on you which I shall read, 'This morning the above-named inmate refused to come out of the dormitory for work.' Is that correct?"
>
> Worley: "Yes."
>
> Mr. Madigan: "Why did you do that?"
>
> Worley: "You have probably read the statement to the Warden, which I signed. I really have nothing to say in addition to that."
>
> Mr. Madigan: "No, I haven't read it. I'd like to hear your reasons."
>
> Worley: "Well, very briefly, they are two. First, I believe that I have been wrongly imprisoned and I do not wish to cooperate with that wrong by working for the system that enforces it. Second, I believe that prison, itself, is an undesirable institution in that it tends to destroy character and does not rehabilitate men, that it is not worthy of my services."
>
> Mr. Madigan: "Do you have anything to say, Lieutenant?"
>
> Lieutenant: "No! It's obviously the same hashed-up business that Parker talked about, and there's no use in going into all that again."
>
> Mr. Madigan: "Do you have anything, Doctor?"
>
> Doctor: "No."
>
> Mr. Madigan. "Step out of the room please."

I had no more than left the room when the bugger called me back.

Mr. Madigan: "Worley, the court has decided to place you
in Administrative Segregation. You will be given your meals
and a bed. You will be allowed correspondence privileges and
will be permitted two one-hour exercise periods every day.
That is all."

I rejoined the other boys who were now taking their daily exercise period out of doors. One by one the others were called into court
and asked if they wished to return to work. The four who were in
segregation because of their protest in the coke incident apparently
agreed because they didn't return. The other three, however, were
original "O1ers" and replied in the negative. We five misfits now
maintain sole occupancy of C2. So far I would refer to our situation
as a welcome diversion. I have made a schedule of reading, writing,
and exercise. Mr. Madigan did not say we would be permitted library
privileges and so far we have not been provided paper for creative
writing (just now provided). However, if these things are not provided all five of us will be on a hunger strike very shortly. I do not question the authority to segregate us, but will never accept conditions
which would make our lives a vacant hell of boredom. However,
I expect that full writing and reading privileges will be given us.

Am reading *The Last of the Mohicans* as it was left behind by
one of the other fellows. Have drawn up a reading schedule for the
rest of this year as follows, assuming we will get a book each Tuesday
and Friday:

10/2   *Agriculture and Farm Life* (Harry Phillips,
         Edgar Cockefair, and James Graham)
10/5   *Five Acres and Independence* (Maurice Kains)
10/9   *Darkness at Noon* (Arthur Koestler)
10/12 *The Oxford Book of Light Verse* (ed. by W.H. Auden)
10/16 *Modern Poetry and the Tradition* (Cleanth Brooks)
10/19 *U.S.A.* (John Dos Passos)
         This trilogy includes: *The 42nd Parallel, 1919,*
         and *The Big Money*
10/23 *The Arts of Leisure* (Marjorie Greenbie)
10/26 *The Importance of Living* (Lin Yutang)

10/30   *Crime and Punishment* (Fyodor Dostoyevsky)
11/2   *My America, 1928–1938* (Louis Adamic)
11/6   *Middletown in Transition* (Robert S. Lynd and
        Helen Merrell Lynd)
11/9   *The Magic Mountain* (Thomas Mann)
11/13   *Freedom and Culture* (John Dewey)
11/16   *The Mansions of Philosophy* (Will Durant)
11/20   *Grey Eminence* (Aldous Huxley)
11/23   *The Future of Industrial Man* (Peter Drucker)
11/27   *The Economy of Abundance* (Stuart Chase)
11/30   *War and Peace* (Leo Tolstoy)
12/4   *Apes, Men, and Morons* (Earnest A. Hooten)
12/7   *Walden and Other Works* (Henry Thoreau)
12/11   *Anthony Adverse* (Hervey Allen)
12/14   *The Education of Henry Adams* (Henry Adams)
12/18   *On Being a Real Person* (Harry Emerson Fosdick)
12/21   *The House of Earth* (Pearl S. Buck)
12/25   *The Confessions of St. Augustine* (St. Augustine)
12/28   *The Wisdom of China and India* (Lin Yutang)

I may not be able to meet the schedule but will try, so if you want to tie in anywhere, I'll try to be there.

Got a letter last night from Sen. Kenneth Wherry, reply to him from Col. Lewis B. Hershey. The last paragraph had the Colonel, I quote, "No additional action deemed necessary . . . in the national interest as to avoid an injustice." Ain't that a b---h?

Just finished dinner: two meatballs, potatoes and gravy, buttered carrots, ketchup, four slices of raisin bread, tea.

Betsy, why don't you write to Vivian Roodenko and ask her to send you carbon copies of her letters to Igal (her brother). Then you could relay them to me and we could both keep up with the latest developments. It was Igal's idea.

Got a receipt last night showing $10 received. Did you send it? It would be a good idea to mention such things in your letters as a safety measure.

Just came in from our outdoor exercise period. I ran a mile. I think two hours of exercise plus a half hour in the cell each evening is going to be about right. Our books came from the library while we were out and I got the one first given on my list. So far I'm right on schedule. Am doing easy time, Honey. Wish you were here. Guess I'd better write to someone else this week or they'll be cutting me off.

Lots of love,
Chuck

To Betsy from Prison

Betsy, your tender charms
No longer press so firm
Upon my memory.
Your bright eyes, slender arms,
Sweet lips, endearing terms,
Endure not vividly.
But ever nearer grows
The marriage of our minds
In common loyalties.
And this, remembered, shows
Why separation finds
You still more dear to me.

◻ ◻ ◻

October 11, 1945

Hi Good lookin, wots cookin?

What do you know, I'm getting short. In prison vernacular . . . How was the conference? 'Spect I'll be getting a summary one of these days, complete in one paragraph. Funny thing how I manage to spread the nothing I do so much of every day out over so much more ink and paper than you do your unrestricted life in the free world. Guess it's just my gift of gab. Well then, let's have some small talk—mighty small.

Quite unintentionally I made the doc blush today. He sat writing in the day room as we in turn trooped out for our suppers. I was feeling easy and breezy (as I sometimes get) and, just for the h--l of it, saluted him. Then's when he reddened and said, "Oh, come now, I'm not that hard on you, am I?" I was hoping he'd ask me about the dental floss (I'd asked him for some the day before to keep clean a rather nasty crevice between two teeth). And what do you think, last night one of the officers, with all due solemnity, gave me, all properly sealed in a prescription envelope, six inches of dental floss. So I use the six inches of dental floss two or three times a day, wash it off, and hang it up to dry. Reminds me of the old gag about how Lindbergh knew when he was over Scotland.

Last night also, as we returned from taking out our dirty dishes, the same officer saw Mal pass me an envelope. Deeply wounded, as though he had just uncovered a plot to pilfer the crown jewels, he explained, "Here, what's the idea, trying to pass things! Give me that." Mal did. It contained a piece of bologna that Mal, not liking, had promised to me.

Yesterday our little family got a new addition, a "queer" who had trouble in his old home, hence was sent here for safekeeping and to act as orderly. He reports that in court it was decided they needed an orderly up here because they couldn't get any work out of those "do-right boys."

Got quite a letter from Howard Buffett the other day. I quote:

> This is to acknowledge, etc.
>
> I have been very much disturbed by the trend in this country towards a militaristic society, and I'm afraid that we may yet see ourselves the victims of the Roman victory described by St. Augustine when he said "The conquerors became ever more like those they conquered."
>
> Today for some millions of Americans the inalienable rights of "liberty and the pursuit of happiness" have been suspended. This suspension has been more severe in some cases than in others, and, of course, you are in the group who have received the most severe suspension of these rights.
>
> Without knowing more about the CO set-up, a subject on which I hope to become informed in the near future, I am not able to commit myself regarding the possibilities for solving either the problem generally or your own specific situation.

I am disturbed about it, however, and you may be sure that
I will try to become fully informed, and upon so doing take
such action as I deem appropriate.

Sincerely yours,

Of course, the last half of the letter doesn't promise much, but
the first half sounds hopeful.

I was sorta amused to hear that you are contemplating traveling 3,000 miles to go to school for one month. You must have a very
high regard for their teaching powers there. But of course it would
be a nice trip. However, you know better than I what you want to do
and I'm much in favor of your doing what you wish.

OK! OK! OK! I take it all back. Your two nice long letters just
arrived, for which I return a nice long kiss. Butler's letter is not bad.
Was also glad to get A.J.'s remarks and the official letter from the
conference. In all humility, your summary was excellent—much more
than a couple of brief paragraphs. That offer of the Moormans just
makes my mouth water. She might be a good person to keep in touch
with. We may be neighbors some day. Who knows? But for the present I'm still very much right here.

The name is Igal.

Cecil Hinshaw (finally located that name in my memory) was
one of our patron saints when Gerry and I landed in jail in Wichita,
way back in 1943.

Some of your remarks, e.g., ". . . was very relieved that the administration thought you were worthy of it (Administrative Segregation)," reveal a woeful misunderstanding of how things work in
prison. Wise up, gal.

Have been doing some more reading—*The Oxford Book of
Light Verse* and *Progress and Poverty* (again!), also a few efforts at
writing (Exhibit A below).

It occurred to me that there are lots of farm bulletins you might
find very worthwhile. (They are one of the things I'll give the government credit for.) Write to the Secretary of Agriculture, United States
Department of Agriculture, for a complete list of all bulletins. The
bulletins may be obtained free through a senator or representative.
Studying that farm book, I made a list of about 60 I'd like to have.

Goodbye, Honey. It's about time for lights out and I want to read my letters again.

Lots and lots of love,
Chuck

The Rain (for children)

I like it when it rains
And little silver rivers
Trickle down the window panes
With jerky little shivers.
I like it even when
The grumbling thunder roars.
Unless it come too close. Then
I'm a little scared, of course.
And just the very minute
I see the rain is gone
I beg and beg to go out in it
To wade around the lawn.
The mud's so cool and oozy
The air so fresh and yummy.
And when the wind blows though the trees
Drops shake down on my tummy.
I like it when it rains.

◙ ◙ ◙

October 17, 1945

Dearest Wifey,

Gosh this has been a lovely day, Sweetheart. During our afternoon exercise period the sun was too deliciously warm to be wasted by maintaining a vertical position. Assuming the horizontal against a south wall, I closed my eyes and took another hike through the Florence hills, the sumac and woodbine and elms.

The only frosty impression of the day was created by the officer in charge of us, who apparently doesn't approve of dealing genteelly with non-conformists and found it hard to hide the thought. He even "shook us down" when we came in from "yard." Why? Oh, looking for submachine guns and armored cars, I suppose. Maybe for the welfare of our post-prison life—so you will always act discreetly and walk the line with eyes averted—I should tell you about the dangerous person that I am. We five were denied salt and pepper because these items can be thrown in an officer's face, leaving him at the mercy of an assailant. And when our food is brought in it is first thoroughly examined—for death-dealing weapons, escape plots, etc., I presume. So don't go getting too independent and forget who's who in the C.V. Worley family—see?

But the officer regularly in charge of us (this was his day off) is really a swell guy, good natured and friendly, a credit to the institution. He says he gets a kick out of his five little intellectuals.

Betsy, I hope you don't get the idea that there is anything sacred about the sum 1,000. Money is only a means to an end, and that end is Abundant Living—a process that goes on today, and today, and today. And every day should be rich and creative. So don't deny yourself for a future that is always uncertain.

Latest news from the War Resisters League office, received tonight, stated that no statement has been forthcoming re: COs in prison but that something is cooking in the Attorney General's office and should be served not later than October 24.

I read the October 1 *Newsweek* the other day. The military is certainly riding high. Their suggestion for control of the atomic bomb would almost turn your stomach. As I recall, the high points were: penalty for revealing information pertaining thereto not to exceed death, governmental right to appropriate any persons or property deemed necessary to its production. And the diplomatic maneuvers with comrade Joe seem to be going just about as I expected—head on.

Yours and Mammy's letters came last night, making the evening considerably shorter. In reply to your question, we do not receive mail on Sundays. I admire your recent resolution regarding letters but won't hold you to it as it seems rather stiff.

On your suggestion, I'm working on a poem for Christmas but may have to start over since what I've started may be a little hard going for some of our friends or kin. Regarding presents, in the past the number of recipients has been determined by my material status.

In CPS and Tucson, e.g., it was greatly restricted. Some little thing to our nephews and niece would be appreciated I think, and some little personal remembrance to brothers and sisters, mothers and dads, and grandparents. But use your own judgment in the matter and don't make it too hard on yourself.

About the "Charles situation," wouldn't it solve the problem and avoid the charge of prejudice to put another, more efficient, Negro in his place—probably someone suggested by the Urban League so as to preserve their goodwill and understanding.

Maybe I shouldn't, but I'll quote an overly sentimental poem that seemed to express a mood of some days back. For the proper effect, however, it must be read slowly (musingly) with pauses in the proper places.

Sweetheart, I'm Lonely

I'm lonely tonight, Honey,
Why don't you come
In a dream . . .
In a dream . . .
Steal in softly
And turn out the light.
Then cuddle up close to me
Just for tonight
. . . for tonight.
With your head, your soft hair
On my shoulder at rest,
Your lips at my cheek,
And your arms on my chest,
My heart would stop aching,
My spirit be blessed
. . . be blessed.
Oh, Sweetheart, I'm lonely,
Come gently to me,
Come gliding to me,
Come riding a beam of the moon
. . . of the moon.

> My poor heart is aching
> So won't you come soon
> In a dream . . .
> In a dream . . .

Tsch! Tsch! It has an awfully lot of "I," "me," and "my" in it, hasn't it?

Feeling rather sharp last night I wrote to Bill Stafford. His clever style is a challenge. John and Frank are still unapproved. In case of your changing address, let me know enough in advance to go through the necessary red tape in the office here.

Give my love to Mammy and Pappy. I was glad to hear from Mammy, had begun to think she was mad at me, or sumpin.

The *World-Herald* clipping didn't come.

Kathy is an FOR member.

G'night, goodlookin'.

You Loving Husbing,

Chuck

◙ ◙ ◙

October 23, 1945

Dearly Beloved,

Your very entertaining letter came Saturday. I must say I think your letters are getting better all the time, and they have all been better than any you wrote to other people when we were living together.

So Doug Corey is trying to put me on the spot, is he? Why that ornery little rat. Well, I'll fix him. I'll just wait 'til I get out of here to answer that question about whether a married man or a single man does easier time. The very idea, that dirty . . . Ha! Ha! Ha! I just said that to see what you'd say.

Honey, I'm not going to write Doug a letter through you—that would only waste precious space. You can tell him all the salient facts about things at Sandstone. But I will give my authoritative opinion on the "doing time" question. Unfortunately, harrumph, one cannot give a simple Yes or No answer to the question of whether having a wife makes things better or worse for a prisoner. Too many other factors can arise to complicate the situation. For instance, if one's wife was lukewarm towards the convictions that put him in prison, or, as happens in some cases, actually hostile towards those convictions; or if one didn't have faith in his wife's fidelity; or if his wife was sickly or had a half-dozen little kids to support; then, I'm sure, he would probably do easier time without one. Glenn Smiley, for example, with a wonderful but sickly wife and three kids is probably doing it a little rough. But in my own case, where my wife not only shares my convictions but is doing a darned good job of pinch-hitting for me; who is not only well, and has no children, but is very capable and able to take care of herself, and even has loving and sympathetic parents to fall back on, well, now that is an entirely different situation.

Furthermore, a wife like mine can do hundreds of things I wouldn't be willing to ask anyone else to do, things that a prisoner cannot do for himself; for example, write letters to guys like Corey, bring pressure to bear on matters relating to his imprisonment, attend FOR conferences, etc. Furthermore, having a wife like mine (or like Doug's) gives one a greater feeling of security, of belonging. Also, for a person who wants to be married (not all people do) to have a wife while in prison is a definite advantage because he has that very difficult, hazardous task accomplished, and upon release he can start living right where he wants to without wasting time hunting for a wife. As far as the question of sex is concerned, personally (and it may possibly be different for others), I am not doing harder time on that account now than when I was single and in prison. As a matter of fact, I think the situation is easier now. In other words, I suspect Doug had the best of we gay young blades down at Tucson. It is true that I did it a little rough here for a while, but it was despite the fact that I was married, not because of it. Chiefly, I think it was because I hadn't settled down to prison psychologically. Also, I had no bosom buddies here to make it easier; also, the work was a drudge. Now, however, I'm doing it easy—just coasting along.

Give Doug and Rae my regards, and, incidentally, Honey, if we still have three extra bathmat sets why don't you send one to Gerry and his wife. He was one of the best friends I ever had and I don't want him to forget the fact. You could even send a cute little note about why we are sending that particular item—that we don't expect to have four bathrooms, or something to that effect. I don't have his address but a card to Paul or Lucille could secure it, I think.

Though J. Swomley hasn't been approved yet, I was permitted to read a letter from him yesterday and also authorized to answer it with a special purpose letter, which I did today. John didn't have much to say but he did remark about my wife's insight and . . . shucks, I've forgotten the exact words now, but anyway it was to the effect that you are not only OK, but on the beam. An opinion which I share without reservation.

Checked out *Importance of Living* today but am still reading Durant's *The Mansions of Philosophy*. It is really good, profound and provocative, but still sparkling with wit. Hope it doesn't make Lin Yutang's book seem petty by comparison. Am also studying *Better Eyesight Without Glasses* by William Bates. Parker and I are both going to give it a try. Wish me luck.

I was tickled at your reaction to Grandpa's materialism and would kiss you if I could strain my neck that far. The library incident is an example of the fun one can have not being ashamed of his convictions—a shrinking violet.

I am glad that you have decided to go to Suffern. I have often thought of going there myself, you know—before you were my wife. I agree that they have a lot to offer and when you find out all about biodynamics, at least write and tell me what the word means. Don't know just how severe you meant it, but it sounded very severe when you said, "Also . . . I'd rather you didn't get *amused* at my notions. I'm not exactly witless, you know, even if I do act it at times." Wow! Not only do I apologize on my knees, but I also plead not guilty— not guilty of intending to give the impression you apparently got. I'll admit I was "amused" at the idea that . . . well, you go to grade school for nine years to learn how to learn, then you go to high school for four years to learn what you want to learn, then college for four years to learn to teach, then you go to New York for *one month to learn how to live*. Praise the Lord and Amen. However, I promise faithfully to never again be amused at anything you think, say, or do. Amen. Also, if I catch anybody, man, woman, or child, saying that you are "witless," I'll punch 'em right in the nose, so help me.

I'm very sorry to hear that Mammy has (I hope it's *had* by now) the flu. If I can write another letter this week, i.e., if the special purpose one to John doesn't count against my quota, I'll write and tell her so. Oh yes, I wrote to Frank and Marie Sunday as they have been approved.

Your very, very sober, serious, and unamused but loving husband,
Chuck

◙ ◙ ◙

October 29, 1945

Dear Wifey,

Hi, gal! I'm beginning to appreciate how hard it is to discuss rather subtle philosophical and psychological ideas by letters, as I sit trying to write this one—especially on two pages. Looking back over your recent letters, I am amused to find that of two plans for future action one leaves you hot and me cold, and the other vice versa. But in a way I'm glad because it shows that we each retain our own personalities. Remember *The Prophet*'s advice—to grow side by side but not in each other's shadow (or sumpin' like that). But I promised to add my bit to the discussion, so here goes.

First, about the idea of going to live with Mil. In the first place, whatever I say on this score may be very wrong since my attitudes are based on very slight acquaintance with the problems and personalities involved. Your remark that I "have seemed a little dubious about too much contact with Mil and her ideas" was something of a surprise to me since I don't recall expressing that feeling. But on analyzing my feelings I found it was true. (You women can read between the lines too darned well. How can a man stand a chance?) So I says to myself, "Well, why do you feel that way?" The answer is (I think) that I am always leery of anyone who says, "This is it and that's all there is to it," also of putting too much stock in one man's leadership. Remember Mohammed's remark, "There is but one God and Mohammed is his prophet." I guess that's the way Mil strikes me: "There is but one Answer (decentralization) and Borsodi is its prophet." If the School of Living is (contrary to what I think) merely an agency to disseminate R.B.'s philosophy, then I don't believe it would interest *me*. Also, if Mil had invited *me* to come up there and the purpose was to acquire skills for subsistence living, I'd be very interested. But if I thought that it was to help promote the cause of decentralist propaganda . . . well, there are other causes (conscription, race relations, war, etc.) which strike me as more immediate (if less fundamental, possibly) and more exciting. From what you quoted of Mil's letter I get the feeling that she is more interested in having you there to help propagandize, but maybe I'm wrong. However, it is very possible that you could acquire more practical subsistence farming skills there than anywhere else. You should know more about that possibility than I. And at least it would give you more of a feeling of belonging in a farm environment, with animals, etc. So there I am with one leg on each side of the fence.

Now, as to the Mel-Chimes idea. Here, too, I want to do some qualifying. I know almost nothing about the plan or the possibilities. However, from what I have been told, my attitude has been one of mounting enthusiasm. Why? Well, firstly, I don't believe I'm quite ready to be tied down too tight just yet. Probably won't be for a few years, or at least until little Worleys begin to put in an appearance. If we were to strike off cold on a place of our own in a totally strange environment, we would be pretty thoroughly tied down—at least if we were living on a subsistence basis. So along comes this idea which is beginning to impress me as the *perfect apprenticeship*. Not only would there be a chance to get first-hand experience in farming, recreation, building, etc., but land here is the real advantage. We would not be so completely on our own. It would not be a case of sink or swim because there is greater strength, greater security, in numbers; we would make up for each other's deficiencies, the group could smooth over individual mistakes. Second advantage: We would be freer to travel around, experiment, and, in general, sow our wild oats (of our own, gentle variety). Third advantage: Going through such experiences with the group of persons being considered would enrich and greatly deepen the philosophical values derived. It could be a school not only in subsistence farming, but also in cultural growth and psychological experience in living with others. It would help to deepen and clarify our own aims and ideals. Likewise (though I don't know the fellows' wives), I will say that Gerry, Chimes, Mel, Emma, and Lucille are all absolutely tops. I feel sure that my own personality would grow by going through such an experience with them.

I think (this is pure egotism) that I can understand your doubts—your feeling that you might "resent any claim they might have on me," that "you'd kinda like to have me for yourself . . . cause you still love me."

God bless you, Honey, I still love you, too, and wouldn't want anything to disturb that relationship for 50 years, at least. From the way Emma and Lucille sometimes write, I imagine that you can just see them taking over poor little C.V., saying, "Let's do this," and "Let's sing this," etc. I assure you that no one but you has ever had or will ever have any "claim" (of any kind) on me. And if the personalities involved were as real to you as they are to me (instead of just a name and address), I think you would agree that your feeling is groundless. Will Durant (who doesn't claim to understand women either) says that a woman "lives only when she is loved; attention is her vital medium." But on the other hand it seems to me that something very vital would be lost from a marriage in which the persons tried to possess each other. Again, let me cite *The Prophet* on "marriage," or God's relationship to man. Do you remember that poem? "He who binds to himself a joy, doth its winged life destroy," etc.

Aren't I getting to be quite a philosopher! Of course, I still don't know many essential details for making a final decision—cost, when I'll be out of here, etc. What is your reaction to my reaction, also Mammy's and Pappy's ideas on the subject?

Gosh, here my space is all gone. Got your Friday letter a few minutes ago. Am sure enjoying your new resolution on correspondence. Youse is a good wifey. Also got a scintillating letter from Bill Stafford. Will relay parts in next letter. The news about Glenn Smiley was welcome.

I did dream of you last night, Honey. We were just smooching like everything and you said (this will slay you), "Gee, you're nice to me today. You must have an ulterior motive."

Lots of love,
Chuck

◘ ◘ ◘

November 4, 1945

Dear Lizzie—How issie?

(My latest poem, pretty sharp, eh?)

Thought I'd try writing Sunday in hope that you might receive the letter the same week (seeing as how the one I mailed Tuesday, October 23, took six days to travel 500 miles). Ah well, only 100 years ago that would have been considered wonderful service, wonderful service. It's too late to blame such delays on the war, but I trust it can be explained by some strike or other, or maybe the Mississippi washed out all the bridges—who knows.

Ol' Man Winter came blustering over the wall Friday and left an inch of snow on the ground—he had permission, no doubt. And the cold wind that has been blowing ever since would seem to indicate that he is still lurking out in the woods nearby.

I must tell you about a new game that is very popular here now. I haven't been asked to play yet, but it looks like it might be lots of fun—at least it is very amusing to watch. Not knowing the official name, we call it "Jr. G-Man." However, it may be only an adaptation of that old childhood favorite, "Cops and Robbers." Like all children's games, it requires some imagination for full enjoyment. In this case the player must assume that every prisoner is concealing somewhere either: a) an atomic bomb, b) a plot to control the potatoes market, or c) a rocket ship capable of flying non-stop to the moon. With this in mind, a thorough search is conducted at all times. Player holds bread up to the light, examines bottom of food tray (spilling coffee in the prunes during the process), searches prisoner before and after leaving room, etc. The players really got enthusiastic Saturday and when we came in from exercise, blankets, mattress covers, towels, everything was piled helter-skelter on the beds. Then the head player made a little speech in a tone of stern paternalism. Not wishing to spoil the game, of course, we all acted very much impressed. Oh, it's great fun.

Got a letter from Frank Friday. I quote:

We are very pleased with Betty. We feel that you have a good
wife—the kind you deserve. [!, C.W.] We are anxious to have
her with us. We hope she will have time to spend with us here
in Chicago. Always feel that where we are, Chuck, that it's
a home for you and Betty. We will consider it a privilege to
have either or both of you at any time. Betty need never feel
that she would be imposing on us by staying at our place.
To even come in the middle of the night is perfectly OK. And
if she can come she doesn't need to feel that she has to hurry
away. She can do just what she wants to. On the other hand,
we wouldn't want either of you to feel duty-bound (or something) to visit us or stay longer than you would want to at
any time. We want to extend our hospitality with a complete
range of freedom.

Frank is doubtful about our plans for simple living; says "there
is a point to which the *simple* life can go that it becomes *complex*."
Also says people are unwilling to change their way of living. (I wonder what he hopes to accomplish then by preaching!) I've just done
a song using Frank's "Zambeezie" song as the chorus. Will try to get
permission to send it to him for additions, improvements, etc., in my
next letter. Wouldn't it be swell if we could get it published?
Let me quote this paragraph from Bill Stafford's letter:

Faulkner had a story to tell about "being out on a fire with a
bunch of San Quentin (Calif. prison crew) men and a bunch
of soldiers back from battle but not yet discharged. Harry, a
prisoner, and a soldier were huddled around a fire up on the
fire line one cold night. Harry asked the soldier what he got
the decoration for and the soldier replied, 'For killing some
50-odd Japs.' The prisoner kicked at the fire, shrugged, and
said, 'I killed a Jap, too, but I guess mine must have been out
of season; I've been in 15 years for it.' The soldier said, 'No
kiddin', is that what you're in for!?' And the prisoner said,
'Yes, but if you think that's funny, here's a guy'—turning to
Harry—'who's in because he won't kill Japs.'"

Oh, irony. Bill also says that Clancy Bunyan is now at Bethany
Hospital in Chicago. That is right across the street from Frank's

seminary. You could meet Clancy and compare notes on prison, etc., if you visited F & M. Maybe you could arrange to meet Emma, too. Milwaukee isn't so far and she might come down on a weekend. I'd like to have her meet F & M and the Thomsons, too.

Was very glad to hear of Pop and you getting together on a letter to the Hon. Tom Clark. Letters to congressmen help but the policy is pretty much determined by the Attorney General. "A letter a day wears resistance away." (Original C.V.W.)

Had a hard time writing a Christmas poem. Wrote a long one first and then didn't like it. Finally ended up with the one below, which expresses my sentiments but may not express yours, or may be a bit too subtle for some folks. What do you think? Is it OK? Personally, I'm against sending anything trite. There's too much of that as it is.

Thought for a while that your letter addressed, "Dear Screw," was delivered to me by mistake. Perhaps you didn't know that in prison parlance, the term "Screw" is used to refer to an officer.

Read Lin Yutang's chapter "On Lying in Bed," lying in bed this morning. He is very witty, no? But I liked *The Mansions of Philosophy* better. Incidentally, if Pappy and Mammy have never read the latter, I think it would make a swell Christmas gift, but you may have something else in mind.

Yours from the same old place,
Love,
Chuck

The Nazarene

A Nazarene there was more humble than
A weed. On speaking terms with God and man,
He walked the dewy path on sandaled feet
And found rare blossoms nursed by desert heat.
Beneath the shade at noon his healing hand
Was raised against a cancer in the land.

The twilight hours have faded into night.
But piercing through the deepest dark a light
Still shines from throbbing hearts; like seeds of grass
That wait in earth for snow and winter winds to pass.

■ ■ ■

November 11, 1945

Dear Wife,

Hi, Sweetheart. Did this arrive on your birthday? Happy Birthday! If I could have permission to send you just one birthday gift, do you know what I'd send?—probably not anything you'd want very badly—but my first choice would be to send—*me*. Maybe you think I should have tried to write a poem in honor of the occasion, but I don't. Poems are never written to one's wife, only to a mistress. Now, I suppose you could quote Lin Yutang as saying that any married woman without children is a mistress. But I think we must differentiate between those women who don't have children because they are too sophisticated, and those whose husbands are in prison. Of course, it's really your parents who deserve all the thanks and congratulations. It was they who went to all the trouble and paid the bills and "raised you up" and what happens? Pow! I come along and collect all the benefits. (Thanks, Pappy and Mammy.) Of course, at the time they didn't know I was going to do that. Hmm, come to think of it, neither did I. As a matter of fact, if someone had told me my future wife was being born, I probably wouldn't even have stopped riding my rocking horse, or fighting with my brother, or whatever I was doing at that time. At the age of 23, Alexander the Great sat down and wept because there were no more worlds to conquer. If you should have any similar ambition, please get it out of your system while I am still here because, frankly, I'm not interested in any such project.

It was at the age of 23 that I obtained my first government lent job. Four years ago yesterday I arrived at Magnolia, Arkansas. The next day we had a holiday and Morris Keston (whom Bill Stafford says has just been awarded a $2,500 Guggenheim scholarship) read a very clever parody on the Bible which he had written for the occasion.

Did you finish *The Importance of Living* yet, Betsy? I did, and liked it more and more the further I read. Some chapters I thought were especially good: "Who Can Best Enjoy Life," "The Feast of Life," "The Enjoyment of Travel," and "Relationship to God." What did you think of "Yuanming" and the "Half-and-Half" philosophy? Personally, I thought he spoke to my condition. Also very touching were the two brief stories in which those fellows told of their wives and their lives together. And that journal about the old fellow who went on his travel was just priceless. Lin's statement as to "Why I Am a Pagan" expressed my own sentiments so well that I wish you'd pass it on to my folks so they will understand my position better. Didn't you think the book was poetical? I did, and humorous, too. Sometimes I'd just roar with laughter and then bother Mal by reading him the passage through the ventilator.

Yesterday I finished Richard Wright's *Native Son*. In the introduction, Dorothy Canfield Fisher says it will "harrow up" one's feelings. It more nearly plowed up mine. Gosh, it's powerful, and incisively critical of pink tea social work. Now I'm reading John Dewey's *Freedom and Culture*, and next on my list is *My America*. Am finally getting the liberal education I heard so much about in college.

So you all are riled up about what the Navy is doing with Austin. Personally, I am much more riled up about what Austin is apparently trying to do to the Navy. Does that impudent young upstart wish to change the very basic nature of that great tool of freedom, that right hand of God? It is not the Navy's purpose to provide free educations for little boys, but rather the stern task of making the world safe for democracy. And in that process such minutiae as individuality, personality, etc., must be sacrificed for the greater goals. Mowing lawns and sweeping streets is apparently just what that young whippersnapper needs, and when he has learned lesson No. 1 (i.e., unquestioned obedience to authority), when he has forgotten his own selfish little ego, then perhaps he may go on to more noble tasks. And if he is talented and disciplined perhaps he may even someday have the supreme privilege of wiping out a whole city of miserable beasts with a clean, kind atomic bomb. Besides, does he think the Navy has nothing more important to think about than him? Right now the Navy is extremely busy trying to convince our stupid American people that huge conscript-military forces are necessary for their protection, that only by armed might can we survive—a fact clearly demonstrated by history, by Sparta, Rome, Napoleonic France, etc.

Besides, the Naval officers are probably very busy helping to bring freedom and enlightenment to those poor, benighted Huns and Japs. Furthermore, since ignorant civilians do not always understand military strategy, the Navy now feels it incumbent upon itself to explain (or at least conceal) some of the facts pertaining to our glorious victory over the Japs at Pearl Harbor.

Also, the Navy is very busy right now fighting for its very existence so Austin and millions of other Austins can say proudly that they belong to the *Navy,* not to the *U.S. Combined Services* or some such inglorious title. So, tell that young man to buck up. Let him recall that he has the supreme honor of being a part, however small, of that noble organization through which God's kingdom is being built. Let him mow for decency and sweep for democracy. Amen.

It was one degree above zero here Friday night. Don't know what it's going to be when winter comes.

Got your letters last night. Am very glad to hear that Mammy is feeling better. Also got a letter (special purpose) from John Swomley, but it didn't bring any news.

Betsy, why do you try to make me play the role of critic regarding Mil? You quote something and then say, "Now, do you have a bone to pick with her on that?" I do not choose to play the part I'm being cast for.

Once you mentioned borrowing Phyl's typewriter. I think it would be better to buy one as we'll want one eventually anyway, and there should be lots of good used ones on the market now, or soon.

Have fun, Honey. I love you muy muchisimo,
Chuck

◉ ◉ ◉

November 13, 1945

Dear Betty,

It's really your Mom's turn for a letter so this is cheating a little bit. Hope she won't mind too much. For Mom's (mine) information, I have tried to adopt the following schedule of correspondence: one letter to you every week, one to our moms every week alternating, one to one of my other four correspondents each week. If that isn't OK, about the best I could do would be to cut someone off my list and I don't think Mom would want me to do that.

But to explain why Mammy is getting gypped out of hers this week; well, I got a letter from Paul tonight. He has been sick and needs an appendectomy and is broke. He said that he had written to Pop and Cecil to borrow money. Since you don't know Paul you probably can't appreciate the significance of that statement. Paul almost never asks favors of anyone. (Though he is very willing to help someone else out of a spot as, for example, when he paid my lawyer's fee in Los Angeles (some $65) when I was broke and going to prison. He gave some flimsy reason for my not having to pay it back but I've forgotten what it was.) Anyway, now he's in a spot and I feel that I'd like to help him out. What do you think about the situation? Since we have always sort of considered our property as being jointly owned, I wouldn't want to do anything that didn't meet with your full approval. But if you agree with me, then I'd suggest that first you call the folks to see if they were able to send any cash. If not, I'd suggest that you wire him $100 at his new address: 334 N Berendo, Los Angeles 4, Calif. If they were able to help out, I'd still be in favor of wiring him $50 so he could rest easy. If you see eye to eye with me, I'd suggest that you act as quickly as possible.

Your letter from Doane also arrived tonight. Guess I'll have to admit that I can't imagine you going around blowing soap bubbles but I'm glad to hear it. I greatly approve of people acting free and natural. Guess I don't need to apologize any more for reading children's poetry, *Alice in Wonderland,* and the like.

Wasn't it good to hear about Don and Mary planning to get married? Hope you can think of some way to express our pleasure and welcome them into the fellowship of married folks. I don't have any suggestions on the spur of the moment. The lights went off about three minutes ago, and this light is barely bright enough to write letters by.

Will you love me just as much if I mail this half of a letter? There is nothing new to write about anyway. I made a chess board the other day and have been playing Mal through the ventilator. He plays from memory and still beats my socks off. Chess seems to be just another one of those things I'm not very good at.

Started on *My America* today. Looks like it might be quite interesting, and much more readable than John Dewey's book *Freedom and Culture*. I managed to wade through the first chapter of the latter and am greatly interested in the theme, but don't know whether I'll make the grade or not. I think there are parts of it in the book you have there, so you can try it out if you wish.

Speaking of that book reminds me that I have been intending to say that I certainly hope Mammy and Pappy feel free to use any of the stuff we have there in any way they can. If they would like a change of pictures, for instance, and can use ours, or if they need another floor lamp—hmm, come to think of it, we don't have much stuff anyone else could use. But you get the idea.

Gormly and I each did 150 consecutive deep-knee bends today. So if you think I might be deteriorating physically, I suggest you try it. Another of my favorite exercises is to walk two lengths of the corridor (about 100 ft.) on my hands, and another is to jump and touch the ceiling, which is nine and a half feet from the floor. I can touch it with either hand but not with both hands together.

Bye, Honey. Trying to read this will probably be even worse than trying to write it. The light I am writing by is on the prison wall about 75 feet away. It gives about as much light as a full moon.

Lots of love,
Chuck

■ ■ ■

November 19, 1945

Dear Wife,

Hello, Sweetheart. Over in B1, just across the volleyball court, the JWs are singing one of their JW hymns. As I stood by the window a minute ago looking out at the cold, black sky and the very real immensity of reinforced concrete on all sides, it seemed rather unreal that I was about to sit down and write to one with whom I had exchanged vows on sharing our lives. Somehow, it rather seems like that . . . spiritual flower, which grew out of our relationship to one another, which war nurtured by the interaction of our personalities, which had its roots in that soil where our beings merged, has quietly receded back into the bulb. Would it have still been blooming, I wonder, had our personalities been intertwined by five or six years of mutual experience instead of five or six months? Probably not . . . as warm and bright as the sun is, still the plants derive no benefit from their memory of it, once its rays have been shut off by the horizon. But then I am consoled to remember that the bulb is still very much alive, is, in fact, only waiting, like the sleeping beauty, for the kiss of our personalities to bring it back from the land of dreams. Haven't you had the same feeling? I hope that expressing the feeling as I have instead of in cold prose has not led to misunderstanding. Anyway, Honey, I love you, and look forward to the day when our flower can again put forth shoots and leaves and richer flowers than we have ever seen. And even now I know that the roots are growing deeper and stronger.

Thanks lots for sending the clipping of Howard Buffett's speech. I was rather surprised that you hadn't commented on it. Personally, I thought it was rather worth getting excited about, worth a strong letter of congratulations and support. For a politician to make such statements on the floor of Congress is evidence of courage and conviction. Especially so for a congressman coming from the conservative atmosphere of Omaha.

If the Jensen clan has the contemplated get-together, I'd give anything to be the invisible man present but unseen at all the conversations. Wouldn't that be fun?

I liked your Christmas card idea but it looks like an awful lot of work to me—way more than I'd ever be interested in doing. However, since you would have to do the work, that is your consideration. I greatly approve of the idea of sending it without envelopes. As to connecting "on speaking . . ." with dashes. Well, you may if you wish. But to me it is such a totally independent thought that I think it might lose more than it would gain by the connection. Probably the initials would be a good idea. How would it be to omit the title—maybe put "Christmas 1945" in its place. This is only a suggestion. Also, since there is such a definite break between the two stanzas, would it not be wise to separate them by a row of dots. You have probably seen examples of what I mean in other poems.

Funny thing, rereading that poem, I don't like it nearly so well as I did. Which seems to be the same reaction to other stuff I've tried to write—possibly explaining why I've written so little. Or possibly the reason is that I seem to be in a state of flux right now. I have a feeling that *The Mansions of Philosophy* and *The Importance of Living,* etc., are affecting my attitude toward life somewhat, but can't put my finger on the change.

Have about 200 pages more to read in *My America.* Didn't you like the story of Cantrell? Or did you read it? I think the chapter "Workers" is very good in that it helps clear up lots of the bunk, the misunderstandings we get through the newspapers. Read a very good war play today, "What Price Glory." The language is especially realistic and the antiwar propaganda very subtle.

We have a new game now. Unlike "Jr. G-Man," we play this one. Someone stuffed an old glove with sawdust and we have been using it during our outdoor exercise period as a football. We play "touch," two against two. So far I have always been on the winning side. Am feeling fine but think I have a couple of teeth that are decaying. They may get around to looking at them one of these days. Parker is busy making himself a slide rule—without even the aid of a common ruler. First, of course, he had to figure out how a slide rule was worked out. Besides being a swell guy, he is undoubtedly something of a genius—particularly along mechanical lines—has an IQ somewhere around 150. At present he isn't headed in any particular direction, but I think he will probably make a real contribution to life, maybe not 'til later years, however. People's personalities still intrigue me. All five of those up here have lots in common and yet are very different. Physically, all but Parker are very thin (me being next to heaviest built). I am the youngest, Adam is 28, the five all 31. Only Adam and I are married. Ah, but I haven't space to describe them.

Did you subscribe to *The Conscientious Objector* yet? You may be able to act more effectively towards getting your hubby out of the clink if you know what goes on, and they carry rather complete reports. Address: 119 Nassau St., New York, NY; price, $1 per year.

Would like to work out a correspondence system whereby we might have a complete exchange of letters in a week. That's why I'm writing this letter Monday instead of Sunday. Will save the remaining space to comment on your letter in case one comes tonight.

Hon, the mail just came but none from my wife—just a short one from Mom. "Ah well," to quote from your last letter, "such is life." Well then, I'll use this space to discuss an idea that's lurking in my mind right now. I'm contemplating going on a complete fast from December 24 through January 1. Chief purpose, of course, would be to arouse public attention to the fact that political prisoners are still in prison—through newspapers, etc. However, in thinking over a statement on the matter, don't know why we couldn't mention the new light being increasingly shed on our recent debacle, and even put in a plug for feeding starving people in other countries. Don't know but, in view of the total situation, if fasting wouldn't be more appropriate than feasting as a means of commemorating Christmas and New Year. What do you think of the idea?

Goodbye with a nice, long kiss.

Chuck

◘ ◘ ◘

November 25, 1945

My Sweet Blond Betty,

I feel good this afternoon. I feel like writing a letter—maybe because I think of lots of things to write about. I feel like doing things—something different—going to a concert . . . no, maybe that would be a bit too tame . . . well, then, taking a long hike through "snowy woods," or going ice skating.

As you probably know from my letter to Mom, we five "crack-pots" concluded a fast this morning, a fast that started after lunch last Tuesday—13 meals all told. I won't go over the details again. Whether or not it does any good to protest the petty authoritarianism in this way, I don't know, but at least one feels better about it. I did the fast easy, as a matter of fact, felt quite healthy and normal this morning. That hot, sort of gnawing sensation in my stomach had quit bothering. Another peculiar physical effect of fasting is that after a day or two it makes the lights go out if one stands up suddenly— but even that phenomenon seemed to be receding on the fourth and fifth day. Frankly, I think that I missed food more psychologically than physically. It is one of the things that breaks up our unvarying stretch of time and seems to give order and a sense of progression to the day. At no time did I feel very weak, could even jump and touch the ceiling on the fourth day. Wouldn't surprise me but that such a fast might be good for a person; gives one's system a chance to get cleaned and pressed. I even noticed that my voice was cleaner and more flexible—quite enjoyed a private songfest Saturday night.

However, not everything is perfectly clear sailing yet. Though Gormly and Adam have washed off the soap marks, they are still denied their privileges until court meets. Though they were told in court that privileges would be restored when the marks were removed. Another cloud on the horizon comes from the fact that our CO colored friend is in the hole for refusing to work. Why he is in the hole with inadequate food and no privileges instead of up here with us is hard to say—some of the fellows think it is racial discrimination, but I am more inclined to believe that they feel Paul is only trying to get away from the "work privilege," and they are using coercive measures to change his opinion. Or maybe the fact that he is all alone instead of with a group has something to do with it, or maybe they intend to have him in the hole just long enough to scare off others.

In Mom's letter I mentioned an article about Sandstone in the Minneapolis papers. Now it appears that it was not just one article but a whole series of them (in the *Minneapolis Star-Journal* rather than the *Tribune* as I said before) and from what rumors sneak through to us, it would seem that the articles are very fallacious and libelous using actual names and giving false information. I am told that they state that the COs were trying to start a rebellion here and that "Worley and Parker refused to work because it was raining slightly. . . . " a falsehood that can be absolutely refuted by the fact that we quite willingly worked out in the mud with the other boys, as can be shown by the court records here. Please have Mom get this whole series of articles from Eva and if some of the other boys in prison population (many of whom are mentioned by name) don't get the matter thoroughly corrected, there is going to be something poppin' when I get out of here. Also, have Eva watch the papers for my retractions. The author of the articles, who was thoroughly hated by everyone and was even forced to move from the dormitory because the "thieves" hazed him so, was a stool pigeon of the first water. Everyone called him "Warden Williams" because of his obnoxious and officious attitude. We suspect that he wrote the articles right here in prison since he had a private cell in the quarantine block, and was the only prisoner on record to secure an institution typewriter for his personal use. Ah well! He is probably only an example of successful prison rehabilitation. But please try to get all the articles.

I found a new use for the capitalistic system the other day. Went up Friday and had a nice, big, new filling put in. The dentist is a little rougher than most I've been to, but he does a good job. But do you know, I wasn't nearly so proud of that filling, didn't rub it curiously and lovingly with my tongue—'cause why?—well, I think it was 'cause I just went up and had it put in—no waiting, no appointment, and *no bill.* Not knowing about the fact, he suggested I treat the filling gently for 24 hours. One of the good-natured guards who brought our food around kept asking me jokingly if that filling was ready for use yet.

So you are with the Rosses. I can imagine your frustration. Hope you didn't want me to change your address—I don't even know what it is. I've got the perfect thing to get that stodgy taste out of your mouth—Read *U.S.A.* by John Dos Passos. It presents the other side of life with extreme frankness and realism—no holds barred. I'm about halfway through it—about 1,400 pages all told. With your sheltered past you probably wouldn't even understand all the cuss words, but they're all there. Not only is it written in a very different style, but it has some darned good propaganda against war, etc., and gives what I think is a very realistic picture of life in the lower class, working strata of society. The other book in my possession right now—*The Rise of American Civilization* by Charles Beard and Mary Beard—is two books in one, 1,700 pages altogether—so maybe you think I'm fixed for reading for a while?

Was glad to get Banning's letter, also Chimes's. If you wish to write to Banning, hop to it. I haven't any suggestions as to what to say. As to Chimes's letter, I was impressed that he and Mel have really put some thinking into this thing and really mean to make a go of it. They are both darned good guys, and capable. Remember when Mil wrote that Chalmers Johnson fixed up their beehives—well, that's Chimes. If you are for the idea, I am. However, in writing to them about it, my future is still very indefinite. I could be here for another 30 months. There is still no clear-cut evidence to judge from. Of course, I don't know how we'd get up 2,000 bucks, unless we borrowed some. Don't think much of that idea myself, but might be OK on a purely impersonal basis from the A.F.S.C., for instance—if they are making such loans.

Gosh, I could go on for another page yet, but have six other correspondents now, including John S. (though only you and Mom wrote to me last week). Despite all the local competition, you are still my best girl. Fact is, I'm rather fond of you and will prove it some day. Bye Sweetheart—don't get in the groove.

Love,
Chuck

■ ■ ■

December 3, 1945

Dearest Wife,

Please don't take what I am about to say too seriously. To get the idea across, I may state it more sternly than I intend. But the fact is that when you write to me that you are bored, it makes me . . . well, to use your phrase, mad enough to spit. When any person 23 years old, healthy, intelligent, well-educated, and absolutely free to choose his environment lives a bored existence, that person should have his (or her) pants kicked . . . hard. It is bad enough that half of our family should be bored; that the whole family should be that way is intolerable. In fact, I personally believe that to be bored is just about as much a sin as any of the things mentioned in the Ten Commandments because it indicates that we are not expressing our own personalities in life, are not being true to ourselves.

To be true to ourselves—that, I am inclined to think, is the real aim of life, not any "ism," or even to "save the world." And that is a thing to remember when thinking about any specific job; e.g., teaching a class of subnormal boys. If that is the thing by which you can best express your personality, go to it; but if not, steer clear. This is no selfish philosophy. Rather, I think it is probably selfish and egotistical to throw oneself, however heroically and sacrificially, into some task for which one has no personal bent, regardless of how fine a cause it might be. There are a million fine causes right there in Omaha, but our job is to live our own life. Seems to me Thoreau said something along this line. So, for gosh sakes, Honey, how about getting the lead, or the cobwebs, or something out of something or other. Spend a few hours some day thinking about you and what you want to do, and then do it. And personally, I don't think your bored feeling started at the Rosses'.

I don't know, of course, what you really want to do, but I can think of thousands of possibilities—ranging all the way from doing a year's reconstruction work abroad to hitchhiking around the country. If it's subsistence farming, there are many now in operation where you could go, in almost every part of the U.S., including Aunt Mil's. If you want to stay at home, there is still lots you could do along that line. I mentioned once, for example, the farm bulletins that are probably the greatest wealth of information about all phases of farming in the country and can be obtained for little or nothing. Did you ever send for any? My gosh, I'll bet you can't even ski, or play a Beethoven sonata. I'll bet you don't even know what the inside of a big industry looks like, or how the lower economic classes actually live, and you are bored . . . well, I hope you get the idea!

I am just starting a new hobby—ornithology. Friday I got a book from the library which is truly amazing. Entitled *Birds of America,* it gives complete information about every bird in this country, and even has pictures of most of them. If you should ever find a secondhand one in a bookstore, grab it.

Today we went outdoors for our afternoon exercise period—first time for several days. There is about five inches of snow so we had fun playing "fox and geese." Seems to me like it has been a couple of months since we had a sunshiny day. I even wrote a silly little poem entitled "Grey November." Guess I might as well quote it. Will also include one that somewhat expresses the feeling about Europe, etc., which I mentioned in my last letter to Mammy. It was surprising to me to get a letter the next day from her—a letter which was written in almost an identical mood. What Mammy said about the church, combined with some thoughts of my own, gave me an idea for another poem, but I haven't worked it out yet.

Thanks for quoting the U.S. Pardon Attorney's letter. I received a similar one a few days before. Am in the process of drafting an objection to it on the basis that special circumstances arising should merit immediate attention. And I think the war's end makes a very special circumstance as far as COs in prison are concerned.

Am wondering what and how some of our friends are making out. Have you ever heard from Jerry, or the Hirabayashis, or the Don Larsons, or Lucille or Emma, etc., etc.? Gordie Hirabayashi should just about be out of McNeil Island Prison by now.

Have you written to Mel and Chimes explaining our situation? About locating a farm, I think it would be a good idea to contact A.E. Morgan and other persons interested in the field, as they might know of some very suitable places near some suitable city.

We are looking for reinforcements soon in "crackpot row." Otherwise, no news. I'm feeling fine. Have heard we five are not permitted to receive Christmas boxes. Protest to Warden if you wish. Makes little difference to me.

Bye, Sweetheart.

Love,

Chuck

Grey November

November, drab and dirty grey,
Were you hiding out when they
Passed out everything that's gay?
Gone is autumn's rich array
Still you stand there in the way
Blocking out the bright display
Winter flings in riotous play.
Grey November, blow away!

Reconstruction

"Light a candle," a wise man said.
Perish a candle! The gutters are red,
And millions of people are starving for bread,
And searching through ruins with sickening dread,
And wandering homeless with snow for a bed,
And . . . "Light a candle," the wise man said.
"Darkness can only be conquered by light."
But Christ! Can a candle diminish the night?
Can a candle spot hope in a forest of fright?
Can a candle burn out the fierce cancer of might?
Can a candle . . . "Can only be conquered by light."

* * * *

Great God! I'm upset by the stench of the dead—
("Light a candle," the wise man said.)
And wish I were blind to this horrible sight.
("Darkness can only be conquered by light.")

◨ ◨ ◨

December 9, 1945

Dearest Sweetheart,

I know what you mean when you say you "don't feel like a much married woman." I've almost forgotten what it means to have a wife.

Oh, there's that girl I write to, and I still remember enough about her to know that she's a great gal; but mostly my memories of her are mental, conscious ones. A short absence may indeed make the heart grow fonder, but a long absence makes the heart forget, I fear. At any rate, it is consoling to think that I have a wife who shares my philosophy of life and with whom I know great love. And what a wonderful experience it will be to rediscover that love, that spiritual affinity. (But maybe I'd better not write too many letters like that last one, which may have been somewhat unjust. Will probably get her reaction Tuesday or Wednesday.)

I hope your optimism bears fruit. For instance, your "Yippee!" regarding conscription's state of health. John Swomley wasn't any too happy about the situation in his letter of December 1, and I have a hunch it is still a long way from being a dead letter. The fellows here agree that I was unduly optimistic in predicting release of COs from prison by January 1947. If we get out before then (or even by then) there'll have to be more hell raised than there has yet been. Hutch's dad quoted in a letter a strong editorial in *The Christian Century* demanding their (our) release by Christmas. You must have never had our subscription transferred back to your address or you'd have surely mentioned it.

Well, Hank has become a part of our group now. He occupies the cell between Gormly and me, which has been the only one vacant on the east side of "crackpot row." He is planning on joining the co-op farm group at Macedonia, Georgia, when released. From their description (his and Art Wiser's) it sounds like a good deal. The effort there is to include as many of the local folks as possible in the program. Another fellow here who, with Parker's assistance, has evolved some new and better ways of making cuts for printing, is also planning a model community to produce their product and find the good life. I understand he wants to sell me on the project. Don't think it appeals to me as much as other plans, but apparently there will be plenty of places for us to serve an apprenticeship to subsistence farming, even if the Mel-Chimes plan doesn't develop, or we are too late to be included.

I'm reading a book, fairly interesting so far, entitled *Enchanted Acre*. The author has an acre and a half near New York City. He makes part of his living by freelance writing and raises the rest on his place. He is against what he calls "subsistence homesteading," his argument being that to deny the advantages of our economic system is stupid. The thing to do is make the system work—unfortunately, he doesn't explain how this is to be done.

I've also read a couple of plays lately that are ripping, absolutely ripping. "Of Thee I Sing" is a very funny satire on our political system.

But the one I nearly laughed myself sick on was Aristophanes's play "Lysistrata." Have you ever read it? The plot is that the women, tired of the war which has been going on for about 20 years, decide to end it by withholding themselves from their husbands until peace is declared. They have a hard time keeping the pledge, but succeed for a few days and, of course, end the war. It is in the Athenian Senate's discussion of the problem that the punch lines, with an uncanny modern ring, are found. Consider a few selected at random:

> President of Senate: "We are the seven who would die for our city."
>
> 1st Senator: "But since we don't die, we live rather well."
>
> 2nd Senator: "No one can complain if we spend all the money since Athens has ships and the soldiers have food."
>
> 3rd Senator: "All this we do without pay or reward."
>
> Chorus of Senators: "Except the commission we make on our soles."
>
> 1st Senator: "One talent for Athens and two in our pockets. Now what could be fairer?"
>
> 2nd Senator: "My department is wheat, I send bread to the Army. Sometimes it is pure and sometimes there's an error. And frequently, as the sacks move toward the front, a dozen or two fall behind at my warehouses."

Another Senator is robbing them blind on his leather contract.

> 2nd Senator: "I was a farmer in a fairly big way but I never rose up to a place of importance. I was ignorant then of political skill but when the war came, I foresaw that my neighbor might turn out a spy. So I came and denounced him, took over his land, which was richer than mine, let two of

the Senators have their way with my daughters, and now I've become a ruler of Athens."

Chorus of Senators: "We owe all to the war, the war must go on."

1st Senator: "For if the war ends, all the laws we have passed, emergency measures to keep us in power, will become null and void and we'll have to go back to the work that we did, which wouldn't be pleasant. I'd be a fish monger."

They mention how they always remind the people that "Athens is democratic, while Sparta, our enemy, is utterly different. It's ruled by a small group of military leaders," etc. They wonder what to do about the women's strike and the soldiers' growing hostility, and one of them concludes the discussion by saying, "Let's appoint a committee." Gosh, but isn't it all there, Honey, and to think that it was written in 411 B.C.

I designed another house yesterday—a very peculiar one but I think it might have some advantages. With the front door pointed due south, there would be a maximum of light and sunshine in the main rooms, especially during the winter. It's just another way of amusing myself.

I think Carlberg's idea is OK except I think it would be more fun to use leg instead of motor power (what would you do if the motor failed 100 miles from nowhere?). Also, I'd prefer to hit regular hostel trails. I think one starts at Chicago and goes through southern Wisconsin. Also believe there is one starting at St. Louis and going through the Ozarks. However, the trip Marie has in mind should help develop a spirit of self-reliance, which, in our soft, sheltered civilization, is often woefully weak.

Sometimes when you have room on your letters, why not include words to some song so I could learn them. You know how hazy my memory of words can be sometimes.

I apologize for the poor writing, but sometimes I can't make out some of your words either, so we're even.

Have fun, Honey.

Lots of love,

Chuck

◼ ◼ ◼

December 23, 1945

Dearest Betsy,

Sometimes after the mail comes around in the evening someone has an item of general interest which he shares with the group by standing near the door and reading loudly. Last night Gormly announced a "flash" and then read an item from Abe Kauffman's (WRL secretary) letter that sent a cheer up through "crackpot row." I quote: "I received a telephone call today from Frieda Lazarus, who had seen Mr. Clark this morning. He told her that within the next 20 days they will release on parole all men who are over 26 and who have served one-third of their sentence. The procedure, he said, will begin to operate tomorrow (the 19th). Restrictions as to type of work, pay, and residence will be lifted." The provision is expected to release about 1,500 of the 5,200 men in prison.

Well, that's the big rumor, but don't get too excited about it because there may still be a number of jokers in the deck. I was at Tucson when the press announced with glowing optimism that a new parole plan (8641) would see several hundred COs released in a few weeks. And I saw the special panel board, set up to start the new plan off, classify about 6 men out of 40 COs and 125 JWs as IV-Es—the rest as I-As. Another possible catch is that maybe not all the men eligible for parole would be willing to accept it, and I can see good reasons. After all, if it is admittedly unjust to keep us in prison, then why should we be kept under the supervision of the Bureau of Prisons, required to make out monthly reports, not move without permission, etc. To acknowledge the Bureau's "right" to keep control over me might very well seem to acknowledge the justice of one's imprisonment—which I don't. Also, it may be decided by the Bureau that non-cooperators are not entitled to release by parole. Gormly, for instance, in one of the slimiest pieces of chicanery I have ever seen, had his parole denied through the efforts of local officials when he quit work in protest to Parker's and my punishment for refusing to haul in the officer's coke. Though such discrimination might set up a protest that might embarrass the Bureau of Prisons. Well, one-third of my time isn't up until June 19, 1946, so we have lots of time to think about it. Anyway, it would seem to appear that the pressure is beginning to be felt by a rather unliberal, unsympathetic administration.

I suppose Mom told you about the other current rumor (not as well founded) to the effect that our non-cooperation group is to be split up by shipping us off to different prisons. (I never know how much to repeat in my letters since none of you ever tell me who all reads them.) To be transferred would be sort of fun, though it is hard to know what conditions a non-worker would receive. However, I trust you all would be on the alert to see that they were not too onerous.

I'm glad you had fun out of Christmas shopping, since that is the only justifiable basis for giving things. I've received 20 Christmas cards so far. Only three of them are from people I know—Harold Kauffeld, Bob Pope, and Jarroth Harkey. Bob's was good, but I think the one you sent was best (pat, pat). Am glad you put it in somber colors—more impressive and in keeping with the idea of the poem. Incidentally, if you get in a letter-writing mood some day, send one to Bob Pope—Apartado 426, Rio Piedras, Puerto Rico. Tell him about the set-up here, our plans, etc. He is a good guy. To how many of my old CPS/Tucson gang did you send cards?

Was happy to hear from Phyl. Send her my love—filial of course. I felt very honored to be ranked with Austin as compared with the local yokels. But that old line about being her favorite brother-in-law doesn't fool anyone. I'll bet I'm also her most disliked brother-in-law, the most disreputable one.

Also, got a letter from Frank just two days after I wrote asking him if I had been crossed off his list. He mentioned getting a letter from you but didn't have much to say. Despite Frank's opinion to the contrary (I suspect), I believe I'm probably learning lots more in the school of hard knocks than he is in "the house of God." But then, every man to his own tastes. At least I think I've learned never to be "bound by any studied system" of dogmas, as Blake says.

Am reading *Main Street*. Oh, the tyranny of small town life. You should read it.

There are about 20 "chukars" (some kind of quail or partridge) playing around on our Fox and Geese track. It's fun to watch them.

A JW acquaintance from Tucson arrived the other day and we've been exchanging experiences.

Be sure to let me know in advance when you move so I can change your address in the office. It takes a few days.

Lots of love, Sweetheart.

—*Chuck*

Here are a couple of . . . hmm, well, a piece of imagery and a jingle, which I should never have included.

Pounding through the night . . . churning the darkness . . .
    fleeing across
The frozen wastes, a train soars toward the south.
A Cyclops of straining steel charging with one bright eye . . .
Seeking the cities of men.
Suddenly flung from its aching lunge, a bellow of anguish
Shatters the mute air.
Fragments are hurled over the river . . . over the wall . . . past
    steel bars.
Fragments that pierce through my reverie . . . and lodge in my
    heart.
In my heart! Ah, what's the affinity there?
Why does that cry of doubt and despair pull like a magnet . . .
Tug at invisible cords in my heart?
Ours is the bond of loneliness.
Southward I too would go . . . over the frozen wastes . . . past
    the long night.
South to the cities of men . . . to a pair of soft eyes as blue as
The summer sky . . . to a smile that warms my heart
As sunbeams stir bud in the spring.
Ah, but the walls are cold and stern.
How can they know my heart's longing?
Only the train's lonesome cry can hurtle the wall . . .
Can push through the bars.
Hear now how it fades in the distance . . . vanishing
    southward . . .
Into the night . . . over the frozen wastes . . . seeking the cities
    of men.

Dear Santa Claus

Dear Santa Claus,
I know you're awful busy
What with shortages and all.
(They say the stores can't buy a thing
'Til excess taxes fall.)
So I won't ask for something new
Or something hard to find.
Just fill my stockin' up with that
Sweet little wife of mine.
(P.S. Please find sock hanging
just outside of Cell No. 35.)

◙ ◙ ◙

December 30, 1945

Dear Betsy,

Just last week I had a hard time filling two pages in a letter to Mammy and now I have so much to write about that I'm going to have to put Mom's letter off 'til next week. Will you explain to her that we had so much "family" business to talk over that I couldn't get one to her this week?

Speaking of Mom reminds me of your question about her in your letter. I am not surprised to hear of her increasing emotional instability. Unlike Mammy, Mom's whole married life has been tied up in her children. She had no outside interests, no creative outlet. So I imagine she feels frustrated, useless, and insecure. And with her inferiority feelings the problem is made more difficult. Also, she seems to be interested in the world situation, the suffering and all, but doing nothing about it—that, too, is a source of frustration. She would be helped psychologically by "lighting a candle." But I'll be darned if I have any concrete suggestions. If the folks could get a place of their own where Mom could have a flower garden, or a dozen chickens to take care of, that might be a start. It would be good for her to take a good long trip, I think. If she could go out and be with Paul and Mary Ellen for a month that would be great. Of course, Paul and

Mary Ellen haven't a place for her now, but I think she could get along some way. She could meet some of my friends—Lucille, Jerry, etc. It might give her new interests in life. What do you think of the idea? Maybe Paul could think of some way to swing the deal, he's good at that. Pop could stay with Jane and would get along swell. Mom could spend the month of March or April there and come back in time for the Nebraska spring. What do you think?

About the Christmas present from us to us—well, I've thought about it some and can't think of a thing we are in very urgent need of. How would the idea strike you of buying a little international goodwill with the money, a little human love? In other words, how about giving it to one of the several worthy efforts being made to feed starving people—the AFSC, FOR, the Catholic Church, the Protestant Church, *Politics* magazine, and others could all use the money to good advantage, I think.

The big rumor (of 1,500 men being paroled) is beginning to develop some of the complications I anticipated. Seems now that the National Parole Board doesn't think much of the idea and hasn't approved of it yet. (Do I have any friends who haven't written to the President requesting my release? A letter a day keeps defeatism away.)

I'm glad that you witnessed to the SCA gang. Youse is a good little Wifey. I was beginning to fear that your pacifism might be getting sort of lukewarm.

Got a letter from Buffett on our letter to the President about feeding. He was with us, in fact, enclosed a *Congressional Record* reprint of a speech of his. Regarding the government's refusal to allow private relief in Germany, he says, "Mr. Speaker, I protest a government policy which forces 10,000,000 Christians in America to stand by helplessly while eight or ten million old men, women, and children of their faith die needlessly in Central Europe." He also includes a good editorial from *The Christian Century,* November 28.

Parker and Dyer decided to keep going on from our Christmas Day fast and are still at it. They plan to stop on New Year's Day. Dyer is getting rather weak but that darned Parker still plays Fox and Geese as hard as ever. I ran a mile yesterday and he ran the last half right behind me. Both of them look a little hollow-eyed. Before

I leave this cloistered, carefree situation I'm going to have to take a week of fasting as a scientific experiment.

I've been feeling fine (though it feels like I might be getting a cold tonight). On most of the exercises which we do I hold the record—150 deep-knee bends, 45 push-ups, walk 100 feet on my hands, etc. I'm probably in better physical shape now than when I was "enjoying" the "work privilege." Everything seems to be going pretty smoothly right now. Another Trenton AWOL, Dave Newton, sentenced with Dyer but given a month's stay of execution while his wife had a baby, arrived a couple days ago. We are hoping he joins us in C2.

I was surprised to hear that you bought us a new copy of *Birds of America*—happily surprised—or rather Pappy did. Quite a book, isn't it? I think a book like that would have meant a lot to me as a kid. I hope some day we have kids of our own to enjoy it. Am also looking forward to taking some really rugged camping trips with boys of my own some day.

The other day I got to reading *The WPA Guide to California* (The Federal Writer's Project) and the thought of those great big trees, lofty mountain peaks, remote lakes, etc., all waiting for me to see them just made my mouth water. I'd like to take a month and hike 100 miles or so there. Do you think you would be interested in, and tough enough for, such a jaunt, or would you prefer a more civilized vacation, letting me take some male companion on the trip?

Will include another Christmas poem. Somehow I'm not satisfied with it yet. May try to rewrite it. Haven't been doing much reading lately. But have finally read half of *The Rise of American Civilization* and have learned a lot more than in all the history courses I've ever taken in school. Beard analyzes all the forces behind social change very well and assigns to each its importance in the tides of time. Good book.

This letter ought to hold you (and the censor, poor fellow) for a while. I love you, Sweetheart. Marry me some day, will you? What are your plans now that you've quit the Rosses?

Love and kisses,
Chuck

Contrasting Christmases

Lulled by the false security of might,
Our politicians nurse the flame of hate
By stern decrees, then hurry home to wait
By cheery firesides on Christmas night.

Our boys in khakis, many a weary mile
From home, in lands by war's crude fingers torn,
Share their own Christmas gifts and food—and warm
To see sad, frightened little faces smile.

◼ ◼ ◼

January 1, 1946

Dearest little callipygous Wifey—

Surprise, Sweetheart, also Happy New Year! Surprise letters are
in order—I got one last night from me. It was addressed to you and
dated December 16. Apparently the postal authorities couldn't read
my writing (the first "3" was not too clear) because the letter was
marked "No such address." I thought the "3" plain enough but they
were probably confused by the fact that your last name was different
from the folks at that address. So, call off the dogs, Honey. I'll quote
the parts of the letter that are still pertinent.

Dec. 16, quote: "This has been a busy day for 'crackpot row'—
we have been copying and addressing letters to senators, representatives, the President, and his Cabinet—some 64 in all. Incidentally, I
am the author of the letter; it reads as follows:

Federal Correction Institution
Sandstone, Minn.
Dec. 16, 1945

An open letter to President Truman

Dear Sir:
As this holiday season approaches, rich in traditions of happiness and festivity, we, the undersigned, sincerely hope that

the rejoicing at home may not blind you to the unprecedented hardships and suffering shrouding a war-torn world.

Rather, may the true spirit of Christmas—a spirit of love and compassion—enlist your efforts on behalf of the homeless and starving masses abroad. Let it not be said that they were delivered from the bonds of tyranny to the freedom of death. Nor may your efforts know any as "friend" or "foe," but rather recognize in all the common victims of a mutual enemy—man's own inhumanity.

For our country to be concerned with this problem is not a matter of mere altruism, but of serious national policy. How will America fare in the judgments of tomorrow if we do not respond to this crisis in the spirit of sacrificial goodwill? To be unselfish now is only to be prudent.

Being in a federal prison and thus incapable of rendering any active service ourselves, it is nevertheless our intention to fast on Christmas Day as an expression of our deep concern. But to make this concern effective, we must depend on you and our other elected representatives.

Yours very truly,

Charles Worley 2473
Glenn Hutchinson 2380
Edward Adamowicz 1974
Malcolm Parker 2501
Henry Dyer 2566
Walter Gormly 1940

Though it isn't as timely now, I wanted you to send copies of the letter to Herron, A.J., Bill Stafford, Mrs. Popowski's brothers, and the *World-Herald*. If you and Mammy think it would have a good effect, why don't you do so even now.

(Quoting again) "Yesterday was a red-letter day. Hutch got a clipping from *The New York Times*. It is a long write-up beginning as follows: "An appeal for grant of amnesty to the 3,000 COs now in federal prisons was sent to President Truman yesterday by a group of 62 leading clergymen, education leaders, and other professional men acting under the initiative of the ACLU." The article scores the discriminatory discharge, etc., applied to COs and makes the following specific recommendations: 1) That the government restore full civil rights and commute sentences of all COs in prison, 2) That COs be given the same parole rights as other offenders, 3) That the War Department review all court-martial CO cases, and 4) That a point system on equality with the Army's be set up for COs.

The list of signers, all of whom denied being pacifists, included several authors, college presidents, magazine editors, etc.—such names as Von Passen, C.C. Morrison, L. Adams, D. Taylor, John Dewey, etc.—even a former American Legion commander.

Betsy, could you stand to write another letter? I have some books at the CPS camp at Beldon, California. Since the camp may be closing up one of these days, would you please send them our address with the request that the books be returned when they close up?

(Still quoting) "Guess this is my last chance to wish you a Merry Christmas, Sweetheart. My theme song this year should be 'I Can't Give You Anything but Love, Baby.' And can't give you that very well by mail, but inasmuch as I can, Honey, it's all yours. Am also enclosing an assortment of hugs and kisses—all of them much better than those I gave you last year. I only wish the other fellows here had such a wonderful memory of last Christmas to fall back on as I have. And this year I can be thankful for something I have never had at any other Christmas—a loving wife and another swell family."

Well, Betsy, I made myself another calendar last night but only up to October (that's a clever way of coercing them to let me out before October 1, don't you think?) Trouble is, I also made out another book list. It has over 100 titles and now I don't know what to do. Suppose that they try to force me out before I finish the list? Should I resist? And if so, how? Please advise.

Would you, could you write another letter, this time for four of us . . . Hank, Hutch, Parker, and myself? We would like to take the "Small Community" course that Arthur Morgan puts out. We are in no position to make the arrangements ourselves, so would you write to him, acquaint him with our situation and, if he is willing to give us the course, ask if he would contact Warden G.W. Humphrey and make the necessary arrangements. (Gosh, Honey, I'm sure loading you down with correspondence. Do you mind too much? I'll kiss you some day for being so good to me.)

If you haven't written to Chimes yet, please revise upward the estimated amount of cash necessary to get started. If we got along on a bare minimum I think we could get it all started on about $3,000, not $2,000 as I said before. Are you doing any thinking on the suggestion? Am interested in you reaction.

What with a new year starting, I've also been wondering if it wouldn't be a good idea to re-inventory our mutual aims, goals, etc. What were the things we hoped to accomplish during this separation and what progress are we making? For myself, I really don't feel that I've made any spiritual progress to speak of. Maybe I "know myself" a little better and have cast off some more of the artificial "crustation" thrust upon me by society, but nothing positive has taken its place. On the technical side, I have read some good books on gardening, farming, horticulture, beekeeping, and dairy cattle, and have books on my list on gasoline motors, woodworking, wiring, poultry husbandry, plumbing, biology, and botany. But book learning by itself isn't very practical—it must go with the practice to be really useful. One of the things we will need is a good library of books, pamphlets, etc., on the various phases of farming, construction work, etc. Why don't you start accumulating such a library? Find out what the best books are on various subjects and then, if you should have a few extra minutes downtown, stop in a second-hand bookstore. What with new ideas always coming out, I wouldn't be in favor of putting out much money for new books, but keep your eye open for bargains. State and federal agriculture departments put out lots of good stuff. You could probably get some very useful bulletins from the University of Missouri Agriculture Department.

Got a letter from Mom last night. She can't seem to get it straight that I'm eating big, healthful meals every day.

Bye, Sweetheart

—*Chuck*

◉ ◉ ◉

January 8, 1946

Dearest Betsy,

Most of the contents of this letter were included in a letter which I mailed to you Sunday and which came back to me last night with a note attached from Mr. Domrese. I quote:

> Worley: The content of a letter should be addressed to the authorized correspondent you are writing to only. You may not write two authorized correspondents in the same letter as you seem to be doing in the attached. You should write your letter to your wife or Durand but not to both in the same letter.
>
> Letter may not go out.
>
> —Parole Officer

Ah, you poor, dear, innocent girl. To think that you are married to a man whose criminal tendencies seem to be hardening into habit—twice convicted of refusing to sanction the "kill for freedom" campaign, and then on top of that to perpetrate such heinous offense against our free and glorious state as this. You see, Honey, what I had done was finish my remarks to the Durands on the bottom of the letter in such a way that it could be detached! Please pray for me, and for the Bureau of Prisons, and the nation, and the U.N.O. so that no international crisis may be precipitated by my dastardly and felonious indiscretion, Amen.

I continue, this time addressing my remarks solely and entirely to you, Elizabeth Ann Worley, alias 2473 S.S. I am sure, however, that you must sometimes tire of my traditional type of letter, which progresses in a more or less orderly fashion from one point to the next. As a surprise, I am varying my style somewhat.

Freedom for COs would have been a severe threat to the war system and the principles upon which it rests. By complying with the Conscription Act which assigns them to forestry work, COs simultaneously accept and cooperate with the government's conscription of other men for war. Is it a matter to be taken lightly that the "peace churches" have actually helped to establish a tradition of enslaving men, with no compensation or care for dependents, and of putting them at work of little social importance? How does this differ in principle from German concentration camps? What splendid traditions to get started in a day when the mortality rate on democratic institutions is so high!

Now, about the Brethren's recent decision: According to Win Osborne of NABRO and two other sources, the Brethren decided to continue sponsoring CPS because they didn't want to affect Selective Service—because they wanted to be permitted to sponsor an alternative program in case of peacetime conscription—because otherwise they were afraid of losing their 18- and 19-year-olds from the church tradition. Believe me, if that is a measure of the Brethren's peace witness, they might as well close shop right now. Verily, verily, if Brethren youth are reared in a home environment of love, goodwill, and democracy, they can't turn out wrong; then government-sponsored conscription camps would probably turn out more Brethren pacifists than church-sponsored conscription camps. What the Brethren apparently believe is that they can make pacifists of their young people by authoritarian indoctrination. I've seen that kind of pacifist and truly believe they do the cause more harm than good.

If you should just happen to see the Durands, Betty, would you assure them of my un-abating affection and beg forgiveness for anything offensive I may have said? I know they wouldn't want me to be silent or to hedge on the truth in a matter that seems so important to me. I'd like to suggest that they have a bunch of friends in to discuss the matter and that Clancy Runyan and Fred Smith, both working at Bethany Hospital, be invited to present the "con" side.

I am in complete agreement with some of your recent comments: [1] As to your conclusions from living with the Rosses, let's you and me resolve to A) live to the end, B) live by our own labor, not by exploiting someone else's labor, and C) let's put the emphasis on things that count; [2] I also amend your comments on brown ink, and your anticipation of what I might say about a 23-year-old girl who allowed her body to "go to pot" through lack of exercise.

Paul seems to be having a little personality problem with himself. I wrote to him this week. Would you drop a postcard to Mom explaining that I had to put her off for another week—she has a habit of worrying, you know.

So Marsh wouldn't give you an opening—the coward.

Pappy's note in our book was cute. Was glad to hear from him. Also got a letter from my pop last night, and one from my wife. I always appreciate hers, even if she does sometimes have two "gobs of fun" and one "gobs of food" in the same paragraph. Were there any gobs at the PF party?

Did you hear from any more of our friends over Christmas: Trav and Florence, for instance, or Scaff, or the Scotts, or Butchie? Did you get any of the letters sent that I asked you to write (Chimes, Margan, Belden, etc.)? Please understand that I wouldn't blame you if you didn't. After all, I married you for my wife, not my secretary. But I like to know when you can write letters for me or when you can't so that in the latter case I can get them out some other way if I think them important.

Just finished Peter Drucker's *The Future of Industrial Man*. Some parts of it are very thought-provoking, particularly his discussion of freedom, its relationship to government, to majority rule, etc. We're starting a series of weekly discussions next Monday morning exercise period and will probably discuss some of his ideas then. Am now reading *Apes, Men, and Morons* by Hooten. He does a good job of making anthropology interesting and entertaining. I may give Mammy's suggestion a try—outlining discussions from some of my reading.

Have you done much thinking about what things you hope to learn or accomplish at Mil's? Would be interested to know your specific aims. Unless we have such aims pretty well in mind, I fear there is a tendency to lose sight of them in the maze of routine daily living—n'cest pas? (That's French, you know.)

This reservation goes on a five-day/week work schedule and a seven-day/week mail schedule this week. The former doesn't affect me much, of course, but the latter means we can both send and receive mail on Sunday henceforth.

Will give you a couple of song titles I'd like words for if you'll promise not to let songs interfere with the things I really want to hear, what you are doing, thinking, planning, etc. "The Ash Grove" and "The Londonderry Aire" will give you a reserve until I think of others.

Have lots of fun in Chicago—go places and meet people and tell me all about it. I especially recommend that you get well-acquainted with Frank and Marie and their progeny—they are real folks.

There are no new rumors. I'm feeling fine, eating my share of the food, etc. We've gotten about 20 replies from government officials on our Christmas letter. About feeding, Dos Passos has a good article in the January *Life*. The editorial is also good.

Lots of love,
Chuck

◙ ◙ ◙

January 16, 1946

Dearest Betsy,

Hi, Honey. I'll write now but don't know when I can mail it as your change of address hasn't been approved yet—'cause you didn't notify me in advance about leaving for Mil's as you had promised.

Shucks, Honey, you don't need to apologize for your letter writing. I'll grant that it isn't your long suit, but you do OK. I think partly the trouble is that you can't project yourself into this situation enough to know what to write about. You see, every day and all day long, we are confined to the same grey walls, the same few faces, the same very limited range of experiences, so anything beyond that is new and exciting—travel, meeting people, your impression of the big wicked city, etc., etc. You mention long bull sessions with the D's but no word of what you talked about, their reaction to my letter, etc.

But I was sort of disappointed that you felt "insecure" just because someone wasn't there, Johnny-on-the-spot, to meet you in Brookville—tsk, tsk, what a pioneer! How far is it to Mil's, 5 or 6 miles? Personally, I hope you had to walk. We don't become self-assured and independent as long as we always have someone else to lean on.

Now I probably wouldn't say a naughty thing like that but my P.A. has been down several points of late. This solitary seems to bring out one's moodiness. I thought maybe it was just me but Mal confessed the other night that he has lately felt the same way, and he's one of the most healthy-minded guys I've ever met.

We are quite confined now since Calloway, our contraband agent, has been transferred. No more newspapers or magazines now, and Monday they went through and took all the extra books which we had accumulated with so much care and ingenuity. We're down to one book each now. I hope Mil takes some good liberal magazines and papers so you can send me significant clippings occasionally.

This institution has been calmly appropriating some of Gormly's personal magazines so he protested to the Warden. The letter said he would check on the matter and went on to say that in his opinion our status compared favorably with Administrative Segregation as practiced elsewhere, that in some places it was more liberal and in others more stringent. Apparently he wants to carefully avoid being listed among the more liberal and progressive wardens. But I don't see where he gets it that this is a middle position. According to Win Osborne, who has visited COs in the other prisons, and according to what other news we get, our position is more niggardly than any of the others. We have sanitary facilities and food, two hours of exercise daily, and two books weekly and correspondence, and that is all. At the other extreme, in Danbury the men receive full privileges and are right out in prison population except during work hours. Among the things we are denied are a commissary, movies, radio, newspapers and magazines, worship services, educational courses, standard clothing, full use of the library, musical instruments, and recreation. He also said that he was going to Washington soon and would talk the matter over with the Bureau officials—which, I hope, gives you some ideas.

This place still suffers from "rumortism." Yesterday all S.S. cases of men over 26 with a third of their time done met with the Parole Office and they say that many will be paroled soon, that Bill Berg is to leave Monday, and that 50 JWs were paroled at Ashland to do "pioneering." They'd better be careful—some day one of those rumors may hit the jackpot. After all, even the most crooked machine pays off occasionally. But apparently the new deal isn't intended for us illegitimate sons up in the C2 garret because neither Adam or Gormly received any notice, though both are eligible.

Got another note from the Pardon Attorney yesterday. He doesn't agree with me that special circumstances have arisen that justify the immediate consideration of my application. Just for the h--l of it, I may write to Buffett and Butler asking them to put the heat on the guy.

Paul Gamble, our colored CO, has been in the hole for over two weeks now. He has some physical ailment that makes work outside in this kind of weather miserable but they accuse him of malingering. Just now saw Paul outside—apparently released. After reading Hooten's book I am beginning to wonder if we are justified in expecting men to act like decent, kindly, intelligent animals. After all, only a couple million years ago they were swinging through trees, scratching fleas, and looking for berries. And yet, on the other hand, I've noticed that one officer here always seems to be very busy elsewhere when there is any dirty work going on, shake-downs, etc. Maybe if God is patient, in another two million years we might be less contemptible creatures if there is still a remnant of "homo sapiens" alive by then.

Yesterday I asked to be permitted to order *The Bible of the World* and *Climate and Man,* but no reply as yet. Also asked if I might order a bunch of USDA bulletins.

Got a letter from Jane Monday—nice, huh? Mom is really wising up. Jane quoted a newsy letter from Lucille mostly telling about people you don't know. Lucy says that Emma has a steady boyfriend in Chicago—ain't that sumpin. Wish you could have met Emma, she's a great person. Lucille is urging me to accept parole—ain't that a laugh?

I wonder what happened to the first of Frank's letters. It never did come. Did you think my comments on CPS and the Brethren were unjustified? If so, in what ways?

Latest flash—says *The Grapevine*: "Conscription will be permitted to die a natural death in May." Also, John S. says that the Army's plan for a year's training is dead.

Gosh, the moon is beautiful tonight, Sweetheart, wish we could be viewing it together.

Give my regards to Uncle John and Aunt Mil, also Dyer's, who says he has stayed at their home twice. Also, the boys all send you their love—and me, too.

Bye, Sweetheart

—*Chuck*

◘ ◘ ◘

January 21, 1946

Dearest Betsy,

No, Honey, Ahm not forgettin Ah got a fat 'n sassy wife waitin' fo' me—Oh, 'scuse me, you said, "sassy, yeller-haired," didn't yo'? Guess that's the result of those Rye Crisp ads Calloway used to show me. But shucks, that's OK, Honey, if you weigh over 165 when I get out, why maybe we won't have to buy a team of mules for our subsistence farm—ain't I a stinker! I admit it, Honey, but gosh I sure love you and would give anything to be able to tell you so right to your face—smack, smack—two big kisses.

Did I make sarcastic remarks about your last R.B. summary? I'm sorry, Sweetheart—but it seems to have had a very good effect 'cause your summaries this time are excellent. Probably better than the originals, with all the meat and none of the bone or gristle. Should I make a few comments on the letters? Send the one or not, as you think best. Hal: sounds like he's still "out after souls." God bless America! Marie G.: "The Robe" wouldn't have to rank very high to outrank Douglas' other works, would it? Every man to his own tastes, of course, but personally I thought the whole middle part of the book could have been omitted with no great loss (too much of it being pure propaganda), and the last part—Marcus picking cantaloupes, etc.—sounded like something fresh from Hollywood to me. Helen G.: I thought her letter very interesting—lots of human interest. Having rubbed shoulders with the proletariat myself, I could appreciate it. But when she started telling about the "Itinerant Minister," I thought she said "Itinerant *Merchant*" and was looking for something quite different. And that Methodist minister who had seven wives—are you sure he wasn't a Mormon? Eula: Must you tell about all those swell hikes—curses, curses. I've figured out that "stone walls do not a prison make" line. It takes a few "cons" inside those walls to make it a prison. Marie C.: "Job" for what you are doing is too mild. Sounds more like a "career for life"—re-planning Omaha—whew! Good luck. Mary M.: Why don't you camp in Pushing Square—it worked for the soldier, and there's no place in the world so rich in material for sociological research. Incidentally, I think Frank's idea, about getting wrapped up in a case and ending up in Europe, is a good one. One year of social work in Europe right now would probably have as much educational value as ten years at U.S.C. Kathy: Sounds positively immodest to me, a girl of your age and family background having 300 children! Ah, but what a wonderful dean she should make—how well she should understand the personal problems of the students! Frank: "Tanks for dem kind woids, Buddy. If you tink youse is chagrined, how about me?" It was a tough fight but it looks like we're winning. I'm happy to think that I may have been a molecule, well, an atom anyway, in the balance opposing conscription. But I'm willing to leave prison anytime now—even though my wife may not be able to support me in the manner to which I have become accustomed.

Am enclosing herewith most of the verses to a parody I made today to that old song about the Army. Hutch, Hank, and I may try to work out a trio arrangement of it tomorrow. Unfortunately, a couple of the best verses are unquotable.

Speaking of songs, I got a book from the library Friday that's a dilly—*A Treasury of American Song*—chock-full of folk songs. I'm planning to memorize words and music to about 25 of them so you won't need to send any songs for a while. Thanks for "The Ash Grove."

Enjoyed the propaganda in your first letter from Mil's. Keep it coming. I'm eager to know what you learn and think. I recently finished a book on poultry and now have one on gasoline engines, but it's rather "cold turkey" as all theory and no practice. Among other skills, be sure to learn how to get up and build fires in the morning. You see, I'm getting in the habit of getting the room warm before getting up by simply reaching down to the foot of the bed and turning a little handle, which turns on the steam.

Got nine letters last week so two had to go back, and had only three the week before. Wouldn't that make you cuss? No? Well, it did me. I hope they fire 'em right back as I probably won't do so well this week.

No new rumors of importance. They say the racial-segregation issue is stirring again out in population. Also, some of the boys are trying to think of some way to protest this flimsy excuse for a solution to the COs-in-prison problem. No decision yet. An amnesty committee is being formed in New York, same address as the WRL. The JWs will probably accept parole now if it's offered 'cause Brother McClelland gave them the word the other day that it was OK with Jehovah.

Tsk, tsk, your letter didn't come tonight.

Goodnight, Sweetheart.

Your loving husb'ing

—Chuck

> I'm doing time in prison
> To pay my social debt.
> I got a three year contract
> Just isn't finished yet.
>
> *Chorus*
> Oh, I don't want no more of prison life.
> Gee, Ma, I wanta go home.
>
> They say the guards in prison
> Are quite intelligent.
> If that's true, when I get out
> I'll be the President.
>
> *(Chorus)*
>
> The crud they serve in prison
> They say is mighty fine,
> And if you cannot eat it,
> They throw it to the swine.

(Chorus)

The work you do in prison
Is s'posed to save your soul.
And if you don't believe it,
They throw you in the hole.

(Chorus)

You write home to your sweetheart
And make a funny crack,
But the censor's heard that one before
And sends the letter back.

(Chorus)

On Sundays there's a preacher
That comes to sing and pray.
He says that Jesus loves you
And then he goes away.

(Chorus)

They say the Warden loves you
And treats you very well.
But if this is just like heaven,
Show me the way to ----.

(Chorus)

* * *

January 27, 1946

Hi, Honey,

Or as we say in French, "Bon jour, ma cherries" (that's French,
you know). A request for your picture was acknowledged the other
day and I have been reminded all over again of how lovely you are.
As Hank said when I introduced you, "Hmm, I can see why you
married her." But even before the picture came I had somehow felt

nearer to you lately—why, I don't know, whether it is due to some psychological change in myself, or in you, or both of us. Anyway, it is wonderful to have such a darling wife. I love you much, Sweetheart. I'd been sailing smoothly through the ideas you've been writing about (relishing the imagination of myself eating a huge slice of hot, whole-wheat bread smothered with butter, etc.) when all of a sudden I banged headlong into those 11 points of R.B.'s —and whoa! Whew!! Wow!!! Did they ever stop me. Verily, I seemed to hear a voice from heaven saying, "Unto us a child is born, unto us a son is given, and ye shall call his name R.B., for verily he shall tell the people all the answers about life and explain all the mysteries thereof for ever and ever, Amen."

Honestly, Honey, does R.B. think he's actually getting at the answers to those 11 points? Reminds me of the guy who jumped on his horse and rode off rapidly in all directions.

But the amazing thing was that you, my own dear wife, should quote such a list and ask naively if pacifists are trying to get at all of them—and all without cracking a smile. (And to think that you have read *The Importance of Living,* too. Tsk, tsk.) Please, Honey, promise me you won't learn the answers to all 11 points. Learn how to bake bread, shovel manure, milk cows, chop wood, anything you want to, but don't learn all those answers. 'Cause if you do, you will naturally feel restive and out of place tied down to a poor little ignorant, earthbound husband and go off to join the angels—and I wouldn't blame you at all. How does R.B. stay on earth? Seems to me God would offer him such an attractive contract as general manager in heaven that he just couldn't turn it down.

"Determining what is true," "determining the purpose for living," "deciding on the nature of man and the universe." Wow! Alongside of R.B., Jesus, Plato, Buddha, and all those boys were strictly pikers of the first water. To think that some of the world's greatest thinkers have spent a whole lifetime on just one of those points! Jesus, for instance, claimed some knowledge in matters of ethics and religion, but was rather modestly quiet about the economic system, medical science (except for that healin' trick of his), government, natural science, etc. I can just see Jesus and R.B. meeting in a synagogue and disputing as to who gets to make a speech. Jesus says, "I am the way!" And then R.B. flashes those 11 points on him. What can Jesus do but retire in doubt and confusion, muttering in his beard, "I am the way, I am the way."

No, Honey, I don't know any pacifists who think they are trying to answer those 11 problems. If they are uncharitable toward R.B. it is probably because he gives them a terrific inferiority complex. Though they needn't feel that way, for there is no conflict between R.B.ism and pacifism. The former gives the answers, the solutions to life. The latter only offers a way, a path for approaching those problems. Pacifism says the best way to find the answer to one of those 11 points—"determining what is true," for example—is by the approach of love, kindness, respect for the personalities of others, etc., rather than by coercion, hate, etc.

Though I hope to go into small community life sometime, it is not with the belief that it is THE answer, but chiefly because I feel I can best express my personality in that field. I think there is not one, but many answers, and naively believe that a person does the most good when he finds the one that best expresses his own personality— be it in political activity, recreation, religion, or street cleaning. The enormity of R.B.'s 11 points reminds me of a little poem by Tagore. "The learned say your light will one day be no more," said the firefly to the stars. The stars made no answer.

Hank and Art Wiser both want us to think about joining the co-op group at Macedonia. It's in the foothills of the Great Smokies, has lots of land and plans. May be worth learning more about. The problem of immediate plans when I get out is not real simple. If Chimes isn't interested in our idea, maybe it would be something to think about—not necessarily as a final step but as a first step, a start.

About the bookkeeping—I had hoped you'd be interested in that—you know me, Ah hates it. I suggest you file our income tax and returns, both salaries have to be figured in anyway.

A million thanks to Mil for her letters, also for yours.

G'bye, Sweetheart,

Chuck

Davey's Ambition

When Davey was three'n-a-half, goin' on four,
He wished he could hurry and grow up some more
And get bigger than Dick—a hard thing to do,
'Cause each time he got bigger, Dick got bigger, too.
But at least it was some consolation to know
He was bigger'n their dog and expectin' to grow.
An' 'longside of a worm or a bug or a mouse
Davey felt like he really was big as a house.
And, oh, it just tickled him ever so much
To know molecules, microbes, and atoms and such
Were so little you couldn't even see 'em at all.
Why, alongside 'a them he was ten miles tall.
Davey din't know for sure what he wanted to be
When he grew up, except, he was certain that he
Wouldn't be an electron when he was a man,
'cause there's nothing electrons can be bigger than.

[to be read slowly]
My heart is full of sighs tonight,
of untold yearnings
longing to be sung.
My heart is full of sighs
and yet the cleansing, burning rhythms
cannot come.
Be still my heart—
in stillness and in perfect time
the stream of life
will bear your slender, pulsing rhyme
down to an all-embracing sea
where throbs in might peace
the tender music of eternity
that swells . . . and fills
. . . and flows . . . and brings release.

◉ ◉ ◉

February 4, 1946

Dearest Wifey,

Gosh, Honey, do you remember how at this time a year ago we were fussin' around fixin' to get hitched up? I remember; and I remember our wedding just as well, and how beautiful you were, and the thrill of realizing for the first time that you were my wife, my partner in this crazy business called living; and I remember, too, the thrill of going home with you—to our home, and of undressing and going to bed together, and how sweet and soft and lovable you were. I was just plumb intoxicated by it all—and still am for that matter.

And to think that now we have been married for a whole year. I can't understand how I ever got along without you—it seems so absolutely proper that I should have someone with whom to share life. Our first anniversary finds me at a loss for something suitable to say. Maybe I can best "say it with flowers." Please find enclosed herewith a large bouquet of Mertensia fragrance—selected to match your eyes.

Certainly this occasion finds you deserving of heartiest congratulations—for being willing to marry such a no-account shrimp with a shady past and an eclipsed future, and for sticking to him for a whole year of thick and thin—and not much of anything else.

I'm glad I had sense enough to ask you to be my wife. Of all the contracts I have been a party to in the past four or five years, this one with you is the only one I'm really proud of. Unfortunately, in so many of the others I have been forced to play the role of an unwilling bride, and somehow it just doesn't seem natural.

Maybe in the year ahead I can be more of a husband to you than has been possible this year—I hope, I hope, I hope. Though the immediate future doesn't look too bright right now. R. Domrese, the Parole Officer, was up to visit "crackpot row" last week and said that we non-conformists were not eligible for parole. Actually, his statement didn't make me feel at all bad because for some time now my convictions have been crystallizing against the idea of accepting parole—for a number of reasons.

I'm preparing a more detailed statement of my views. but briefly they are somewhat as follows:

> I do not believe that I have been justly imprisoned nor that it is right to accept and cooperate with this injustice. I am placed in prison and held there by physical coercion, but by accepting parole I would be willingly and voluntarily accepting the terms of that minimum for imprisonment, and thereby acknowledging the justice of it.
>
> If it is now proper that I should be released, then I should be released entirely. The very philosophy of parole is that the person can't be fully trusted in free society, and therefore has to be supervised, and they can throw him back in prison at any time. COs are not criminals but political prisoners, imprisoned for ideological reasons. Parole was not intended for that type of prisoner. Our continued imprisonment is either right or wrong, but the government wants to meet the public demand by dodging the issue.
>
> I am unwilling to agree to any of the conditions of parole: one must first obtain the Parole Officer's permission to A) change his residence, B) change jobs, C) go outside of the judicial district, etc., and D) one cannot go into business for himself but must work for wages.

And another purely personal reason is that when I get out of here I want to feel free to go ahead with our plans without having prison hanging over my head. When on parole, the Parole Officer can have you put back in prison for any reason whatever, or for no reason at all, and then you must serve out not only the remainder of your sentence, but also the time spent out on parole.

I'm figuring out a campaign to put the heat on the Pardon Attorney to get me out of here. The idea is to get lots of letters from individuals and groups urging immediate commutation of my sentence. Will send the plan to the folks when I get it worked out and may ask you to request letters from our personal friends. Will let you know.

Morgan's letter was excellent, but I haven't heard from the Warden about it yet. Am optimistic though since Hutch was recently permitted to take a course on creative writing. Will let you know if I receive our copy of *The Small Community,* or anything else you can do.

Gee, Betsy, I'm hitting so many snags in your "program of education" that maybe it'd be best for me to shut up and let you go ahead. Specifically, I disagree with your idea that "Henry George" or something is the fundamental approach. To fully explain why would take pages. I'd suggest you read Huxley's *Ends and Means* as it has some good things to say on this point. You forget, I think, that the strength or weakness of any "system" is the people and their philosophy of life. Also, I think you greatly misunderstand the purpose of the pacifist movement. Reread very carefully the FOR's "Statement of Purpose."

I also totally disagree that a symphony is either "an elaborate buzz" or a "symbol of our centralized, highly organized society." Bob H. would apparently condemn all group activities as "symbols of . . . , etc." And to think that they call me an individualist.

I also disagree with R.B.'s attitude toward saying grace. I heartily agree that adults need to play, but I'd call that self-deception and hypocrisy rather than wholesome, constructive play.

But to your idea about the desirability of raising a batch of healthy, freedom-loving kids, let me voice a thundering Amen.

Have been doing some interesting reading. Will tell you about it some time.

Got your "clippings" from *Fellowship*.

No, I never did get a withholding statement from Farmers Union.

G'bye, Sweetheart, I love you much.

Chuck

◙ ◙ ◙

February 11, 1946

Dearest Betsy (or is it St. Betty or St. Elizabeth by now?),

I hope you will forgive me, Sweetheart, for writing to you at a time like this. I'm sure that if you are going to learn everything mentioned in the syllabus you'll be much too busy for either reading or writing letters, at least I would be, even with a whole lifetime for the course instead of just two weeks. Judging from how much response my recent letters have elicited from you, however, maybe just reading this one won't take too much time. Guess you must be getting used to my line of bull, no?

You were wrong about my reaction to the syllabus, Honey. I was not annoyed—only amazed. So was Parker when I read it to him. He suggests that you find out for sure Borsodi's birthdate so we can begin to reckon time thereby . . . so many years AB or BB. He and I have been visualizing a new Bible with a "Book of Betty," and, if he and I can get in on the ground floor, possibly a "Gospel According to St. Parker" or a "Chuck's Letter to the Scandahoovians."

A strange thing happened last night at about 7. A voice suddenly called up through the ventilator, "Hey! Upstairs there!" "Yeah," says I, hastening over to the telephone. The voice: "Do you know if Bailey is still at this institution?" Me: "Yeah, he's still here. As a matter of fact, I hear he's thinking of joining us up here in Administrative Segregation. Do you know him?" The voice: "I used to know him at Springfield; I just came from there." Me: "From Springfield. Say, what's your name, Podner?" The voice: "John Hampton." Did it ever floor me! What a coincidence, one of my old Tucson buddies in the cell right below me.

John's prison career has won him the reputation of being CO problem child No. 1. Trouble is that he refuses to accept his imprisonment in any way— refuses to obey the petty regulations, refuses to be intimidated, and even destroys government property that interferes with his comfort and convenience. John, like all other inmates from Springfield, is full of atrocity stories—beatings, short rations, strip cells, etc. He, himself, has been beaten up a couple of times by inmates who had no grievance against him. One of these inmates had good time restored four days after the beating took place. John gathered evidence, which he thought sufficient to convict the officer in charge, and filed a court writ against the officer. This writ may explain the transfer to Sandstone. Or it may be that they'd had enough of him at Springfield and wanted a rest. Anyway, it looks like we may have more company upstairs here soon.

John brought with him some curious information. He says that the Parole Officer who brought him here said that they were supposed to parole all S.S. violators over 26, whether in Administrative Segregation or no. He also says that at Springfield the COs got out so many writs against the administration that they were finally granted almost unlimited and unrestricted correspondence and visiting privileges.

They brought a colored CO up here Sunday, a good, religious, Baptist boy who was having trouble out in population. They moved him downstairs today before we could contaminate him. He and I discovered that we had the same birthday, although I am a year older.

Speaking of birthdays, thanks for your little greeting. I thought it was very sweet. Apparently it had trouble getting through the censor's office though since I didn't get it until the 4th, and then it arrived with a note from Mr. Domrese, which I enclose herewith.

I finished a hard job yesterday—completed my statement as to what's wrong with parole. It turned out to be quite an effort—six and a half pages. I'll try to get permission to send it to the folks along with all the other stuff pertaining to my application for Pardon, and request that they send a copy to you. My idea is to get all the people we can to write in to the President during the month of March urging that my application be accepted immediately and explaining why. Maybe my folks and your folks and Paul and you can be a sort of committee to put the campaign across. Maybe it would be best for you to contact all of our friends except those who live in Omaha, but maybe it will be best for the committee to decide who does what. If we can get letters from all our friends, a few groups in Omaha, Sen. Butler, Rep. Buffett, and your Col. uncle, I think we may swing it.

We had a delightful spring rain last week that completely changed my attitude toward the weather. It has seemed like spring to me ever since, though the thermometer still goes down in the zeroes at night.

Haven't heard anything from the Warden yet about the "Small Community" course.

Doesn't seem possible to me that we've been married over a year, Honey. I'll bet there aren't many people who have been married such a short year as we.

Pockets of privilege! Cesspools of desperation! Bless Borsodi!
And Baby, I love you.
—*Chuck*

P.S. Honey, would you mind dating your letters so I can refer back to them more easily.

◙ ◙ ◙

February 17, 1946 (Have you noticed how pretty the moon is now?)

Hello, My Sweet,

I think probably you are right, Betsy, that I may have criticized R.B. unjustly. But there may be a couple of reasons. In the first place, I didn't want you to be too uncritical in your acceptance of everything the School of Living (or any other school) may believe, but to accept what seems true and reject what seems false to you. I'm sure they couldn't be 100 percent right or they just wouldn't be human. Secondly, I actually believe that those 13 points and that syllabus are presumptuous. And thirdly, I think they seem especially so from the way you have presented them and other of R.B.'s ideas in your letters. If you could reread some of your letters I think you might agree. I'll take back anything unjust I've said, but I will never agree that there is *one way* to a better world and that they have *it*.

Hope you had fun and learned lots in NY. It was kind of the folks there to remember our anniversary. It was especially nice of Steve to give you a bouquet, and the way he did it, as if he was sort of pinch-hitting for me. Express my appreciation to him.

Hampton was transferred upstairs (C2) two days after his arrival at Sandstone—for good reasons, no doubt. His presence has certainly had an electrifying effect on our group. He is an active proponent of an approach that is quite new to most of us, new in the concrete at least. John feels that his presence in prison helps the war effort—discourages others, etc.—uses him against his will as a tool to support the war effort. He therefore feels conscience-bound to do everything he can to prevent them using him as a tool; hence, anything he can do to complicate and make difficult his imprisonment, he does. They offer him privileges in an effort to appease him, but he insists these things are not privileges but rights and refuses to be appeased.

The discussion of this philosophy and trying to discover how each of us stands in relation to it has turned nearly every exercise period into a bull session. I am enjoying the quaint feeling of being perhaps the most conservative person in the group. Chiefly, I think, because I feel that his approach, rather than win understanding and agreement, tends to arouse emotional reactions, black thinking, etc. Of course, it is all a matter of degree (our differences), but I feel that John's position, rather than exercise "soul force" or "truth force," actually exercises physical force in a coercive manner. I don't think we really win a person against war (or anything) unless we change that person's life.

Anyway, a couple of the boys are all bet up and three of them, on the basis that they are opposed to assisting in their own punishment, have refused to go voluntarily into their cells when exercise period is over. So the officers have to take them by the ear and lead them in— they don't actually resist. None of us recognize the prison authority over our lives, but up to this time we have pretty much cooperated.

Mixed up with John's attitude is the consideration of our status in prison, i.e., what "privileges" we should have. Paul French recently saw James Bennett about our status and even without John's approach we were expecting our conditions to be ameliorated. We sent in a letter to Mr. Humphrey today, outlining conditions minimal to our best physical, mental, and spiritual well-being, including commissary, visits, church, cells unlocked, recreational equipment, musical instruments, etc. Incidentally, the course in "Small Community" was recently approved and five of us are enrolled. Would you please have *The Small Community* and my copy of *Ethics* by Dewey and Tufts, sent to me pronto?

Am rereading *Walden and Other Works* with as much pleasure as ever.

Hope you will keep in the back of your mind, "Where do we want to start in when I get out of here?" The Durands sent me a family picture last week. You're still my favorite wife.

Chuck

* * * *

We do not believe that peace can be legislated from the top
but must grow out of the philosophy of the people. Because
the people at present have not formulated and do not live by
a philosophy of peace, plans for a political solution to the war

problem are certain to be futile. In considering how pacifists can work most effectively toward preventing a third world war, we would suggest that they concentrate their efforts toward building such a philosophy into the structure of daily life. In their efforts we would have them remember that the use of physical coercion, either by individuals or by the government through the use of police or armies, is a denial of pacifist principles and cannot assure the desired results.

There are two ways in which the great majority of us pacifists are daily working toward war so that we have no right to expect world peace. One way is in our daily occupations, which, for the most part, are in the war-breeding profit system. Each day we spend our major energies sustaining the profit system—the basic warfare—of which military hostilities are only a dramatic aspect. We must be COs opposed to participating in that warfare economy, otherwise we defeat our own purposes—more than counteract our avocational campaigning for peace. There is a prodigious amount of work to be done in decentralization, consumer cooperation, and education for example, so that none of us needs to depend on the profit-war system for livelihood.

A second way in which we are regularly promoting war so as to nullify our spare-time work for peace is by paying income taxes, over 90 percent of which support the military establishment. We want armaments abolished, but we pay to maintain them. To stop paying income taxes raises problems of procedure with minimum wages, withholding taxes, financing certain peaceful government functions and possibly changing our whole mode of living. But we won't prevent war by merely passing out leaflets.

A third thing we need to do is to develop methods of training our spirits into brotherly attitudes. How shall we learn to keep from anger, selfishness, envy, bitterness, resentment, and jealousy? Peaceful attitudes and behavior will probably not come without a conscience training comparable to the physical training necessary to harden a soldier. A few pacifists are pioneering in this field, but more thinking and training in this needs to be done by the great bulk of us.

◙ ◙ ◙

February 20, 1946

Dear Sweetie Pie,

You are probably no more surprised by getting this letter than I was by the occurrence that occasioned it. In my last letter I mentioned that something was in the wind. Well, Monday the angel of Armageddon appeared in the form of a memorandum from the Warden. About 3:30 Mr. Harlin, our congenial officer, unlocked our cells and let us out to read the new emancipation proclamation. I quote it (dated 2/18/46):

> To: Associate Warden
> Re: Administrative Segregation
>
> The Director has authorized the liberalization of Administrative Segregation procedures in certain respects. Therefore, effective immediately, the following will govern operation of the Administrative Segregation in C Cell Block:
>
> Meals
> – Regular main line (This only means full meals, CW.)
> – Inmates to serve themselves from insulated containers at the table in the day room.
>
> Correspondence
> – Three postage paid outgoing letters to approved correspondents.
> – Seven incoming letters from approved correspondents.
> – A reasonable number of necessary special-purpose letters. (There is no change in this item, CW.)
>
> Commissary
> – Orders for stock items accompanied by coupon books to be submitted through quarantine officer not later than morning of sales days (Tuesdays and Saturdays).
> – Orders for special items to be submitted by request to Commissary Clerk.

Recreation
- One hour "yard" in the afternoons under supervision in
  the area between C Cell Block and A Dormitory (seasonal
  athletic equipment to be made available if requested).
- Use of day room following the evening meal until "lights
  out." (Checkers, chess, dominoes, and playing cards to be
  made available if requested.)

Attendance at religious services of choice.

Library
- Two books in possession, exchangeable on Tuesdays and
  Fridays.
- Reference books necessary for pursuit of any study courses
  (cell or correspondence) being taken.
- Newspapers and periodicals for which subscriptions have
  been placed through the commissary.

Education
- All study courses through institutional school.
- Correspondence courses.

Visits
- Members of the family on request previously approved.
- Other visitors on approval by the Director only.

Quarters
- A fully equipped cell.
- Cells unlocked from "arising time" to "lights out."
- Grilled door to day room locked except during meal time
  and during evening use of day room as set forth under
  Recreation.

Ain't that a . . . Gosh, after being locked up like a bird in a cage
for four and a half months it certainly seems odd to be out walking
around just like a regular person. The thing I've enjoyed most so
far is eating at the table with the other boys. You couldn't imagine
how this new freedom feels even if I could describe it. Almost all
of our requests were granted, musical instruments being the chief

exemption; also, daytime use of day room. I'm a social animal again, Honey.

Lots of things built up to the change—yours and Mammy's and other letters, NSB's pressure on Bennett, letters from ourselves and other men in this institution, etc. It's a good thing it happened when it did. With the advent of the Hampton philosophy and the fact that we have a mechanical genius up here, I dread to think of the dire fate that hung over this hapless institution. Everything isn't all pie and ice cream, even yet!

Next step is amnesty—or a pardon. I sent out my plan to Pop yesterday. You may be hearing from them soon. I suggested they organize a committee and that you would probably be willing to contact your and my personal friends outside of Omaha. Suggest you get in touch with the "Freedom for Worley Committee" right away. It's going to take real work for success. You know, with the group thinking that is bound to take place around the table in the evening, I've got a hunch that some red-hot amnesty pressure is going to be emanating from these parts.

I'm glad you got to witness our national megalomaniacs first hand. "An elaborate pile of cement"—no? I'd like to see it sometime but could die happy without that experience. Your friendship with Steve apparently has its advantages as well as its disadvantages. I can't believe you are so artless, so devoid of normal feminine wiles, that you can't keep him at arm's length without hurting his feelings. For goodness sakes, don't let the poor guy fall for you. (It's possible, you know—take me, for instance.) I'm sure that wouldn't help his personality any, or my feelings.

Two more COs saw the light and applied for membership in the "O1 Athletic and Amnesty Club." One of them was immediately judged sufficiently queer to fit in with the general theme in "crackpot row," but the other was sent up to the hospital on probation. The latter, incidentally, has been quite ill lately. His wife recently had a baby and the poor guy was attacked by such severe abdominal pains he had to be hospitalized. The trouble, I am told, was diagnosed as "sympathetic labor pains." Ain't that odd?

Life has seemed very strange the last couple of days. Being out and around with the other boys affects me about like a little boy trying to watch all three rings of the circus at one time. It just tires me out. Looks like my days of hard time are over. I'm going to have to discipline myself to stay in the cell some time every day if I want to get any reading or thinking done. Got a note from the Warden tonight authorizing the receipt of *Small Community* and *Ethics*.

We're getting the news again. There have been some very interesting incidents lately about picket lines appealing for amnesty—50 people marching three miles out to Danbury, folks passing out literature in Los Angeles, etc.

Hope you aren't disappointed that I overlooked Valentine's Day. It isn't one of my national holidays.

G'bye, Sweetheart. Lots of love,

—*Chuck*

◙ ◙ ◙

February 26, 1946

Dearest Betsy,

This has been a rather wonderful day, not that I've accomplished anything, but we've all had lots of fun. We're still wallowing knee-deep and deeper in this new freedom of ours, still slightly inebriated by it all. This morning the eight of us turned out for church, more than doubling the usual attendance—the preacher was flattered. Ah, the power of God is indeed great—even greater, I am beginning to suspect, than the Great White Father, for there in His presence even the bars of segregation dissolved. And there we were sittin' alongside of the other boys singin' and prayin' just like regular people. Then at dinner our happy little group sat down to a meal of fried chicken, candied sweet potatoes and gravy, creamed corn, and ice cream. Raspberry pie topped off the evening meal, after which five of us played a couple of hot games of Hearts. (I won both of 'em.) A little later Hutch and I got in a singing mood so we ambled down to Hank's cell and had the doggonedest song session you could imagine—everything from "The Bells of Saint Mary's" to the "International." After a while, Parker joined us and we really got up some volume—probably enough to be heard all over the prison, especially when at the end of some workers' song, one of us would shout out, "Fellow Workers!" and the rest would respond, "Unite!" We all began to get a new slant on the technique Joshua used on the Walls of Jericho.

More fun! This set-up reminds me of the good old days at Figueroa Spike Camp out in California—except, alongside of these darned radicals here, those boys were pink-cheeked cherubs. We've started a new public service now. As the boys line up in the yard for the work privilege, we give them a little broadcast program of news, inspirational items, etc. We're working up a few songs for the program. My parody on "Gee Ma, I Wanna Go Home" is one. Of course, we plan to include the two verses I didn't think quite proper to send through the mail.

Yes, I know your folks' home was burglarized—Mammy sent me a carbon copy, you know. But things like that can happen any-where—yes, anywhere, even in one of our Uncle's character-building institutions. For example, we rigged up a mail box up here in C2 made out of a Grape Nuts container. The next morning it was gone. Thinking that perhaps there had been some misunderstanding, we rigged up another and marked it very plainly—U.S. Mail ("for SRAS members only"—"SRAS" represents our new official title, the "Sand-stone Recreation and Amnesty Society"), $5,000 fine or 10 years imprisonment for damaging, removing, or otherwise molesting this container. Well, this morning it was gone also. Now we're offering $10,000 reward for information leading to the arrest, imprisonment, and rehabilitation of the culprit.

Another little difficulty arose when the officers began going through at night banging our cell doors. One of the boys woke up a little confused when this happened and shouted loudly, "Grand Cen-tral Station." The idea spread and the difficulty dissolved.

Thanks lots for sending a copy of Bennett's letter. It's wonderful. The most amusing thing I've read in prison. All the boys copied it and we've even shared it with the boys out in population. Our hearts bled when we thought of everyone suffering because we failed to meet our obligations. Just think if everyone would do that—tsk, tsk.

On Washington's birthday, seven of us signed a statement en-titled, "Why We Will Not Accept or Even Apply for Parole," and sent copies to the Attorney General, Bureau of Prisons, Board of Parole, and the Pardon Attorney. It is a modified edition of the personal statement that I wrote out and sent to the folks. Last week I also sent the statement to John S. requesting that it be made public to interested persons, so keep your eye peeled for it—in *Fellowship* or *The C.O.* Incidentally, we're getting *Fellowship* now and have sent in subscriptions for lots of other magazines. I'm ordering *The Call* and *The Country Gentleman.*

Thanks for quoting all the letters. I'd be interested in John Way's if you ever have room for it.

Your criticism of my remarks about Borsodi were so very personal and seemed to indicate such a total misunderstanding of what I was trying to say in a playful way that I think we may both be happier if I make no further comments. I have felt all along that we had enough fundamental beliefs in common to furnish a mutual basis from which we could consider various problems profitably and in a spirit of love and understanding. Now I'm beginning to wonder if we ever had such a basis; if so, what's happening to it, or am I only overlooking it temporarily, or what? Frankly, I'll be darned if I know what the score is.

Your letter of February 23 just arrived. I have one of the tax forms for figuring a joint return. Think I'll do it and see if our return would be greater that way. If so, I will send it in instead. Returning it to you for signature of course.

Read your letter carefully; will do some with *Interpreter* clippings and *Inflation Is Coming* if you send it. (I'm sure the library would accept it but better send it to me.) R.B.'s comments on education are the same general, unspecific thing you've been sending all along. What thinking or actions of my own am I supposed to change? What do you want me to believe? I don't get it.

Lots of love,
Chuck

◨ ◨ ◨

March 5, 1946

Dear Wifey,

Hello, Honey Bunch. I hope you still love me. I meant to write Sunday but couldn't think how to say it. So I wrote yesterday but so many exciting things happened that I didn't get the letter copied and sent. Since last Tuesday until yesterday, we in Administrative Segregation have been locked up 24 hours a day in solitary (explanation later) and I had lots of time to think but I can't say that my thinking got anywhere. One of the problems that has been bothering me most is one I mentioned somewhat in my last letter, i.e., our relationship to one another, our ideological rapport (that's French, you know), or more specifically, why have some of the things you've been writing about aroused a sort of unpleasant, almost antagonistic response in me—especially since I asked you to keep me informed of your ideas. The problem doesn't seem as acute now as it did a few days ago, but I think it is very, very desirable that we understand each other, so I'm writing to you about some of the queries that have been tumbling round and round in my mind. Maybe if we think about them together we can get at the bottom of things. I'm sure you've been troubled by my reaction. But by all means, let's try to be objective and openly honest because when you criticize me personally, unobjectively, it hurts.

Well, then, how to explain this uneasy attitude I sometimes felt about some of the ideas you write about (me thinking on paper): maybe I'm just intolerant, maybe I don't really want Betty to follow her own light or think for herself, maybe I don't really respect her personality, but selfishly want her to think just as I do. Undoubtedly, I disagree with many of the impressions I get from her letters.

While my concept of life and its problems and solutions seems to be getting broader and broader, hers seems to be getting narrower and narrower. So when she says that such and such seems to be the basic problem, or so and so the answer, I think, Whoa! But is it desirable that a man and his wife think alike about things? Yes, especially if they are the kind of people who act on their ideas because different ideas could require different environments, different ways of living. But what do you mean, C.W., by "different ideas"? I think that this subsistence farming business was your idea, too. Yeah, it is, but something is still wrong. Well, maybe the trouble is that you're jealous of Betty's loyalties; I can see why you would be. After all, when a guy is selling his life (three years of it, in this case) for some cause, he quite naturally craves support and understanding. I know she's 100 percent for me personally, but how about this cause; am I all alone on that? Is she slipping or wasn't she ever in it with me? Or maybe I'm only afraid that she may be naively and indiscriminately swallowing everything somebody else believes, afraid that when I get out of here I won't have a wife with a personality of her own, but rather a junior edition of the School of Living. Or maybe the trouble lies in Mil's and R.B.'s approach. Certainly they aren't overly tactful and they certainly give me the impression that they think they *know* all the answers and anyone who disagrees is just a poor, bewildered sap.

Undoubtedly I rebel when someone tries to make out that they *know* something, because frankly, I don't think anyone KNOWS anything. I truly believe that man's puny grasp of truth is like a grain of sand on the seashore. Those three points, for instance; I still think they are presumptuous. And those questions Mil asked about John Hampton's ideas. I got the impression that she asked them not to get our answers, but rather, like a first-grade teacher would ask her little kiddies some questions, let them have fun trying to guess the answers, and then when they got done guessing, she tells them all the right answer. Whenever anyone gives me the impression that they think they KNOW something, I don't even care to talk to them. That's one reason why I don't give much credence to the first query— I abhor intolerance, it comes from this attitude of positive knowledge. I also resent it when I think someone is trying to sell me some idea. Nobody can decide what is true for me but me. If they want to share their thinking, that's fine, but if they're trying to persuade me that they're right, they know the truth, Whoa! Or maybe I'm just getting frustrated and hypercritical in prison, but I don't seem to be so toward the people around me. Or maybe it's just impossible for two persons in such totally different situations to maintain their feelings of unity, maybe that's what has me upset and confused. But anyway, I still remember at times how absolutely sweet and lovely and unselfish my wife is; I still remember how happy I was living with her, how I loved her and how strongly I was attracted to her physically. (Incidentally, while you're learning all about living, I hope you won't neglect sex. I feel that we're still novices, and in such a wonderful field of activity we ought to be artists. Unfortunately, our library here very carefully avoids the topic.) About the actual skills Betty is getting, my attitude seems to be better. I hope she learns lots and lots, but even here I hope she won't get intolerant ideas, get the idea that there is only one right way to do a thing—the Lane's End or Suffern way.

I don't know whether this unorganized rambling makes heads or tails to you, Sweetheart, but if you can help me solve this problem, please do. Maybe your attitude toward some of my ideas, some of the things I've said, etc., would shed light on the matter. You know, just having written about these doubts makes them seem less important, sort of unburdens me. Maybe it's a good idea for us to let our hair down, to take stock of each other once in a while.

So, maybe until we improve our mutual understandings a little bit, maybe I won't comment much on some of the recent clippings and things you've sent, though your last two or three letters have set pretty good with me. I've read two or three of Beston's articles in *The Progressive*. It has that delightful, nut-like New England flavor, like Thoreau and Frost, though he doesn't perhaps probe as deep as they.

I'll follow this up muy pronto with another letter all about the past week's excitement.

G'bye, Sweetheart. You are very dear to me.

Very much love,

Chuck

◼ ◼ ◼

March 6, 1946

My very sweet, buxom, callipygous wife,

Hi, Baby. I love you much and miss you. Also, I seem to feel better since I wrote that letter yesterday—I must have got something or other off my chest.

I promised to let you in on some of our recent excitement, so here goes. Shortly after our new deal started, we sent a note to the Warden requesting that we be given access to the day room during the day, too. It didn't seem very important to me, but we all signed it. The answer was no.

So what happens? Well, when the officer came up to lock the huge, iron gate to the day room on Tuesday morning, Feb. 26, the darned thing had plumb disappeared. Of course, our theory was that an angel of the Lord had taken it, or else this vandal who'd been swiping our mail boxes at night. Now, the ability to lock a man up is the most sacred thing in the world to prison officials. They were greatly concerned. Mr. Madigan, the Associate Warden, said, "You may think this is funny but it's very serious." Hampton quips, "Oh, we agree that it's serious, but it's an insignificant thing compared to locking men up for their religious beliefs." Finally, after going through the place three times they found it under a bed in the day room and for some reason jumped at the conclusion that we did it. They asked us to put it back on (so they could lock us out of that nice sunshiny room—can you beat it?). Well, naturally we didn't think we ought to do that, so we didn't. A few minutes later our private nursemaid (a good guy) and a congenial lieutenant came up and asked us to go to our cells to be locked up. Well, even a pig has more sense than that, so one at a time we were dragged away gently but firmly and locked up. When my turn came each of them took hold under an arm and away we went, my feet dragging along behind in one long, graceful swan dive, me saying meanwhile, "You can't do this to me; I'm a CO."

What a time! Well, some of the boys, since they were treating us like dogs, renamed it the "Sandstone Kennel Club," and every time one of the "attendants" came around they got down on all fours and began barking—even at their food that way. Of course, we continued our very fine broadcasting programs out the windows. Parker got restless, at least so he says, and a strange thing happened—everything in his darned cell came apart, desk, bed, wash bowl, everything. He accidentally broke his toilet and since they wouldn't move him, some very amusing developments took place, as you can imagine. Hamp's room suffered a similar fate. Some of the guys, every time the food

came, would pick up their trays and start for the day room, others
wouldn't go out in the hall at all and made the guards push the food
in. Oh, what a time, what a madhouse.

Then Friday, two little 18-year-old Quaker boys (after enjoying
the "work privilege" two days) joined us in Administrative Segregation. They're both sharper than firecrackers. Makes me feel good
to have a couple of kids around. Next to them, I'm the youngest
up here. We gave them the best reception possible under the circumstances. They're great kids, plenty wised up, very critical of the
Quakers.

Well, we were in solitary six days. On Monday they let us out
for baths and I had to be dragged in again. The officers were different
ones. They were gentle still, but not greatly pleased.

Then on Monday afternoon, everything busted. John and Mal
were taken away to court. A little later, two more new members,
Roodenko and Taylor, arrived. What a cheer we gave them; wow,
even cheered the captain for bringing them up. Of course, we had
been expecting them. After no one from population joining us for
five months, it made us feel like we'd just conquered the world.

About a half hour later the guardian angel (our officer) came and
turned us all loose. The only thing that dampened our joy was that
John and Mal were put in "the hole." I finally shaved off my week's
growth of whiskers. Back in the hole, things immediately began happening as John went industriously ahead remodeling the prison. Park
is laying low this week, but if he isn't out soon I am looking forward
to major alterations. That guy is a mechanical genius.

So, we're back in all our "privileges" again, still broadcasting,
making plans for amnesty campaigns, writing letters to important
people about prison and related subjects, and in general having a
big time. Gosh, it seems funny to have such a big family up here.
These new boys will never know the experiences of the original
O1ers though.

That five months of semi-solitary was a terrific experience but
I'm glad it's gone. It's great to be out bathing again, but it's hard to
concentrate. When I want to write to my Sweetie, I have to go in my
cell and shut the door. Our bunch up here is militant now, and the
old days of bowing (or even nodding) to the prison system are gone

forever. Freedom is for the people who are willing to be free.

This is only the barest skeleton of all that has been going on. What a time, what a time.

The books from home came last week, muchas gracias, Querida.

Have you heard from the Worley Pardon Committee? I think the folks (mine) didn't understand it or the full consequences very well, thought I was just interested in my own private release. What I want to do is punch a little hole in the dam dam. If we can do it, the dam dam will wash away. The parole business is turning out to be another beautiful farce of 120 men (figures are approximate) here eligible, 10 have received replies from the Parole Board, 5 granted, 5 denied. Ain't that a -----.

Got your letter last night (of March 4). See you're still going strong on this one-basic-problem and answer, or we're-right-and-they're-all-wet idea. Better think it over.

Much love, Honey.

—*Chuck*

◘ ◘ ◘

March 13, 1946

Dearest Betsy,

Hello, Sweetheart, isn't it a coincidence that just when you decided to do a little self analysis, I did too, and our letters passed en route? So while we're "talking serious," I might jot down a few further reactions. I largely agree with your analysis of the situation and, as I suspected, it will probably help us fit the various pieces of this puzzle together. Because you were on the defensive, it made it impossible for us to talk things over as a husband and wife should— with perfect confidence and love. I had the feeling that Mil and R.B. were coming between us, and that instead of thinking with me you were thinking at me.

I am sorry that you felt defensive, but it was probably my fault. Maybe if we had previously discussed our differences more freely and openly, it wouldn't have happened. That I am five years older and have had quite a bit more training in the hard school of experience are undeniable facts. You have had a fine, democratic home life, but a certain amount of stern responsibility, even adversity, seem necessary to develop the full confidence that dispels inferiority feelings. On the other hand, I have been on my own for years and have known some strenuous times, consequently I have an advantage in self-assurance and independence. I think we both recognized this from the start, long before we were married, but I felt then, and still feel, that it need not cause any difficulty and will gradually taper off if we truly respect each other's personalities. I am certain that I have often failed to be truly tolerant of your right to say, think, or do things that I may think to be mistakes, though I fully appreciate and try to remember the fact that we grow by our mistakes.

The solution, I think, is for both of us to be openly and lovingly honest about our deepest feelings and feel free to discuss them. We are bound to make mistakes in our relationship but they shouldn't cause any damage if we discuss our problems in a spirit of love and mutual confidence. In this connection, I think it tends to destroy our mutual confidence when we discuss our problems with others before we discuss them with one another—as though we didn't trust each other.

Maybe I should mention at this time that the main thing I had hoped might be accomplished by our separation was that the gap in our range of experience might be narrowed and that you might thus gain greater self-confidence. That is probably the chief reason why I was not enthused about your going to Mil's—the fear that you would tend to lean on her instead of taking responsibility fully on your own shoulders.

As for the actual ideas you have been writing about, I think there is really very little conflict—as you can easily see if you just remember things I said before I ever heard of Borsodi. It isn't that I am more receptive to one person's ideas than another's; I am receptive to ideas that seem true to me. As mentioned before, I disagree with anyone who thinks that he *knows,* that he has found *the* way. Simple living, raising and processing your own food, making your other necessities, etc., etc.—all of those things I agree with, though I think we should always remember that these things are not an end in themselves, but are only desirable in that they can contribute to the real end: free, creative living. I believe in eating wholesome, healthful food, but I would rather eat straight starch and be free than eat healthful food and be enslaved to food.

Lots of exciting things have been happening around here lately. Parker got out of the hole last Friday after not eating for nearly a week and sleeping on the bare concrete several days. Hampton is still there, however, proceeding merrily on his own program of being a bad tool. He blocks his door so it can't be unlocked, smears cereal on the walls ("cerealistic" art, he calls it), etc. Unfortunately, some of the officers seem to take his actions personally. One of them got so angry that, according to John (and I fully believe him), he hit him several times with his fists. Two theories were circulated to explain this beating: one was that John attacked the officer, who hit him in self-defense; the other, and apparently official one, was that John fell on the floor and hurt himself. As far as I am concerned, such flimsy whitewashes are much more serious than an officer's getting angry and hitting a man, in that in effect they constitute official approval. The chief reason John throws food on the walls (and even at the doctor's window) is that they are feeding him a starvation diet to try to break his resistance. Whereas I don't go along with John's program, I think the hole and the conditions there are barbaric and inhumane and should be changed.

We've had lots of "shakedowns" lately as the guards continue to play Junior G-man. Apparently they think we're smuggling things in to John some way. I don't know what could give them such a "pecooliar" idea. Yesterday three of the boys were called into "court" and threatened with being locked up because food was found in their lockers. When will they ever learn that threatening or even punishing us isn't going to stop us from running our own lives?

Adam was supposed to leave on CR Monday, but instead had good time taken away for the time he has spent in Administrative Segregation (44 days). We are writing to Bennett for an explanation.

Did I tell you that the books came from Mammy? Also, that according to my figures, we have $106 coming from the government on our income-tax returns?

Looks like the pardon campaign is in full stride. If this doesn't work, there are other tricks to be tried.

G'bye my love. I care for you very much.
Lots of love,
Chuck

◉ ◉ ◉

March 15, 1946

Dear Betsy,

I hadn't intended to write to you again this week, but here I am
starting another letter for the third time and finding it very tough
sledding. I had just begun to think that we were getting our misunderstandings ironed out and then your letter came Wednesday night.
For some reason or other, it hurt me deeper, made me more unhappy
than anything has for many years. I know that wasn't your intention,
but you couldn't have succeeded better if you had tried deliberately.
In fact, it set me off on an emotional jag that kept me awake half that
night and only now is slowly ebbing away.

I sincerely hope that some day I may think back to this experience and think how silly, or stupid, or selfish, or all three I was, but
that will no way invalidate the reality of the experience. Trying to
find reasons for my reaction is not easy chiefly, perhaps, because
it was primarily an emotional rather than a reasoned response.
However, maybe I can put my finger more or less on a couple of the
worst spots.

One, undoubtedly, was your remark that, "I'm not sure now
that I would make the same decision you did for myself, but I'm
happy that you made the decision and are standing by it." That, to
me, seems to be trying to say gently that you wouldn't have made
the same decision. And yet, as you point out, there were only two
choices—"cooperating or prison." Just what decision would you have
made? And why? I can't imagine you lining yourself up with the destruction of war even though a clever person might get a safe though
more dishonest and cowardly position. You say, "War is the wrong
method for solving the problems that beset mankind." But I honestly
can't see how it can even be called a method for solving problems.
What problems has this war solved, for instance?

Maybe I am too sensitive about this matter, Honey. But as you know, I've been on the firing line for about five years now and have met lots of people who were openly hostile to my position and me, and lots more who were tolerant, but I had certainly hoped for something more than mere toleration from the one person in the world whom I hold most intimate and dear, the person whom I chose as my companion for life. The statement that you are happy that I made the decision I did doesn't seem to me like it will hold water. If you don't personally accept the position, I don't see how you can be happy about the heartache and loneliness it causes—to me at least. I'm sort of disappointed, too, that you would be willing to give up something which I regard as valuable without at least giving me a chance to defend it. It would be lots easier for me if I could feel that I was taking this stand for you as well as for myself, that it was your cause as well as mine. But if it isn't, I hardly feel justified in asking you to do things for me all the time—as though I were just imposing on our relationship. Aren't you willing to give me a chance to defend this ideal, Sweetheart?

I think that is one of the most maddening things about this whole business. Here I am locked up in prison a thousand miles away and no way to defend myself or the ideals I value except through a few paltry letters. I must feel a little like that fellow in "The Pit and the Pendulum" as he lay there unable to move with that huge pendulum swinging ever nearer. What makes it worse is that you apparently don't understand or else refuse to consider even what things I do try to say. I write what seem to me to be just, valid, and reasonable criticisms, and to you I am only emoting. Worse yet, you accuse me of being vehement when to the best of my knowledge I have never in all our relationship acted or spoke vehemently toward you—not even in this letter. If I have given you that impression, please forgive me. I assure you that I didn't intend to. I am very sorry that you got that impression, that you would think I would be that way toward you.

Not only do you seem to not understand me, but you even seem to have completely forgotten the ideas, attitudes, etc., that we shared freely when we were together. Instead of thinking of me as an individual, as your husband, you seem to identify me with pacifists or the pacifist movement.

I don't feel any obligation to defend pacifism or anything else. The only things I feel obligated to defend are things that seem to me to be true. It was you, not me, who tried to tie up pacifism as Borsodism. The idea seems stupid to me, as though Borsodi and Mil had a persecution complex. Seems to me like you could remember that I used to be and probably still am more of a humanist than you, yet you hope your attitude won't alienate me. And so on and on and on.

It is probably entirely unreasonable, Honey, but I think it seems to me that I am losing at least a part of my wife. Sort of as if our paths crossed and went along together for a little way and now were branching off again and I am unable to do anything about it. Maybe I am afraid that the breach may get wider and wider and we may never be able to close it. And to me the real marriage, the kind that can make the very fullest, richest life, is one in which there is more than a mere marriage of bodies—a marriage of minds and even spirits as well—not identity but completion of one's full self.

I greatly fear that you are going way overboard in one particular direction, swallowing one line, one approach to life, hook, line and sinker. Your resolve to evaluate everything critically is noble but, I fear, inadequate. When you eat, sleep, drink, and breathe the same line 24 hours a day, perspective is impossible. It's like being in the middle of a forest and resolved to be critical. You may notice that some trees are shorter, some taller, some diseased even, but you will never be aware of the prairies or the mountains or the ocean.

Sweetheart, I sincerely hope nothing I have said in this letter hurts your feelings. I truly hope I may sometime look back upon it with either shame or amusement. Maybe I was only ripe for an emotional splurge anyway, and your letter only set it off. But believe me, Sweetheart, I could never write a letter like this if I didn't love you so much, maybe too much. Please, Honey, don't sell me out when I am in prison. When I get out I'll take my chances on anything, but please have mercy now.

All my love,
Chuck

◼ ◼ ◼

March 20, 1946

Dearest Betsy,

Hello, My Sweet Wife. Isn't it the darnedest thing, Honey, the way our correspondence seems to have gotten on a regular teeter-totter. I send a letter to you full of doubts and misunderstandings and then a day later I get a letter from you that helps iron things out. Your letter gives me greater understanding and confidence, and I write to you expressing same. But in the meantime, you've gotten my first letter and it raises doubts in your mind that you express to me. And so it goes—up and down, up and down. Your last letter put me very much on the upswing and I don't doubt but what mine put you on the downswing. Maybe if we can do the thing we both mentioned as important (i.e., be objective or, as you say, use an intellectual approach to the matter) and at the same time not confine our discussion to a few surface differences when we have so many basic agreements, then perhaps we can stop the teeter-totter and hit a happy level of loving confidence and understanding.

Please know, Sweetie Pie, that the emotional splurge I wrote about has subsided and I once more feel that I still have a swell and loving wife. I can subscribe without reservation to Mammy's contribution to our conversation. If you can, too, then it would certainly seem that we have been making mountains out of molehills. That you read lots more into my letters than I ever intended is obvious, e.g., your remark, "Then when you rejected it so strenuously, I felt rejected, too." I certainly didn't mean to give you the impression that I strenuously or otherwise rejected all of Borsodi's ideas. I thought you understood from all the thinking we have shared together that I very largely agreed with his ideas; don't you remember that I was interested in decentralism, simple subsistence living, small community life, etc., before I ever met you? What I could not accept was the impression I received, probably unjustifiably, that it was supposed to be the only answer, or that it was the answer for everyone. Since we all have distinct personalities of our own, the same way of life will not fit any two people perfectly. It is my concern that everyone express his own personality as completely and honestly as possible. Any other attitude, I think, can result only in frustration, intolerance, and eventually unhappiness. When you apparently saw a conflict between pacifism and Borsodi's ideas, I never did, and said as much in one letter long ago when this discussion first started, remember?

So you are a little bit confused as to my attitude toward prison. I can see why you would be as my attitude has changed a little lately. I had intended to write about it sooner but there were so many other things to be said (some of which probably shouldn't have been) that I haven't had a chance. I think you may understand, however, since my new resolve is to live as normally as possible. When we were all locked up for a week, guilty and innocent alike, I wrote a letter to the Warden explaining my attitude toward prison but didn't get it mailed as we were released the next day. I will quote a part of it:

> I should like to assure you that I have no animosity or ill-will whatever toward you or your employees. Most of the guards here have always acted like gentlemen toward me, and even if they should not, it is still my intention to act like a gentleman toward them. Unfortunately, you have taken upon yourselves the job of imprisoning men who violate the Selective Service Act, men whose only crime is that they have chosen to follow their highest ideals. This role makes your job part and parcel of the Selective Service itself; you keep in custody those who cannot conscientiously serve in the Armed Services or the COs' slave-labor camps.

> Since the Selective Service Act not only makes possible stupid, destructive, evil war, but also stands in the way to God [Betsy, by this I mean one's appreciation of love, truth, and beauty] by taking away a man's right to order his own life, I feel it would be wrong for me to obey it. Consequently, I have refused to recognize the Act or to grant it authority over my life. Since your job is an integral part of the Act, I must also refuse to accept the authority of you and your staff. If this should lead to a conflict of interests, I sincerely hope that there will be no conflict of personalities, no misunderstandings or hard feelings.

> But please be assured that I have no wish to coerce you to do anything except what you think is right. If you feel morally justified in imprisoning COs, I shall not cooperate with you

and shall try to persuade you that you are wrong, but I will not take any acts with the intention of coercing you against your own highest loyalties to turn me loose. I will not maliciously destroy prison property or deny your authority just to be mean or contrary.

Rather, I intend to live in this situation as normally, pleasantly, fruitfully, and peaceably as possible. If restrictions are placed in the way of my doing so, I shall feel no obligation to obey them. If physical properties are used to violate my freedom, I shall not feel obligated to respect them. I adopt this stand not in a spirit of defiance but rather in a sincere desire to protect and preserve, both for myself and others, those sacred liberties which are the inalienable right of every individual.

I do not intend to carry this as far as Corbett Bishop, Honey, (incidentally, Corbett was released on March 12) since that, to me, would not be normal living. People who have never lived under a regime which is completely and totally totalitarian probably can't appreciate the evil done to personality by such a system. I don't think I should bow down to such a system since it is doing such a disservice to society; what do you think? Prisons do not operate on a basis of reason but upon a basis of absolute authoritarianism. Last Saturday, six of the boys in C2 were locked up in their cells without any explanation whatever. A few days later, one of the officers said it was because contraband had been found in their cells. One of the boys had a little metal book, one a few slices of bread, one the screen off of his window, etc. And I wasn't locked up though I had all the items mentioned in my cell.

The Arthur Morgan course is here. Many of the books look interesting.

We've had fun at volleyball lately.

Looks like the campaign is going fine.

You're very sweet, my dear; I love you awfully.

Chuck

P.S. Am glad you didn't decide to come with Paul as I'd much rather see my wife alone.

P.P.S. Better send *The Interpreter* to me in letters as librarian says it is wasted over there.

◼ ◼ ◼

March 25, 1946

My Darling Wife,

Hello, Sweetheart. Your letter of March 21 came last night. I don't know just what to say except to caution you not to be too critical of my Sweet Wife. Whenever there is a misunderstanding of any kind, there are always at least two persons responsible. But we probably learn lots more from our failures than from our successes; through misunderstanding, I'm confident that we shall find greater understanding. "Into each life some rain must fall"—and just think how dry that life would get if it didn't. I still think this separation is going to deepen our appreciation of each other and enrich our lives together if we learn what lessons it has to teach—and I think we may be learning them.

Please know, Betsy, that I love you with all my heart. Our little misunderstanding has had the same effect on me as you described— i.e., it seems to have brought you nearer to me, reminding me vividly of how dear you are to me, how incomplete life is without you. I've missed you terribly of late and the effect has been accentuated by the sex drive, which, like many other psychological phenomenon, seems to come in cycles and has lately been very strong. (Maybe it's only this lovely spring weather we're having—a kindred response to the same force that sends the sap surging up through the branches.) I still think of sex as the most beautiful and most intimate of all human relationships, and I sometimes wonder if you feel the drive with a desire similar to mine. Incidentally, Honey, Taylor was telling me about a clinical method of determining very accurately the time during which a woman can conceive—usually a very few days. It is accomplished clinically by taking a body temperature reading every morning for three months. He said his wife had it done and they are very pleased with the results. If you think it's worth checking up on, you might get in touch with his wife in Chicago—Kathryn Taylor, 45 & 8 N. Dover, Chicago 40 (Tel: Sunnyside 7968). She might be a very interesting person to meet anyway. She and John (her husband) are the center of a gang of liberal and artistic young people. They are planning a community of their own in the Black Hills. Incidentally, they have a little boy "3½ going on 4" and his name is David so they were much impressed with that little poem.

But to get back to the above matter, I hope you will bear with me patiently because I am probably over sensitive and over critical chiefly, I think, because for some two or three months I have felt quite frustrated—more so than at any other time in my life. The frustration probably arises from impatience to reach the end of this road now that the end seems to be in view. Consequently, I am not accepting this situation and living as completely within it as is possible; am thinking too much about being out. Partly the trouble may be, too, that I have acquired as much from this environment in the way of personal growth as I can in my present stage of development. Then, too, being in prison doesn't seem to be quite as necessary now—and yet my presence in prison probably means more for the cause of freedom than it has at any time during the war. Because now conscription and its philosophy (that the individual exists for the State) hang in the balance. Now as never before, we need stern opposition to our native fascist tendencies, and yet it seems to me that now pacifists are letting up just because the end is in sight. Hope I don't do that even should I feel like it. Well, anyway, Sweetheart, should my frustration cause me to be overly sensitive or critical, please forgive.

Paul was here for a visit last Friday, but I can't truthfully say that it was a very great success. He got two hours so please be sure to make complete arrangements with the Warden before you come as that may mess up your plans. Paul didn't seem to know anything I haven't already heard, so most of our time was spent with me trying to clear up his misunderstandings of prison, my attitude, how government works, how to work most effectively for COs' release, etc.—not very successfully, I suspect. Adding to the usual difficulty of visiting in prison was that being locked in made Paul so nervous that he couldn't sit still. He must have a latent case of claustrophobia.

After his visit I'm no happier than I was before as to his psychologi-cal well-being.

Paul talked to the Warden but I don't know what all they said. Later Hampton talked to the Warden and said the latter told him my people were worried about my "bitterness." The statement I wrote out about parole seems to be "Exhibit A" of my bitter attitude. And here all the time I thought it was a reasonable statement of a valid principle. Hampton also said that it seemed, from what the Warden said, that I was not one of those persons in the world of whom he is most fond.

Parker is getting *The Progressive* now. It would seem that on the international scene things are going from worse to unthinkable. How people can be so blind and stupid, I just can't understand. If conscrip-tion is continued our chances for getting out soon would seem very slim indeed.

Little things still happen to keep life interesting. Last night the northern lights were quite spectacular. Today our request for a typewriter was granted. We've had lots of fun playing volleyball and the weather has really been wonderful. Our relationships with the of-ficials here is a constant source of amusement and amazement. I hope they get as much fun out of it as we do, but doubt it since our inde-pendent attitude is a radical break with prison traditions dating back through antiquity. Personally, my attitude toward the personnel is more wholesome and healthy than I have ever known since it is one of equality, of man-to-man rather than supervisor-to-slave relation-ship. All of the boys are out of lock-up now except John, who is still in the hole—going on four weeks now. The Warden recently granted our request for a typewriter so maybe our amnesty campaign can get to rolling. We also have full use of the day room on weekends.

Goodbye, my love, don't worry about anything. I think that to-gether we are going to find life a real adventure. This is only chapter two that we're in now.

Much love,
Chuck

■ ■ ■

April 2, 1946

Dearest Betsy, My Wife,

Here it is Tuesday morning already. I have been lying here on my back this morning thinking it was about time I should be writing to you because I love you so much and miss you so much. And yet, I've been thinking how difficult it is to write to you just now because the things we are most interested in seem to be taboo topics of discussion just now because somehow or other we (both of us) have permitted selfish, defensive attitudes to creep in and temporarily assume a position superior to our spiritual unity, our feelings of loving confidence and security through which we should view our various problems. Every time I get a letter from my Honey, my heart leaps with joyous anticipation, but it has been all too obvious that in the last two or three she has assiduously avoided mention of those ideas which led to misunderstanding. I suppose your idea is to wait until we can talk face-to-face and that we can then find our spiritual unity again and iron out our little problems. I sincerely hope with all my heart that we can, but I am not too confident that the conditions of artificial and unnatural restraint which characterize a visit in prison are greatly conducive to understanding. So far I have never felt natural or at ease during a visit. But maybe if we have our questions and doubts clearly in mind we can accomplish something. In the meantime I suppose, since we are not sure of each other's true attitudes, that we must be content with sharing only a part of ourselves in our letters. But at the same time, I can't help thinking how tragic it is that two persons who love each other and who are both above average in education, intelligence and personality should have to set up such self-imposed restrictions.

I have been reading some interesting things in our course on community and would like to share them so that together we could extract what we felt to have value, but avoid doing so for fear you may still feel defensive. Sweetheart, I think it is of the greatest importance that we get back on the beam again so that we can discuss, as a husband and wife should, not only these matters of community, pacifism, prison, etc., but that we may also explore other fields together because I can think of no other way of growing in our love and understanding as long as we are physically separated. The only way we can share and grow in our mutuality under these circumstances is through mutual mental adventures.

Your outline of the semantics course would seem to indicate that it was very much worthwhile. The one point on which I should like to have heard further discussion is point 5—projection. Since no two persons have exactly the same connotations of any one word, and since we seldom if ever know just exactly what a word means to someone else, it seems to me we must all of necessity be victims of projection. How can we converse in any way without assigning our own values to the words used? In general, I should think the ideas brought out in the lessons should tend to make one more tolerant.

We have been having some good bull sessions lately—discussing moral questions (sex, drinking, etc.), social organization, international affairs, and others. Wish I could have some such discussions with you. On Monday nights we read our papers for the "Small Community" course and discuss them. I always did feel that these informal small group discussions were one of the most valuable of educational processes. It brings out one's own thinking better than anything else. We are also starting a drama-reading group and Hank is going to start giving us daily summaries of the news at the supper table.

I recently read the Pacifist Research Bureau's booklet "COs in Prison" and was agreeably surprised how fair and how comprehensive it is. I wouldn't hesitate to recommend it to anyone who wants an objective picture of the question. Most of the boys here agreed, however, that it could have been stronger in some respects, e.g., the situation at Springfield.

Recently a bunch of left-wing pacifists (mostly ex-cons, I suppose) met in Chicago to consider the possibilities of organizing. They drew up a set of resolutions for interested persons to think about. We read the resolutions in a group meeting and discussed them. Though I don't go along with everything they said, I must say that it was the most revolutionary thing I've yet heard about. I hope something comes of it. It would be a shame if something were not done to make use of the friendships and ideals brought about among COs by the war.

The weather has been miserably windy lately. Trouble is that our yard is nothing but sand and gravel, which blows in our cells, our mouths, and everywhere. Our affairs with the administration have been very quiet and congenial. Hampton is out of the hole and along with the rest of us is busy studying, reading, typing (did I tell you that we have a typewriter now?), etc. One fly in the ointment is a recent ruling by Mr. Domrese that our letters urging amnesty must be counted against our regular quotas. If we get a red hot campaign going this may play havoc with our regular correspondence, in which case I hope you would know what to do.

I owe Mammy a letter this week but find writing to her even harder than writing to you, chiefly, I think, because I don't know what you have written to her, nor am I sure just what your attitudes are on some subjects (e.g., your statement that you are "trying to make yourself into something you can't be" puzzles me).

This little poem is just another way of saying "I love you, Sweetheart."

Bye, Honey, hope to see you soon.
—*Chuck*

Springtime in Prison

Why should robins fleck the budding trees
This year, or pussy-willows fringe the lane?
What use of lilac fragrance on the breeze?
What need of violets smiling in the rain?
What good for spring to give fresh form to earth?
These walls will still be naked, stern and gray
And she whose presence lends to spring its worth
A thousand miles, two barren years away.

◼ ◼ ◼

April 8, 1946

My Darling Wife,

Sweetheart, I have always thought of you as a sweet and lovely creature, but you have never seemed so wonderful as in our visit

yesterday. Never have you been so beautiful. All day I've been thinking how gorgeous your hair was, how lovely the contours of your
face, your breasts, your knees, how soft and luscious the touch of
your cheek, how warm and loving your wide blue eyes. I might suspect myself of prejudice were it not for the fact that all the other boys
warmly echo these sentiments. Of course, something they can't appreciate is that your personality is as fine as your appearance. Honey,
I hope this visit marks the change of the tide—that henceforth our
love and mutual ideals are of major importance in our thoughts
so that through them we may meet our problems in a better spirit.
Always remember that I love you more than anything in the world,
that you are not just a person to me, but a most sacred and wonderful part of my own life.

You seemed not only more beautiful but also more mature than
ever before. I am sure that this separation is going to add to the
depth of our relationship, just as *The Prophet* says that our joys are
but the fulfilling of our sorrows and can rise no higher than the other
goes deep. I am eagerly anticipating now the fun we can have thinking and planning for the future. Don't you think it will be fun to get
acquainted with some cooperative-living experiments in the country
and trying to decide if and how we might fit into the group for a
while? Art Wiser's wife, Mary Wiser, will be very happy to write to
you, says Art, about Macedonia, their plans, setup, etc. Her address
is Tr. 3, Clarkesville, Ga. And as I said Sunday, I think Chimes, John
Way, Howard and Ruane Scott, possibly Arthur Morgan could give
us other leads. Lin Brown could tell us about the group she was with
for a couple of years in Zirconia, NC. If there are any groups doing
the sort of thing in the part of the country we want to settle in, that
would probably be our best lead.

What part of the country we want to settle in is another one of
those things we can have fun thinking about. I still think SW Missouri and NW Arkansas would be a good place, in view of my own
love of nature, mountains, etc., and its advantage for subsistence
farming, but there may be even better places. Parker, for instance,
speaks highly of the western slope of the Rockies as a place for
subsistence living. Hank presents an attractive picture of Macedonia.
Some have told me of advantages of the Pacific Northwest, etc. And

if it is our hope that our folks might eventually be interested, then they should be included in the thinking on this score.

About books we could read together, I will make a few suggestions now on the spur of the moment, hoping you will do the same and that we can soon start reading some things together. Some books in the prison library that might be worth reading are:

The Good Housekeeping Marriage Book (William F. Bigelow)
The Farm or Early Autumn (Louis Bromfield)
The House of Earth (Pearl S. Buck)
The Deepening Stream (Dorothy Canfield)
The Story of the Plant Kingdom (Merle C. Coulter)
Crime and Punishment (Fyodor Dostoyevsky)
The Story of Philosophy (Will Durant)
A Living from the Land (William B. Duryee)
The Story of a Baby (Marie Hall Ets)
ABC of Agrobiology (O.W. Willcox)
Language and Thought in Action (S.I. Hayakawa)
Scum of the Earth (Arthur Koestler)
The Rainbow (D.H. Lawrence)
Pigeons and Spiders (Maurice Maeterlinck)
Discovering Music: A Course in Music Appreciation
    (Howard D. McKinney and W.R. Anderson)
Giants in the Earth (Ole E. Rolvaag)
The Last Puritan: A Memoir in the Form of a Novel
    (George Santayana)
War and Peace (Leo Tolstoy)
*Let Your Mind Alone! and Other More or Less Inspirational
    Pieces* (James Thurber)

Then there are a number of books in our "Small Community" course that I think we would enjoy reading together. I have just read Arthur Morgan's *The Long Road* and *The Soul of a People* by H. Fielding Hall, both of which I thought interesting and worthwhile. Would you care to read the text, *The Small Community,* with me? (Marv Graeler has a copy of mine that I wish you could run down.) Morgan suggests purchase of a few of the books for one's personal library: *Holy Earth by* Morgan ($0.25); *Your Community* by Joanna Carver Colcord ($1.00); *The People's College* by Paul Henry

Holm-Jensen ($1.00); *A Business of My Own* by Arthur Earnest Morgan ($0.75). Personally, I think these would be worth buying. What do you think, Honey? I believe that by buying them through Community Service, Inc., we can get them at a discount. I'd also suggest buying Morgan's *The Long Road* someplace; price, $0.25. Other books in the course that I think we would enjoy reading together are:

> *The Lord Helps Those* (Bertram B. Fowler)
> *The Peckham Experiment* (Innes Hope Pearse and Lucy H. Crocker)
> *Leadership for Rural Life* (Dwight Sanderson)
> *Action for Cities: A Guide for Community Planning* (Public Administration Service)
> *Exploring Tomorrow's Agriculture* (Joseph W. Eaton) [This one contains a couple of pages about Macedonia]

Hope all this doesn't overwhelm you, Honey. And I hope you don't feel opposed to this course in community because of your feelings or former feeling about Borsodi. Please let me know. Also, would you like to read the papers I write in the course? Not that I feel any of them are or will be particularly worthwhile, but it may help you know more about what I think and why, and you can tell me your reactions. If so, write to Morgan and ask if he would be willing to return the papers to you instead of to me.

Maybe I should connect a few of the loose ends of our visit. The reason the other boys had to drag Bailey to the door was because he just had on underwear. Remember how he was ducking down? As for the picture, they were only checking up to see if it was the same girl. Sorry I only mentioned that telegram and then didn't explain. Our idea was to sign the names of all the boys up here to it—as if you should know.

Tell Mammy I got and enjoyed her letter mailed last Saturday. Buffett deserves support in his stand on conscription.

G'bye, Sweetheart. Keep me in close touch with that part of you that is so dear and so-o-o far away.

Love and several long ones,
—*Chuck*

◼ ◼ ◼

April 12, 1946

Dear Wife and Sweetheart,

I'm kinda lonesome, Honey, so may I write to you another letter? But is it any wonder? For two sweet hours you were here like a glorious vision. And then you went away, far, far away, and I haven't heard from you for so-o-o long. I know you are very busy and very happy to be in the bosom of our fine family again, and that you are saying lots of things I would like to hear. So, don't you think it would be sorta nice to let some of those things spill over in this direction?

Maybe another reason I'm lonesome is because my correspondents (all but you and Mammy and Mom) seem to have gone on a strike. So far this month I've received four letters and sent six—some average, huh? I haven't heard from Frank for about two months, from Bill for a month and a half, and Paul hasn't sent me a half-dozen letters since I came to prison. Should I try to replace some of this dead wood or just say "to heck with 'em," and send my letters to you? John Swomley suggests I write to you instead of him and that you drop him an occasional note to let him know what's cookin' at Sandstone; and maybe that would be the best way to do. Well, you think it over, Betsy, and if you decide on replacements, you might send out a few feelers (e.g., to such people as Gerry D., Gordie, or Bob Pope), but whatever you decide will be OK with me. It is pretty disgusting to think that when one is as confined and restricted as he is in prison, that his friends won't show any more concern about writing (maybe I'm getting a persecution complex, huh?).

April 15 and 23 are Mom's and Pop's birthdays, respectively, and I am sending them each a number of gifts, all of which consist of things for them to do. Among the things Pop is supposed to do as a part of his birthday present is read *The Soul of a People* by H. Fielding Hall. This is one of the books used in our course on community and can be purchased from Community Service, Inc., but I doubt if it is in the Omaha library. So if you should decide to buy the books I suggested buying in my last letter, would you include this one, too? I think it would be well worth owning. Let me quote you a passage:

So the Burman lives his life and he asks a great deal from
it. He wants fresh air and sunshine, and great thoughts that
come to you in the forest. He wants love and companionship,
the voices of friends, the low laugh of women, the delight of
children. He wants his life to be a full one, and he wants leisure to teach his heart to enjoy all these things, for he knows
that you must learn to enjoy yourself, that it does not always
come naturally, that to be happy and good-natured and
open-hearted requires an education. To learn to sympathize
with your neighbor, to laugh with them and cry with them,
you must not shut yourself away and work. His religion tells
him that the first of all gifts is sympathy, it is the first step
towards wisdom, and he holds it true. After that, all shall be
added to you. He believes that happiness is the first of
all things.

You know, Wifey, when you were here I was so happy to be with
you again, so eager for your love that (as I now realize) I was reluctant to discuss our past misunderstandings lest they should interfere
with the joy of the moment. But now I am aware that there are still a
few misty places in my mind as to just what your ideas and attitudes
are on some of the concerns we discussed in our past exchange of
letters and some of the things you wrote then. I am not going to mention any specific items, partly because I have already done so at other
times and partly because to do so may only add confusion. But please
know, Sweetheart, that I want to know you and understand you, and
I want you to know and understand me, and anything you say which
can contribute to that end will be appreciated, and if you have any
questions about my ideas and attitudes I shall love you much for
bringing them out into the light.

Poor Taylor, both he and his wife had decided not to visit because they did too much hard time afterwards, but since your visit
they are both having a change of heart and I expect Kathryn will be
coming up before too long.

When you were here, I mentioned the amnesty demonstration
planned for May 11. I wonder if you or Mammy or anyone
in Omaha is on the Amnesty Committee's mailing list and if you
get their bulletins, etc. If not, contact Vivien R., Secretary of the

Committee. It is going to take all the families and friends of the COs in prison working together if we are going to get anywhere with the campaign for amnesty. Quite aside from its effect on me personally, I think this campaign has important implications for the welfare of the nation as a whole. For if freedom of conscience is lost, then what is worth saving?

As for the pardon campaign, I don't know much about what has been accomplished. I know some of our friends have written letters. I think it is important to try to get favorable recommendations from Judge James Donohoe, U.S. Attorney Murphy, Senators Butler and Wherry, and Representative Buffett, but especially from Donohoe. Why don't you get all the facts well in mind and call on "His Honor" some day? It should be very amusing even if you couldn't get any-where.

In connection with our idea of joint activities, Honey, if you ever want to contact me by mental telepathy, do so from 10 to 10:30 at night. We go to bed at 10 and I am generally tuned in on your station for about a half hour then.

Vivien sent a list of those sponsoring the amnesty campaign. It must have included nearly every outstanding liberal in the country.

I was copying some notes from a book the other day and was I ever roaring! Must have gotten up to about 60 words a minute for a while. Of course, I made lots of errors but I wasn't worrying about that—it was fun.

It's well I'm near the end of this page. It's about time for volley-ball and we little guys have a grudge battle on with the big guys for today. Yesterday we tied with two games each.

Darling, as my favorite wife, you are way, way out ahead. You are my golden-haired Sweetheart.

Have fun, enjoy the spring for both of us, and don't forget that each little insignificant detail of your life is of great interest to me.

Your loving husb'ing

—*Chuck*

◉ ◉ ◉

April 13, 1946

Dearest Wife,

Hello, my love, it's me again, already so soon. Your nice letter came last night and I was very happy to receive it.

I am glad you told me about Paul's plan for getting me out of prison. You say, "I hope you think it's all right." *I don't!* I am absolutely 100 percent opposed to it. (Though it appears that I may have been presented with a *fait accompli.*)

It is pretty disappointing to think that the ideals I have been living for five years now should have made such a small impression on members of my immediate family that they would sell them out on the basis of pure, unmitigated expediency—or worse.

I would like to be out of prison, naturally, but doesn't Paul realize that I have had ample opportunity to consider this matter of selling out my principles for selfish reasons? Is getting out of prison to be considered the most important thing in the world? I have chosen to live for ideals that I feel have national and international value, and personal, too, of course. And now, with a possible end in sight, he would knife in the back the very values for which I have already done two years in prison. If my first loyalty were to my own selfish benefit, I would never have gone to prison in the first place, or, for that matter, to CPS. And even now I would play ball with this outfit and get out on parole.

Not only would I consider such a plan as the most dishonest and degrading form of compromise, but as outright fraud and dissimulation as well. To give the judge the impression that I am becoming mean and bitter, that my character is going to pieces, that I need "care" in "helping me to adjust"—all that sort of thing would be absolute dishonesty. I can't see how anyone who knows me could think I would be willing to go out on such a basis as that. If anyone has given the judge such a line I sincerely hope that they go to him and correct the impression, or at least let me know what was said so I can write to him *myself.*

I can't even agree that the steps by which Paul arrived at this idea are logical. In the first place, COs were not imprisoned to rehabilitate them or even to punish them, but rather in order to coerce others into compliance with the Selective Service. In the second place, I did not refuse to work in prison because "cooperation didn't get me anyplace" (meaning out of prison, I presume), but rather because I sincerely believe it is wrong to imprison people for conscience and I do not wish to support that wrong by lending my cooperation. In the third place, just what are these things I am doing (because of lack of policy by the prison system) that society doesn't like? Though I have tried many times to explain my position to anyone who would listen, it would certainly appear that I have failed utterly. Honey, would you try to find out what it is about my position that folks don't understand and send me specific questions so I can explain things better?

I do not want to appear ungrateful for the efforts of those who are trying to help me, but I can't exactly consider their services as desirable if it involves sacrificing ideals for which I have given so much and which are an inherent part of my personality. I don't want to hurt anyone's feelings, Honey, or overstate this matter, but neither do I want anyone to not understand just how I feel about it.

Is not the fact that my imprisonment denies freedom of conscience, freedom of the individual to follow the truth as he sees it, to lead his own life, the fact that it is a part of the whole stupid destructiveness of war, are not these sufficient reasons to justify my release? What value in the whole world is as sacred as this?

Sweetheart, won't you sit down and think this thing over good and hard, talk it over with Mammy and Paul, and see if you still think it would be the thing to do? It may be that I am wrong and that you can show me where I am wrong, but my feeling right now is that I would rather die in prison than to deny what seems to me to be true and sneak out the back door.

The peace-caravan idea sounds interesting, and I think you would find heading up such a group a valuable experience, but how would it fit in with your promise to help En?

Betsy, do you remember that little business deal I mentioned to you suggesting you keep mum about it? Well, I've been talking it over with "da boys" and about eight of them think it would be a good deal. So will you write to Vivien about it muy pronto, tell her all you know about it, and ask her to contact Lew Hill to see if he would be

interested in going into partnership on such a venture. Most of the
fellows think, however, that with inflation getting worse all the time,
it would not be advisable to wait—that July 4 may be too late.

It has indeed been lovely today—really warm. Our day room
is just to the left and behind the softball backstop—we now have
choice grandstand seats for all the games. There were three of them
today. We have lots of fun yelling at the players, ragging the ump, etc.

You are right, Honey, that spring always did mean a lot to me.
But don't forget that even if I were free to experience it this year,
I could only do so with half of my senses since the rest are down
in Omaha. And don't forget that beauty is intensified when seen
through the eyes of love. No, I wasn't just flattering you.

The only wildlife I've enjoyed for some time is a little tree frog
I've heard singing out in the compound the past couple of nights. It
sounds good.

I was greatly pleased with the tone of your last letter, Honey.
Hope we can ever more feel free to discuss things, and can do so in
the right spirit.

All my love,
Chuck

◙ ◙ ◙

April 18, 1946

My Dearest Wifey,

Hello, Sweetheart, do you love me like I love you? Hasn't that ol'
moon been sumpin though lately. I enjoyed the little nature touches
in your last letter—the smells, the cardinal, and the bullfrog.

This is going to be a sort of hodgepodge letter with a little bit
of miscellaneous stuff thrown in from hither and yon, mostly quotes.
There is a fairly good story in April *Fellowship* entitled "These Are
the Work Strikers." It presents one side of the story fairly well,
i.e., the prison aspect, but leaves out the other side, the fact that
there are valid philosophical principles supporting noncooperation—
that prison is a part of the war-corruption, denial-of-conscience,
totalitarian system.

Several letters you'd be interested in: Hutch's dad writes: "Senator Pepper has written again (regarding Hutch's application for pardon) and they have given him some definite promises on basis of my letter to him. This from the Dept. of Justice." Don't know just what the "promises" were, however. He also quotes Judge Kennedy (the guy who sentenced Hutch) as writing: "In as much as the war is now over, it would seem to me to be entirely in harmony with a sound national policy to allow this class to be wholly restored to their former status." His dad goes on to say the judge's "position is that amnesty should come to all, but this does not exclude one person who seeks pardon."

Of all men who applied for parole in March, 43 have been granted and 11 are still undecided. About a dozen COs (not counting JWs) made it. Igal and Hank, both of whom applied on the understanding that they would accept no conditions, were denied, probably in part because they were in Administrative Segregation. Art Wiser's wife called on the parole judge very recently and he said that he had just been to see the Attorney General, that they had talked about men in A.S. and that "they now want to get them out via some loophole without making a fuss about it." So apparently the government is worried about the public pressure to get COs out of prison. But they're going to have to come there with something more than parole for members of the SRAS. Honey, I hope you are beginning to see why I am so strongly opposed to Paul's idea, that there are high principles at stake.

Yesterday four of us who will be eligible for parole in June, July, or August went over to a parole meeting in the auditorium. Domrese made a little speech as to what it was all about—mostly he quoted from the same booklet that I used in my statement on parole. When the time came for those who were not interested to leave, we four departed, not bothering to sign the "waivers" they expect you to sign. I had three reasons for not signing it: 1) It may give them the impression that I like it here and want to stay; 2) I don't care to assist them in their job as our imprisoners; and 3) A waiver doesn't explain *why* one doesn't wish to apply for parole.

Igal writes to a sculptor named Barte who corresponds with Harry Lerner's brother, Gene. Small world, no? Gene has just joined the Merchant Marines! Harry is still working in Germany. Gene says Harry is not so gloomy about the situation there as formerly. In view of news reports about cutting down rations in Germany to 950 calories daily I can't see what he has found to cheer up about.

In view of other news reports, I'm not very encouraged by the conscription situation. I suppose you have read that the House has passed a renewal of conscription. Of course the issue still isn't settled but the omens all look very bad.

I composed a resolution the other day which you may find amusing. Though we mean and believe what we say in it, it is still done in a spirit of fun, as many of our projects are. (Plans are to send copies to all persons concerned.)

> *Whereas* members of the SRAS respect all men—not as superiors or masters but as equals, as fellow humans, as brothers, and *Whereas* members of the SRAS shall always strive to express this attitude of respect by being fair and courteous in their speech and in all their relationships with other men, and *Whereas* the use of the title *Mister* as employed at this institution (wherein inmates are required to address the officers as "Mister," while the latter address the inmates by name only) exceeds the bonds of courtesy and has the effect of creating a class or caste consciousness in which the officers are considered as superior to and deserving of greater respect than the inmates, and *Whereas* such a caste system is harmful to the personalities of both the officers and inmates in that it tends to develop in the former domineering, authoritarian attitudes and false superiority feelings, and to develop in the latter cringing, fawning, slave-like attitudes and false inferiority feelings, thus rendering both parties less fit for their responsibilities in a democratic society, and *Whereas* this caste system creates a spirit of unfriendliness between the officers and the inmates and is a negation of ideals of equality and fraternity dear to members of the SRAS, *Be it hereby resolved* that members shall henceforth strive conscientiously to refrain from using the title "Mister" in addressing or referring to officers at this institution, and shall address the officers as they address other inmates, i.e., by name only, or may, if they wish, use some title denoting equality, such as Brother, Comrade, or Friend, and

> *Be it known to all persons concerned* that this practice is being
> initiated as a sincere expression of members' goodwill and re-
> spect for both officers and inmates in the belief that doing so is
> in keeping with eternal verities and that it will tend to benefit
> the personalities of both officers and inmates, and will in this
> way serve the best interests of society.

Don't bother to pay postage for sending my books from
Belden—after all, they had free use of the books for 3 or 4 years.

Have started reading a chapter at breakfast each day from *Ol'
Man Adam*. The guys love it.

Had a short letter from Bill but he said practically nothing.
Think I shall continue writing most letters to you.

Bye, Honey, give my love to everybody. Many hugs and kisses
and all my love,
Chuck

◼ ◼ ◼

April 20, 1946

Hi, Sweetie Pie,

This has been a wonderful April day. I got up before the whistle
this morning. The sun was already shining brightly but the air was
deliciously fresh and cool—just like up in the mountains. Parker
agreed, and he's from Colorado Springs. Unfortunately, it has been
a bit windy and whenever the wind blows it whips up a small dust
storm in the yard.

In response to the article in *Fellowship* which I mentioned before, I wrote out some comments as follows:

> The article in April *Fellowship* entitled "These Are the Work
> Strikers" did a good job of presenting half of the picture.
> Prisons are completely totalitarian—one has no rights, only
> "privileges." The entire program is bound up in a maze of
> petty regulations applied indiscriminately. Most of the work
> has little or no social value and is frequently the most dis-
> gusting and futile sort of drudgery.

Such an institution is a disservice to society. It tends to destroy character, to build irresponsibility, bitterness, and antisocial attitudes. This is true despite the fact that the physical accommodations are (in Federal prisons, at least) usually very good and many of the officers are fine men.

Such being the case, prisons are not deserving of the cooperation and active support of socially conscious persons. All of the fellows in Administrative Segregation at Sandstone, Minnesota, who have cooperated in the past say they feel happier, freer, and more right with themselves since resigning from the "work privilege."

Unfortunately, the article scarcely mentions the fact that many men have refused to cooperate on the basis of larger issues than mere prison problems. In fact, it goes on to say that ". . . these men are the exception." This is certainly not true at Sandstone. To our entire group of non-cooperators (13), prison problems are secondary and the benefits of non-cooperation are strictly by-products. Our main argument is with the war-conscription system.

I can't properly express the position of each person in the group, but in general, it is as follows: We feel that our imprisonment is very wrong and unjust. It is a denial of the most sacred of all human rights—freedom of conscience, freedom to follow the way of life one thinks most true. It puts the nationalistic State in the place of God. Furthermore, inasmuch as it incarcerates Selective Service violators, it is an integral part of the war system. It is a weapon used by the State to coerce its citizens into unwilling cooperation with this form of stupid, inhuman slaughter and destruction.

Our devotion to the ideals of peace and freedom prompt us to refuse to lend our cooperation to the institution which enforces this grave injustice; though, for personal reasons, most of us do cooperate to varying degrees, not choosing to draw the line as fine as did Corbett Bishop. We eat our food, exercise, keep our bodies and cells clean, etc.; but one thing we all refuse to do is to perform slave labor in support of the institution which wrongfully imprisons us.

It seems to us that many *Fellowship* members who have had little personal experience with the war-conscription system have turned a cold shoulder toward men who have left CPS to go to prison, and especially toward men who have refused to cooperate while in prison. We welcome constructive criticism and offer this explanation in the hope that greater understanding may be brought about.

Would you send these comments on to Alfred Hassler at 2929 Broadway?

I checked *The Farm* and *Language and Thought in Action* out of the library. Will start on the former tomorrow (Sunday) and read about 50 pages a day and then read *Language and Thought in Action* between Sunday and Friday, which, I hope, may be about your speed. Can't guarantee what I'll be able to get next but will try for A Living from the Land. By that time our books from Community Service, Inc., may be there and we may want to read some of them next. Hope you knew *The Farm* was fiction. My policy on fiction is to read only one or two by any one author and to read only the best ones. One gets the variety of different styles that way and whatever philosophy the author may have to share.

By this time you should have received my first "Small Community" paper and Morgan's comments. I'll be much interested in your criticism, and please don't hesitate to say anything you think. I have no pride in this paper and no desire to defend it. It is only "thinking on paper," to be blended with your own. I think Morgan's criticisms are OK. I'd still prefer, I think, to try a recreation center near a small town rather than a city. And I entirely disagree with his point about getting on a place of our own immediately. He talks as though life was something to be accomplished. To me, life seems rather a process, a school to be attended, something that should be ever new and ever changing. And I feel a couple years in a group experiment would be a most pleasant, profitable experience—something we would always remember, something from which we could learn a great deal— that, to me, is living at its best. I don't think a co-op group, which one enters voluntarily and is free to leave at any time, could be considered as social regimentation—especially if one were living with a group of persons who respect the personalities of others as much as the folks at Macedonia, for instance. Incidentally, I think Chimes is considering going there. Suggest you ask Morgan for information about the Celo Community. It is in a beautiful section and sounds interesting. Though, for a temporary thing, I feel a more fully organized and going thing would be better; what do you think?

Gosh, here's the end already, Honey. Looks like I'll get to write you another letter to say some more things that have been happening.

All my love, Sweetheart, and some passionate kisses.

Regards to all,

Chuck

◙ ◙ ◙

April 21, 1946

Hello, Honey,

Easter today. I've been trying to recall what we did last Easter but can't—probably because every day was a holiday then. The two years before I recall well, one at Tucson. We COs had planned a brief sunrise service up in the hills but it unexpectedly snowed during the night so we slept it out. And the year before, Jerry and I rode into Albuquerque with the Marshalls on Easter Day—facing a beautiful sunset. We had a very good dinner here today—some delicious ham with raisin sauce on it, potatoes and gravy, creamed corn, buns, chocolate ice cream; and for supper tonight apple pie—good.

Our volleyball games were interrupted today by a couple of fellows who came out on the court and threatened to beat up Hutch for wearing a shirt on which he had printed PW (prisoner of war) on the back; said they had fought for their country and all that stuff. Another foul-mouthed guy hung back, cursing us as he has been doing for several days now. Funny thing is that the guard was at hand and had carefully shooed COs out of the area but didn't even seem to see these fellows. In fact, we later saw him laughing and talking quite a bit with a couple of the boys who had been threatening us. We went on with our game and suddenly, as I was going down after a ball, a rock hit me in the head up by the temple. It didn't hurt me any but bled quite a bit—the guard didn't seem to see the blood or maybe he thought I "fell down and hurt myself."

I gave myself a typing test today and made 52 words a minute—best I've ever done by far. Deducting for errors as we used to do in high school, it came to 45 words per minute.

Six of us just finished reading aloud to the group one of Ibsen's plays, "Hedda Gabler." I didn't think it was especially good. We're planning to read one each Sunday evening. I've suggested "What Price Glory" for next week. It is a he-man, two-fisted one with all but one character males, good propaganda, and some good punch lines—would lend itself well to this situation. The *Ol' Man Adam* book is getting so popular that the boys demanded two chapters today, one at breakfast and the other at dinner. "Soap an' Watch, Country Boy," is becoming common parlance in E2.

Congratulations, Sweetheart, on the rejuvenated intellectual vigor you mentioned. I'm glad. Maybe it will help me get back on the ball as I seem to have been in a slump for a few months now. I haven't kept up with my schedule on *The Farm,* but I have a good alibi—one of the boys had checked out *The Water Babies,* and you know I just can't resist that kind of stuff. I finished it this morning but now my glasses are up in the hospital for repairs because I cracked the right lens one day while Indian rasslin' with Parker.

After cooling off for a week, I am still as strongly opposed to Paul's approach to my release as I was before. To me it doesn't just seem like compromise but *is* compromise—full blown. Your further explanation only seemed to point out a couple more points where I think Paul fails to understand the situation. The first mistake is in thinking that the forces that put me here couldn't be made to let me out. Many of the judges and other government officials responsible for the imprisonment of COs said they hated to do it but felt they had to. There are still a good many persons in this country who think it wrong to imprison men for following their conscientious convictions. Many of the people rationalized it during wartime but are now ready to admit it was a mistake. Public opinion (as shown by the Crespi Poll in 1944) has never been as much opposed to COs as the government (particularly Selective Service) has tried to make out that it is. I wish you had a list of the Amnesty Committee sponsors. It includes a large number of the country's most influential preachers, educators, editors, etc. Government officials do not so much act on a basis of principle as of expediency. Though they undoubtedly want more power, if they see the people believe in freedom and are against something the officials are doing, the latter can and will very quickly find some legal grounds for reversing their position. I could cite illustrations ad infinitum—the Japanese evacuation is a good one to illustrate the point. Our job is to arouse public opinion and show the officials that they are denying ideals the people still hold to.

Paul's idea that I "made my protest" in court and now the only problem is to get out of prison where I can propagandize is also wrong. The trial was only a dramatic incident in my protest. War was not the only issue involved. Basic to war is the philosophy that the individual belongs to the State and that his life and conscience can be appropriated for the State's purpose. There is a big battle going on over this issue. The German people lost the battle to Nazism and we can lose it here unless people who believe in freedom for the individual stand by their beliefs. The job that has been assigned me in this battle may not be the most pleasant one, but I have no doubt that it is one of the most effective ones. I am not so discouraged and beaten that I intend to give up my job for my selfish convenience. In fact, I would rather withdraw my application for pardon than leave prison except from a recognition of the principles at stake. And that recognition is not as far off as Paul thinks it is. And I think all of you need to get in contact with the Amnesty Committee to get courage and a better understanding of the situation.

Wish you would write to Lucille for me, Honey. Mom keeps suggesting that I write through her, but that idea doesn't appeal to me.

Adam leaves next Monday, the rest of us all have a year or more to go.

Much love, Honey.

Chuck

◙ ◙ ◙

April 28, 1946

My Dearest Betsy,

Hello, Sweetheart, I am still groping about without my eyes and finding it a hard go. One of the little Quaker boys thinks I look so funny without glasses (probably in part because of the fact that I have to squint pretty badly to see much of anything) that he starts laughing nearly every time he looks at me. Needless to say I have done almost no reading or writing during the past week. Consequently, I have read only a couple of chapters in *The Farm,* and can't comment as I had hoped to do at this time. But I'll catch up with you before long—I hope.

Gosh, this has been another beautiful day. It makes me do hard time to have to spend days like this locked up in a darned jail. In order to get out for just a breath of the fresh morning air, I went up to the library with "de Hebrew boys" for their service this morning—felt it would be the lesser of two evils (the other being the Protestant service). We didn't stay long because the rabbi from Minneapolis was coming, and since he is a flag waver of the first order, he is persona non grata to Igal and Jack. It's kinda fun sitting there with those black caps on and hear the fellows (a couple of 'em) sing a few Jewish songs.

Which reminds me (though I don't know why) of your comments on the Camb. Club's discussion of God. As I said once before, I think our positions at this time are quite similar—more humanistic than anything else. But I had the feeling from what you said that you perhaps felt that humanism was enough, that "that's all she wrote." Just because we can't "know ultimate reality" doesn't prove anything to me because I don't believe we can positively "know" anything. All of our so-called knowledge comes to us through our senses and it's not hard to show that our senses are very unreliable—e.g., what looks and feels like a heavy mass of steel is probably only a number of minute particles in extremely rapid motion—more empty space than anything else. As William James points out in *The Varieties of Religious Experience,* the reality of God is as real to people who have experienced it as the food they eat or the bed they lie on. Just because they can't smell it or feel it doesn't make it any less real. Though I don't intend to try to force myself into some preconceived concept of God doesn't mean I'm not going to keep my mind and heart open to whatever light on the subject as may come my way. I sincerely believe that this God concept satisfies a deep and fundamental human need. It wasn't just thought up for the heck of it. When everything is going fine, you're in perfect health and all that sort of stuff, humanism (or nothing at all) may be enough. But when adversity comes, problems to which we can see no solution, hardship greater than we can bear, some deeper belief may be necessary to preserve our spiritual and mental health. Even in my own psychological depressions I have often felt a need for something more satisfying, something deeper to rely on than my own little reassuring mind. Whether or not I shall ever have any such security, I don't know, but I'm always going to try to keep my spirit open to the possibility. What do you think of this thought?

The big news here is Adam's imminent departure—tomorrow morning. First one of our gang to leave from A.S. He had three years. He has no intention of complying with conditional release restrictions, monthly reports, etc., so could be tossed back in, though frankly I don't expect it. He's a funny little codger—will probably miss him. He's promised to write to you. Incidentally, some of us drew up a statement the other day that I think you will find interesting. Will try to find space for it in the near future. I'm glad you now know which letters are important.

I suspect that you all sometimes forget to tell me about things relating to me that I'd like to know—whom you've written letters to or gotten letters from, etc. I can think of lots of loose ends I've never heard anything about (or very little), e.g., the pardon campaign, letter to Seymore, letters to personal friends, etc. Understand, Honey, I'm not kicking, you are a loving and dutiful wife, but I do like to know about such things.

Thanks for the big, red kiss, Honey. It gave me a funny little irreverent . . . whoops, I mean irrelevant, thought which was: I wonder how such things as natural foods, healthful habits, good posture, in a word, normal living, jibes with such froth as lipstick, leg make-up, high-heels, and (dare I say it) girdles. The latter especially, for a young woman at least, and me without children, have always sort of impressed me as rather shameful and an unhappy price to pay for a lazy habit—but maybe I'm wrong. Understand, Sweetie Pie, I'm only wondering, not suggesting anything.

Don't believe I can discuss the question of land usage in your terms, Honey. Frankly, I'm not much excited about the idea of land-use reform—not because I don't think it is important—I do. But rather, because I think it is a rather impractical and futile way to work for reform. I look upon it about like abolishing interest on capital—a good idea, but not a very good handle to take hold of. Such institutions grow out of the philosophy of the people, which at present is predominantly crass materialism.

And I think there are other, more effective, ways of attacking that philosophy. Specifically, I don't believe a person is entitled to more land or other kinds of capital than he needs to secure a decent living, and I don't think it right to live off of somebody else's labor. But I don't at all believe that this attitude can be reformed by some law or some system, but must grow from within. I don't think a person should use land in a way that offends others, but to secure his coop-eration by coercion rather than his own free will is to my mind worse than useless.

All my love, Darling.
Chuck

P.S. You tan? No.

◉ ◉ ◉

May 2, 1946

Dearest Betsy,

I feel like a new man. My glasses came this morning—now I can see what I'm writing to you. For the past week and a half I have felt almost as though I were in prison. Isn't it a crying shame that one should be so dependent on some mechanical contrivance!

This is another gorgeous spring day, Sweetheart. Art Wiser left on parole for Macedonia this morning. I asked him to write to you about the setup there. I am inclined to think it is a swell place with a dandy gang of like-minded folks, but I'm afraid that by the time I get out they will have just about reached the optimum population point. Hank says several ex-CPS fellows have gone there recently. Anyway, I think it would be worth our while to find out all we could about it. If we should be able to select Macedonia or some other place to go to when I get out, you could possibly go there beforehand and get in the swing of things, fix us a place to live, etc.

I agree that a cash income on a place of our own would be pretty slim at first. Probably it would be inadequate even if we should be as self-sufficient as is humanly possible. For one thing, it takes about five years before most fruit trees really start bearing. And it would undoubtedly take a few years for a recreation center to even pay for itself. (In that connection I might mention that some of these committees to help COs returning from CPS and prison to get started will make long-term loans without interest.) By living with a cooperative group first for a few years, I think we might be able to accumulate some cash-producing property. If we could go onto a place of our own with a couple hundred good pullets and three or four good mulch cows and the equipment necessary for their care, they might be sufficient to provide most of the cash we might need. For further cash, I might be able to get odd jobs or part-time jobs in a nearby town. But I don't think you should be bothering your pretty little head about ways to make money. You'll have enough to do learning all about raising a family, processing foods, etc. I don't mean to be dismissing handicraft as a possible source of cash income, however. Some of the fellows at Santa Barbara made darned good money that way, and anything we learn in that line will probably come in handy sometime.

I don't see any point in accumulating a lot of stuff (tangible property) at this time, except for things you regard as immediate needs. As you point out, prices are sky high right now. Inflation isn't just coming, it's here. (No, I haven't received the book. Will ask the library if it has been received there. Think I'll try to buy that latest book of Huxley's. I see it advertised in *Fellowship* for four bits.) The less stuff we have, the less stuff we'll have to haul around until we get settled down. Of course, if you should just happen to run across some real bargains on things we need, snap 'em up.

Sent you my second "Small Community" paper last night. It doesn't say anything important. I was interested in Morgan's comments where he told about the directory of community-minded persons being assembled. Sounds like a good deal to me. Would make it possible for folks to travel on a small budget, and I'd personally enjoy being host to like-minded folks who might come our way.

Contrary to my promise to Mammy in my last letter, I thought I'd not send any suggested slogans, telegrams, etc., for a possible May 11 demonstration. Chiefly because I'm not too sure any of the folks there see my position and I don't want to ask folks to do something unless they really agree with it. Maybe I've been making too many suggestions as it is. Anyway, if you all should decide on some kind of demonstration, I think it'd probably be better if it was all your own ideas.

Considering the shape the world is in, and the way courageous, determined action is so badly needed to preserve freedom for the individual, it is hard for me to understand and appreciate it when folks advise compromise and expediency, or when they can't seem to understand my position. Monday night I got a letter from Frank. I quote:

> Personally, I don't think the parole restrictions are so terrible that they restrict one's effectiveness more than you are restricted now. Of course, if it's a matter of conscience I would not advise parole. Frankly, I sometimes wonder if it is a matter of conscience or just plain pride, independence, or stubbornness. It keeps me going to try and discover precisely to what you are conscientiously objecting at any one time. The item keeps changing. I hope the Springfield brother is not selling you too much . . . I see in E2 more fighting for rights than a burning desire to heal a broken world. Please consider parole!

Such a colossal failure to understand or appreciate the issues involved, particularly on the part of such a close friend, isn't very encouraging. I wonder if he thinks I haven't "considered parole," or if I like it in prison. Trying to explain an unselfish, idealistic action seems to be lots harder than taking it. Sometimes I feel like giving up trying to explain, but if you have a copy of the parole statement, would you send it to the Durands?

We are at present drawing up copy for a booklet outlining in greater detail the reasons why parole is no answer to the problem of S.S. violators. It is our intention to have it printed and distributed in large numbers. I'm to write a part of it. *The C.O.* had a short story this month on our refusal to accept or apply for parole.

Adam left on schedule Monday morning. He refused to sign anything but I've heard that they shoved some papers in his pocket and advised him to keep them. I know he will not make any reports or carry a registration card. Funny thing is that *The Call,* which came the day he left, quoted the text of a letter he had written criticizing the prison system.

Have heard there is a new CO in quarantine from Nebraska. According to one of the library boys he has had a letter from Enid some time ago. I hope to be able to talk to him when he gets moved into G2. Understand he's eager for parole so probably wouldn't want to join the SRAS.

Got a receipt for the 10 bucks you sent some time ago. Thanks, Honey.

If you ever succeed in getting a tan, I'll be surprised.

Sweetheart, I love you like everything. How I'd like to kiss your sweet lips right now. Have fun on the farm. Will get going on reading again now.

All my love, Darling.
Chuck

◉ ◉ ◉

May 7, 1946

My Darling,

I woke up this morning longing to have you by my side. You don't know how much I miss you, Sweetheart. I haven't much to write about today either. Chiefly, I think, because I have written you three letters and I haven't yet received any comments from you. And since I do very little traveling nowadays and since my life isn't particularly crowded with activity, there isn't much I can do in letters other than discuss ideas.

But as I get to thinking of how you sometimes fail to make any response to some things I write about, I realized that I must sometimes be guilty of the same thing. For instance, in your last few letters you have mentioned how much you would like to be having a baby of our own—that you think we should get started on a family as soon as we can, and probably you were hoping for some comments on the subject from me. So let me assure you, Honey, that I share your desire very much. Nothing would make me happier than for us to have a little one. Whether we should try to get such a project under way immediately upon my release or not, I am not so sure. For instance, I think it would be best to wait until we are living in circumstances that assure us some degree of permanence and security—a co-op farm, for example. Also, I think we owe ourselves something of a little honeymoon before we settle down to raising a family. But I am entirely willing to leave the decision of when to get our family started (assuming, of course, that it is all going to be that simple) entirely up to you. At the same time, I think you will agree that if persons intend to plan their families, they must arrive at some satisfactory method of preventing untimely or unwanted pregnancies. And, unless you object, it is my intention to leave that matter (contraception), too, entirely up to you—whether we are to use any, none, or what kind. You make the decision. Maybe I'm wrong, but it seems to me that in a sensible division of responsibilities that one should belong to you, sorta like cooking and sewing. You are now in the position where you can learn everything known on that subject and, whereas I am perfectly willing to leave the matter wholly to your decision, at the same time I hope you will not fail to give the matter full consideration. That's my say so, now what do you say—yes, no, or maybe?

I am still reading Bromfield's prolonged essay on American history and rural life, hope to finish it tomorrow. Is there any plot? If so, I haven't come to it yet. What he has to say is fairly interesting but not particularly valuable, I'd say. Yesterday I read all about the physiography in the Ozark region. Am still interested in that section. One of our "Small Community" books, *Family and Society* by

Zimmerman and Frampton, has a rather long section dealing with family life in the Ozarks. Looks very interesting—rather thorough case studies. Will read it and tell you more soon.

Taylor's wife had a two-hour visit Sunday. We didn't get to see her because when the guard came up to get Taylor one of the boys made some remark about gathering at the door downstairs to watch, so the guard made them sit by themselves down at the other end. That is the kind of intelligence that plays the role of God at this institution. Can you imagine grown men stooping to such childishness? I could cite many other recent examples. The guard in charge of our headquarters, for instance, has recently taken to lying in order to gain his ends. The other day he came around and said that Domrese had to initial our manila folders but he'd bring them right back. That was the last seen of them. Parker had the screws out of his window so he could take it clear off and get more air. When we were out at exercise one afternoon, one of the guards came and took it. And the next morning a lieutenant came up and demanded to know what he had done with his window.

The Warden just turned down a request that we be furnished with pants and shirts during the warm weather instead of coveralls. When it gets hot I think he may think he made the wrong decision.

I really don't see how folks on the outside manage to live without having so many omnipotent and omniscient gentlemen to tell them what to do. Two COs and two JWs have been up in the hole for about 11 days now for *not working hard enough* out on the "rock pile." We who do not work have all the conveniences while they who pretty much cooperated with all this petty ---- have only a bed, mattress, and Bible. They have a very poor and inadequate diet (even in violation of the Prison Bureau's rules, which say that they should have full meals once every three days unless prescribed oftener by the doctor).

The SRAS players presented "The Importance of Being Earnest" Sunday night. Gormly did a good job on your old part, Laetitia Prism, and Hank was a scream as Dr. Chasuble. I read one of the two main male leads, Algernon Moncrieff. We got lots of good laughs out of the play.

No, Honey, I'm glad I wasn't a little mouse in the corner when

Doris and Leona got to criticizing their husbands for not being "serious" about things. In this day it is not easy to find a creative place in society, especially for the average person. Just what are these two gals so serious about and just how much are they helping to make their married life worthwhile? I'll bet En has twice as much work and half as many conveniences as the other two, and I'll bet she criticizes her husband less than either.

Well, I'm all fattened up for the kill, Honey. Adam's letter probably enlightened you as to immediate plans. You must have faith in me and in my judgment in this business, Sweetheart, or it is going to be very difficult for both of us. This was no hasty decision on my part, but was thought through for many days. Fuller explanations will be made in due time. Don't forget what I told you shall largely determine the effectiveness of this program. Do everything you can, but *don't* worry.

They are having a hard time renewing conscription. Looks now as if they'll probably settle for a very short extension—four or six weeks. I hope that is the best they will be able to do.

You should see my whiskers. Have been raising them for about two weeks now. Why? Oh, just to be doing something. Parker and I exchanged haircuts the other day. The regular barber was doing such a poor job that we thought that we might as well have some fun out of it ourselves.

G'bye, Sweetie Pie, I love you lots and lots. In fact, more than I can ever tell. Give my affectionate regards to all the folks.

G'bye, Darling.

Chuck

◙ ◙ ◙

May 10, 1946

My Dear, Sweet, Little Betsy,

Hy Dy, Good lookin'! Where have you been all my life, Sweetheart? No, it's not all my life, but just this month that I haven't heard much from you except just a couple real short letters that really didn't add up to one. But already I know the answer, Honey. You have been busy, and I am glad you are keeping busy—up at En's for a week working hard, and then all that mail waiting when you came home, and you with a bad cold, and probably you decided to do something to add to the May 11 protest. Though, if you did, I hope it was not just because I suggested it. Sometimes I suspect that I may have dragged you along into a battle in which you have no great interest and which is not true to your nature—that your loyalty is more to me rather than to the ideas that have landed me in prison. And I am not quite sure that I should constantly be thrusting you into this business if it is not a part of yourself. Probably the reason I am in doubt as to just how you stand on this stuff is because you very seldom express yourself one way or the other, even though, as when you were still at Mil's, I asked you rather bluntly just what your position was. And yet it seems that it was these ideas that attracted your interest in me in the first place. (It certainly couldn't have been my good looks 'cause I didn't have a beard then.) Please don't misunderstand me, Sweetheart, I don't want you to be anything but your own sweet self—it's just that I am somewhat in doubt as to just what that self is, which sort of confuses me. Maybe you are only reluctant to express your thoughts on the subject to a professional war-conscription objector like your husb'ing for fear he may not understand or appreciate your ideas. But there is really no reason to feel that way because I wouldn't want to change you for anything in the world. I only want to know you (in more ways than one, incidentally) and to understand you better. Wish you would help me out on this score sometime.

There really isn't much to write about at this time, Sweetie Pie. We are all quite jubilant at developments in the draft situation. That six-week extension by the Senate looks like the end of it. Wouldn't that be wonderful? It would certainly give CO stock a boost. In that line, there is quite a bit cooking and I'm not sure if you know about it. If the Minersville case ever comes to trial, I rather expect some decisions in favor of the COs on many of the issues we all raised in court—no pay or dependency allotments, illegality of conscription for civilian purposes, military control, etc. Thank God the boys in CPS are finally coming to life. At Glendora the whole camp is on a work strike and rumor has it that the same thing is about to happen at Big Flats, N.Y. Whatever gains are made by the fellows in CPS will react to the benefit of those in prison. Parker received news last night that three fellows at Danbury are on a hunger strike for freedom. I hope they get it.

There's really no use sending me clippings out of *The C.O.,* Betsy, since Vivien sends in the whole paper a page or two at a time. I notice they are in financial difficulty. Suggest you pass your copies on to folks who might find it interesting and perhaps subscribe.

Taylor has introduced a new feature into segregation life. He goes over to the library in the evening to teach the drafting course. He brought back some interesting news the other night. It seems that the educational department has been adding up and averaging the IQ scores. Average score for the institution is 102; Selective Service violators 104; COs 116; and Administrative Segregation 127. Since at least a couple of the boys up here have IQs of over 140, mine must be rather low to help bring the average down.

Thanks lots for sending the lenses, Wifey. They have been placed in my personal property, which is just what I wanted in case I ever break them again.

Finally finished *The Farm*. Though it is only an essay, it is a rather good essay after all, I thought. Farm life, standards, etc., have certainly gone downhill since the good old days and I suspect he is right in blaming it on business—industrialization and our materialistic philosophy. The farm my old grandmother lives on was a fine place 30 years ago.

Have started on Hayakawa. What's next on the program?

Tom Cooney was one of the boys at Tucson—not very radical. He was denied an IV-E. Would have gone to CPS and was released on a hospital parole. He is not a spectacular person, but a rather small, wholesome, happy, cheerful, friendly guy, with a hearty laugh. Was secretary to the AYH in San Francisco at one time, I believe. The fact that he is in New York only means that he has gone home after some five years of absence. Had you sent him a copy of my parole statement? He seemed to overlook the most important point of all, which is that parole does not recognize freedom of conscience; in fact, it continues the implication that the individual is so much property belonging to the State to be used as the State sees fit.

I'm sure you and others, too, must have some doubts and questions regarding the matter Adam wrote about. Why not present them

in your next letter and I will try to explain things more fully. Or, if
you have the matter well in hand, would suggest you mimeograph a
letter, including the statement, and send copies to all of our friends,
explaining, as I did to you, that it is their support which makes such
a program effective or ineffective. I think the *World-Herald* would be
interested. Will send more information anonymously.

G'bye, My Darling. When I say that I love you, I ain't just a
clackin' my goombs, 'cause I really do, Honey, and miss you terribly.
A lo-o-o-ong kiss, Baby.

Chuck

◙ ◙ ◙

May 11, 1946

[A small ad from a newspaper is stapled to the top corner of this letter. It
reads: 110 acres cultivated, 113 woodland, all fenced, water, free range,
2 miles stores, church, school, new boxed house, artesian well, springs,
half acre young apple trees, peaches, barn, poultry house, stone fruit cel-
lar, $1200. Free lists Southern Ozarks Realty Co., Realtors, Clinton, AK.]

My Beloved,

Doggone if you ain't jes' the nicest, sweetest, darnedest wife I
ever had. On Friday morning I send you a letter saying I haven't
heard much from you and what happens? Wham! That very night a
whole great big letter chock-full of interesting stuff. And I outright
ask you just what your attitude is on COism to war-conscription-
fascism, and wham! There's the answer, or at least a part of it. I'm
glad Kirby has helped to bring you back "into the fold." Not that
I think a couple should see everything exactly alike, but I do think
it vastly important that they should fully understand each other's
thoughts and actions. I was rather painfully aware of the fact that
you didn't seem to understand or greatly appreciate my position,
but the worst thing was that you seemed to be unwilling to say so,
unwilling to discuss the matter, unwilling to give me a chance to
explain, unwilling to explain yourself to me. So all I could do was
accept division and misunderstanding where I didn't feel there was
really any basis for it. Even in the recent letters, which you said have

been helpful, I had to address my remarks to Paul or Mammy rather than to you. But that's OK, Honey. I predict that by the time we have been married 50 years instead of just one year three months and two days, we'll not only understand each other but will be able to discuss every problem openly and objectively, and undefensively.

Well, Honey, I am now in the process of missing meal number 1. We ate breakfast this morning, played what will probably be our last volleyball games, but from now on it's freedom or nothing. It will no doubt be a long, hard grind, but be of good cheer, Honey, and keep our chins up. We mailed our statement, signed by five of us—Parker, Roodenko, Zumwinkle, Hampton, and myself—to the President, Attorney General, Director of the Bureau of Prisons, and sent a copy to Brother Humphrey with the request that food not be sent up for us as it will only be wasted. Four of the other fellows are interested in our action and may join us later on. I will be interested to know your reaction to our statement. One of the boys said that he thought it seemed rather selfish to be taking such an action with thousands of people starving. But I can't agree with him. Taking a stand on any issue that affects one personally could be considered selfish, but unfortunately they are the only issues we can act upon very effectively. As for the starving, we should do everything we humanly can to relieve the situation, but our most important moral obligation is to do all we can to destroy the causes of the starvation, and all the death and destruction and hatred that goes with it. And do not these things arise out of war, nationalism, imperialism, and the philosophy that the State is supreme and the individual only a means to its selfish ends? That is the real battle, I think, and that is the battle we are fighting with this hunger strike. As long as people go along, cooperate, and make it easy for the State to usurp their lives, no doubt the State will be very happy to do so. I think we are closer to fascism and chaos than most people realize. Only the most uncompromising resistance can secure freedom for ourselves and our children. If our action can contribute only a little toward that end, I am satisfied.

As stated yesterday, Betsy, the thing that can make our action most effective is constant agitation for our release. If we believe our cause is just and for the welfare of humanity, then we should not be hesitant to publicize it. I think that many times truth has only to be known to conquer falsehood. Tom C. is wrong in thinking that if I were offered a complete and unconditional release I wouldn't accept it. I think that is the most effective thing I could do to bring about the release of others. But parole continues custody, and the principle of imprisoning men for living what they believe to be true is wrong. Following are thumbnail sketches of those involved (except me, whose facts you may know—married, etc.):

> Igal Roodenko—29, single, N.Y.C., BS in horticulture, Cornell University; worked for Dept. of Agriculture in Albany, Ga.; for CIO war-relief committee in Washington, D.C.; for Federal syphilis-control project in N.Y.; 9 months in CPS; 3-year sentence; has served 13 months.

> Malcolm Parker—30, single, Congregational, Colorado Springs, Co.; BA in math, Colorado College; before prison did botanical research in Santa Barbara, Calif.; 18 months at El Reno for refusing CPS; 3 years for refusing CPS; has done 10½ months.

> Richard Zumwinkle—22, single, Quaker, Minneapolis; student of U. of Minnesota when drafted; 3 months in CPS, walked out; 1 year at McNeil; did hospital work in Minneapolis; refused CPS; got 2-year sentence.

> John Hampton—36, married, born in Oklahoma; one year at Oklahoma City University; worked for Oscar Ameringer on the *Oklahoma Daily Leader*; operates own movie theater in Hollywood showing prewar classics; 5-year sentence for refusing induction into Army; has served 2 years.

Was glad to hear the news about Lucille and the Coreys. My congratulations to each. And should you write to Adam, tell him the Mother's Day program is well under way with Hutch going on a 1,000-calorie diet instead. Got a letter from Frank. He made no mention of a gift to Ruthie, and very carefully avoided mentioning the question of parole. Also got a letter from Bill yesterday.

Afraid I can't entirely agree with Werkheiser. I'd say women paint for at least three reasons: 1) Because some men may actually like it, 2) Because it satisfies some women's vanity, 3) Because of advertising, which sells them on most anything. I don't particularly dislike it (especially just occasional use) but can't say I think it improves their natural beauty—too artificial.

Darnedest thing is that we have had some nice warm days and plenty of steam in the pipes. But recently the weather got cold and simultaneously the authorities decided we had to save coal because we were getting low on stock. One of the boys out in population who is not given to just shooting off his mouth says the real trouble is that they have 250 tons on the books that aren't in the coal pile. And one guard said they couldn't buy any more until fall. How the con could secure such information I don't know. The new rule is no heat if the thermostat is 60, and showers only from 7:30 P.M. to 8:30 P.M.

Our pansy is in bloom. It smells very nice. Guess it'll have to serve for hikes in the woods and raising a garden for this year.

About the pardon application: I'm afraid not enough attention was given to working on Buffett and the Nebraska senators. They can put on real pressure if interested. Dyer thinks Wherry might be willing to help.

I was dashing off a letter to Mom when the mail was picked up and had to close in a hurry. Forgot to send Mother's Day greetings to my moms. Please do it for me.

G'bye, My Darling. I love you more and more all the time. You are the dearest thing in my world. Hope to be with you before too long.

Chuck

◎ ◎ ◎

May 17, 1946

Dearest Betsy,

Hello, Honey. There has been quite a bit of excitement here lately, what with daily newspaper stories and radio reports about the amnesty campaign and the five hunger strikers at Sandstone. I had imagined that some mention, at least of the amnesty campaign, might have been made in the *Herald,* but apparently it wasn't for you made no mention of it nor did I find any clippings. The *Minneapolis*

Tribune had a very good picture of the poster walk at the White House, showing Al Kewbrand's (one of the Ashland COs) three-year-old daughter leading the parade with a big sign reading "Let My Daddy Out of Jail." According to Vivien, 135 people took part in the demonstration, but no word has been received as to any practical results of the action. Even as far away as Hollywood the campaign made the radio newscasts. The original AP dispatches also carried news about the hunger strikers. According to these reports, there are eight or ten men in other institutions who are taking the same action. Unfortunately, they got things all messed up and confused our strike with the fast to death of some Irish patriot, Sean McCaughey, a guy none of us had ever heard of before.

Since then the Twin City papers have been giving a blow-by-blow description of the Sandstone strike, and it has been mentioned in at least a half-dozen newscasts. Some of the stories have been good and some putrid. The story in last Tuesday's *Minneapolis Tribune,* for example, was practically one big mistake from beginning to end. (I'll bet Eva and Ray must think I've gone plumb mad.) I counted over a dozen errors in this particular story and will mention some of them as Eva will probably be sending you the clips.

States that we have been placed under medical observation. The truth—the doctor came up for the first time on the fourth day of the fast at the request of one of the fellows who wanted an enema, and stopped up for a brief visit on the sixth day. Neither time did he examine me in any way or inquire as to my health.

Makes much use of the term "draft dodgers," though all of us violated the act very openly and intentionally, even writing statements of our intentions to the government.

Says our fast is also a part of a sympathy movement protesting the death of this aforementioned Irish general, whom none of us had ever heard of before.

Says Richard Zumwinkle is the "ring leader" of the group. Fact is that the idea was conceived before Dick even came to segregation and he was the last to join.

Says we have refused to accept parole. We probably all would so refuse, but the truth is that we have never been offered parole, not even Igal, who actually applied. Says we all have refused to work since our incarceration, when actually three of us did work for a while, Roodenko for nearly a year.

"At mess time, they go to the cell block dining room and sit silently while their fellow prisoners eat." Good Lord, what a laugh. Very seldom do any of us even bother to go into the dining hall during a meal.

"Humphrey said that they perceive in their behavior a form of martyrdom which is difficult to understand. They have become heroes to the other convicted draft evaders, he added." If either statement is correct, I have yet to discover it.

Says Humphrey tried to talk us out of it. Fact—None of us has talked to Humphrey for several weeks. Personally, I haven't even seen him face-to-face since last August 10.

Quotes Humphrey as saying, "They think the government ought to turn them loose as national heroes." Ain't that a b----! All any of us want is out—heel or hero, it makes no difference.

At first we were inclined to blame Humphrey for this lousy article, but a more recent (5/15/46) *St. Paul Post-Dispatch* story would seem to exonerate him of the charge. It is much more favorable in tone and disassociates us from Sean McCaughey.

On the seventh day of the fast I'm feeling fine. Have suffered no hardship whatever, though I did get a bit sick for a few minutes when playing volleyball on the fifth day. (I now know a sure method for reducing one's waistline should you ever be interested.) I've been clearheaded and active all along, though just a wee bit weaker. Hunger pangs pretty much passed away after the fourth day. Biggest hardship is the cold. I put on all the clothes I have and still freeze. We've had no steam all day though the weather is very chilly, and, I understand, they have steam in the dormitories. That Parker just ain't human. He's played volleyball every day and still goes running around in his underwear.

Don't believe I care to make any specific comments for the Round Robin. Maybe one's attitude and perspective become perverted in prison—at any rate it certainly seems to me that what most people have to say in their letters surely doesn't amount to much.

A little superficial talk about equally superficial and meaningless activities, no apparent concern for "what it's all about."

Finished reading *Language and Thought in Action* yesterday. Thought it worthwhile but not startling. Most of what it said seemed to me to be things I have already observed for myself. However, I'll probably memorize a few of the terms so I can appear to be learned in the field of semantics. What book should we read next? How about some of the "Small Community" books?

Hope you are doing some thinking about our plans for the future. Can't count on it, of course, but with the Selective Service Act expiring June 30, and with this hunger strike and all, I wouldn't be too surprised to be kicked out some time this summer.

Have you done anything to find out about co-op communities, etc., yet? A letter to Hanks says Mary Wiser plans to write to you soon about Macedonia. Art says they need lots more people there so it may be a good lead. Climate, topography, type of work, etc., are similar to what we would find in the Ozark section. But I am not sure how interested you are in this kind of experience (i.e., cooperative living). And I'm not particularly interested in "selling" you on it, but would like to have something lined up for when I get out of here.

Sounds like you all put on quite a dynamic amnesty campaign— what with having the folks over for dinner, playing carom, and all. Hope you will see fit to distribute freely copies of our statement, which on May 11 was mailed to Truman, Clark, Bennett, and Humphrey. There's probably no value in working on the Minneapolis papers as Dick's brother is already working that angle.

One good thing about this fast is that it pretty well solves the sex problem. But I miss you anyway, Honey, and dream of eating some of your good, wholesome cooking some day.

Tell all the folks I'm feeling fine physically and am happy to be doing something more to resist the State's encroachment on the freedom of individuals.

Love to all, and something more than that to my Dear Wife.
Chuck

◙ ◙ ◙

May 19, 1946

Dearest Betsy,

Hello, Sweetheart. I am right now in the process of enjoying my Sunday dinner—a cup of black coffee. We hunger strikers have also drunk a few cups of hot tea since it has no vitamins or calories. The rest of the boys are having a very nice looking dinner—pork chops, tomatoes, potatoes and gravy, and ice cream. I found that my hunger pangs pretty well passed away after the fourth day, but the thought of food, the pleasure of eating, is still a very attractive idea. Yesterday I spent nearly the whole day thinking about all the good things I'm going to raise on our farm some day.

Well, we are on the ninth day of our fast today, Honey, and all of us are still well and up and around, though naturally not as strong and peppy as usual. It certainly seems queer to me to feel so weak. Parker is still playing volleyball, but the most I felt like doing this morning during exercise period was walking slowly and sedately around the yard. Also went to church this morning and heard a stirring message by a Moody grad—all about sin, and how God is a God of wrath and the only way to escape that wrath is to accept Jesus as your atonement—all very edifying.

Betsy, Mom is apparently very concerned about my health and wants me to write to her. I will try to write to her later in the week, but since my letters have to be distributed around, would you please call her up and assure her that I am still well and happy and convinced that the effect of our fast is going to be good. In fact, I wouldn't be too surprised to be released sometime this summer.

The doctor comes around to see us just about every day. He is quite friendly and sympathetic. Said the other day that he hoped we were able to win our freedom, that he never could see the justice or logic of imprisoning men for conscience. From the Warden's statements to the press, it is apparently their intention to start force feeding us before long. This will probably be done by shoving a rubber tube down our nose and running liquids through it.

Meanwhile, the movement is growing. Hank Dyer joined the fast Saturday after sending a good letter to the Attorney General. This brings the total number of hunger strikes in federal prisons up to sixteen. Walt Gormly announced his intention to start fasting on June 3.

His mother, Mrs. Anna L. Gormly, 412 N. 3rd St., Mt. Vernon, Iowa, has been quite opposed to his actions all the way along and he is concerned about how she may take this latest step. He asked me if you, or possibly Mammy, would write to her about the matter to soften the situation for her—explaining the value of Walter's stand, physical care, etc. Would one of you do this soon?

Seems like I always sound off on things just a half day too soon. Friday morning I lament the fact that there has been no Omaha publicity and that night I receive three clippings. And very good clippings they were, too. In general, the most favorable of all we have seen. I'm glad Mammy gave them a copy of our statement. Local papers and radios are still carrying daily accounts of the strike. Yesterday's *Minneapolis Tribune,* I am told, published a letter from Dick's brother explaining that we knew nothing about Sean McCaughey, and also printing our statement to the President. Though not all of this publicity is exactly favorable, I think the effect will be good in that it will serve to remind people that there are still men in prison for the sake of conscience, and that is all we can hope to do.

Betsy, I know that I am often impatient when people don't understand my position. I think that this impatience is largely due to the frustration of prison life, and the fact that for 24 hours a day we think almost entirely about one subject—our fight against war-conscription-fascism, and we forget that folks on the outside have other activities and interests to occupy their time. And I am fully conscious of the fact that frequently I say mean little things that I shouldn't and am usually sorry later, e.g., my remark in my last letter about your Amnesty Day activities. Please forgive me, Honey. I don't want to drag you into doing anything except what your own conscience urges you to do. At the same time, since this fight is so much a part of my life, and since our lives are one, I am eager that there be as much understanding and unity as possible. I very much appreciate knowing what you think and do in this matter, and am always happy to get news about how things are going on other fronts. Incidentally, when you and the others send clippings, would you please date them and name the paper from which they were clipped?

I am in the process of writing letters to Butler and possibly Donohoe. Intend to send the former a copy of the parole statement and fast letter. Will send you copies so you will know what I've done.

Think you misunderstand my attitude toward Paul's ideas. It was not my intention to convince Paul of anything, or to criticize him, or anything else. My point was that my battle with the government is still my battle and I think I have every right to run it my own way, and I don't want my ideals compromised.

Bye, Darling. I love you much.

Chuck

◙ ◙ ◙

May 21, 1946

Dearest Betsy,

Hello, my Wifey. It was my original intention to send this letter to Mom as I had halfway promised to do. But there are always so many more things I have to say to you that I hope you will send her the pertinent portions and beg her forgiveness.

Today begins the 11th day of our fast, Sweetheart. All of us are still up and around (though rather slowly), no one has passed out or gotten discouraged, and we are still satisfied with the validity of our action. Apparently something is cooking, though. The doc was up yesterday afternoon to look us over and said he might take Igal, Dick, and myself over to the hospital for a feeding—but he didn't. Incidentally, he told Igal the formula which they are intending to feed. I've forgotten the number of grams of each item, but it consisted of two eggs, milk, cream, orange juice, and maltose. He said there would be two feedings a day, each feeding of about 1,400 calories. Latest rumor from one of the boys who works in the hospital is that they cleaned out the largest ward (10 beds) yesterday—which may be only a coincidence, but I doubt it.

All of us are opposed to moving over to the hospital, if that should be their intention, chiefly because of the advantages of our present clubhouse. Here we have friends to bull with, our "Small Community" books, a typewriter and other office supplies, private cells for sleep and study, and considerable freedom of movement. If we are granted as many conveniences and as much freedom over there, things may go OK, but otherwise I fear the boys will not take such a change without friction.

To keep you posted on how things stand, I'll quote the letter which we fasters sent to the doc yesterday after his visit. He had rather implied that when he wanted us in the hospital, he would only have to say so and we'd come. Well, we didn't think that would be the thing to do, so we sat down and talked it over with the following results:

> Dear Dr. Krombagh,
>
> Your statement today that you would perhaps take three of us over to the hospital to force feed us caused us to consider what our attitude should be toward this procedure.
>
> Please know that all of us like you and respect you personally and do not wish to complicate your job or make it more difficult. But, on the other hand, the very purpose of our fast is to secure our freedom. In effect, we have said that we will not voluntarily maintain our bodies by eating food until we are released from prison; that, if the Bureau of Prisons is going to keep our bodies incarcerated, it must also take care of them.
>
> For this reason, we do not feel that we can honestly and consistently cooperate with a system of force feeding. It is not our intention to actively resist your efforts, but we do not feel that we should voluntarily assist in this process by the performance of such specific acts as walking over to the hospital or lying down in a bed.
>
> We sincerely hope that you will understand and appreciate our position in this matter.
>
> Respectfully yours,

After the doc's visit yesterday, I was taken over to the hospital to have my sore throat treated. The Associate Warden saw me, gave one look at my beard, and called me "Honest Abe." (The boys do say my beard looks like Lincoln's—but it has about stopped growing since the fast started.) I stepped on the scale and how much do you think

I weighed with my clothes on? 124 pounds. Looks like I've lost a little weight, no? About 12 lbs., I would guess. Maybe I'd better not get
too rough with you in this letter since you're bigger'n me now. They
also gave me some pills for my throat, which must have released
some stored up energy somewhere because, whereas yesterday I was
weak as a kitten, stayed in bed 'til 10, and then didn't leave it often,
last night I was just full of pep, slept very little, and got up at dawn
to write you this letter. Right now I feel like a new man, but I know
it's only a temporary and artificial spark. Even so, I hope it lasts long
enough for me to get out and really enjoy some of today's lovely sunshine. All during May we've had lousy weather but night before last
we had a long, wonderful rain, and from the looks of things summer
(or at least something vaguely resembling it) may have finally arrived.

Betsy, don't you think it would be a good idea to send a copy of
our statement along with a brief note of explanation to *Fellowship,
The Grapevine, The Christian Century, The Call,* and *The Progressive*—and don't forget that Henry Dyer's name may now be included
among the signers.

Monday I sent a letter to Butler. A copy is enclosed. You might
like to show it to Pop and possibly to Pat before filing it with your
other letters on the case. Has anyone thought of an "in" with Wherry
yet? And is Buffett doing anything?

Looks like the CO problem is finally coming to a head, not only
in prison but in CPS as well. The fact that about 10 other guys in
prison began a hunger strike on the same day as ourselves certainly
came as a pleasant surprise—purely spontaneous. The CPS insur-
rection seems to be growing. The government has finally decided to
press charges against six of the Glendora boys. I sincerely hope that
they do. If CPS ever goes to the Supreme Court, I don't see how they
could fail to call it unconstitutional—which wouldn't hurt our cause
in the least.

No doubt Mammy knows best, Honey, but I'm afraid she forgets
that you aren't a little girl anymore. If handling En's house and two
kids for a couple of months would be too much for you, how would
you ever be able to handle twice as many of your own? What you
do this summer should be entirely up to your decision, but personally I hope you don't take on something that may obligate you for

the whole summer. If the slim chance of our release should actually develop into a reality, I'd certainly appreciate having a wife to come home to.

Have you done any more thinking about Macedonia, Honey? Personally, I'm getting more enthused about that possibility all the time, but my comments don't seem to have aroused much response from you. And after all, any such decision must be a mutual agreement. I've been thinking lately that before going onto a place of our own, it would be well to wait until someone else, the folks for instance, are ready to take the step. Then, if they are interested, we could pool our resources and probably do much better. What do you think?

You did a wonderful job summarizing all those R.B. letters, Darling. But would you be disappointed if I confessed that I didn't enjoy them much. The real reason, I think, is because they took up valuable space which could have told more about the one person in the world I'm most interested in. Seems like I've heard awfully little from you ever since you went up to En's. We had a pretty good discussion and even a reading program going up until then—what's happened to 'em?

Don't know when I'll have enough pep to write another letter like this, Betsy, but don't forget you can always write the Warden, and after all, he has assumed full responsibility for me.

Tell all the folks I appreciate their sympathy lots, but their pressure on Washington lots more.

All my love, Sweetheart.

Chuck

◙ ◙ ◙

May 24, 1946

Dear Sweetheart,

Just after I mailed my letter to Mom this afternoon, things began to happen. The doc and several of the high officials came over and said they were moving we five over to the hospital. So we packed up our worldly belongings and said goodbye to our buddies. Only Zum

made them carry him over on a stretcher—not that he was too weak
to walk, but rather because of our resolve not to voluntarily assist in
the force-feeding program. The rest of us only insisted that they take
our arms and lead us over so that we could not be said to be willingly cooperating.

Our new quarters are really sumptuous—a nice, big, bright, 10-
bed room which we have all to ourselves. Best part about it is that
my bed is right next to a front window so that I have a view of the
beautiful green grass and the trees and hills off across the river. Gosh,
Honey, you can't imagine how wonderful it is to see fresh, green
growing things again. The beds are much softer, the lights better, and
our coveralls have been discarded for some snazzy brown pajamas
and blue bathrobes, our shoes for bedroom slippers. Furthermore,
the room service is terrific. Inmate orderlies fetch everything we need
and probably will clean the rooms.

Well, no sooner did we get over here than we began making
ourselves at home—putting up our pictures, arranging our possessions, etc. I stripped and stepped on the scale—115 lbs. flat. About
that time the feeding started. Parker was first, I was third. Most of
the other boys had a pretty hard time getting the tube down their
throats, but it went very easily for me. It hurt a little going through
my nasal passage, but not too badly. I was even able to joke with the
doc as they poured down the 1,000 cc's of yellowish liquid, made
up of milk, cream, eggs, maltose, orange juice, sugar, and salt. That
combination of milk and orange juice reminded me of Grimes Gold-
en apples every time I belched. They say we'll get two such feedings
a day from now on. The effect of the food was felt almost immediately, all of us perked up and felt much stronger. I'll probably be back
to normal weight soon. The only things I don't like about our new
setup are:

- No typewriter
- No outdoor-exercise period
- Bathtub instead of shower

But the administration has been quite reasonable and I think arrangements can be made to meet at least the first two objections since
I'm sure they wouldn't want us to become too restive in the hospital.

All of the big and little shots had to be there, of course, to witness the first feeding (probably so they can describe to other inmates how horrible it is). But I'm afraid I didn't give them much of a show. They tried to persuade us to drink the stuff first but we all refused. So it looks like we're started on a new era of prison experience.

Wednesday *Inflation Is Coming!* was delivered to me accompanied by a note from the Warden. The note said that the book had been placed in my personal property and suggests that henceforth such books be accompanied by a note stating what disposition is desired to be made. I have read it and think I agree largely with the contents. I am not fully convinced that a runaway inflation and devaluation of the dollar are as certain as Borsodi says, but can see grave indications of it. I have rather felt that there might be a temporary decline in prices first, but may very well be mistaken. So maybe your idea of buying up a few of the things we need would be a good idea after all. Especially such things as we can get at wholesale prices. Can't Pappy buy electrical appliances wholesale at Nebraska Power? Probably we ought to have some things like an iron, toaster, hotplate, etc. Whether we move to the Ozarks or Macedonia, I'm sure we can count on cheap electricity. You said once that we ought to have a mill for grinding our flour, cornmeal, etc., and I certainly agree. Where can the best one be bought? If Sears and Roebuck handle it, Frank could probably get it at a discount for us if you wrote to him immediately—provided, of course, that would seem right with him.

Also, Honey, I can't help but think that we are going to need a vehicle of some kind. If you agree, I'd suggest that you go see Tom Neff, who, I am sure, would be glad to help us out and who frequently runs across a bargain. A second-hand pickup truck would probably be the most practical thing to buy (station wagons would probably run lots higher since so scarce), and I think we could afford to spend as much as $200 for one. I'd much rather trust Tom to make such a buy than myself. You could arrange for him to call Pappy and have him buy it for us with our dough in case you should be in Kennard. Don't feel bound to do this, Honey, but I personally think it would be a good idea. You might also ask Tom if he would be willing to pick us up secondhand or wholesale a few of the most essential car and carpenter tools—jack, pump, tire irons, pliers, a few wrenches, hand saw, hammer, brace, and an assortment of bits, square, level, screw drivers, etc. I think if you assured Tom of how much we'd appreciate it and of our willingness to take whatever he finds that he'd be willing to do it.

Betsy, I've been thinking more and more strongly about Macedonia. Am enclosing a copy of a statement by Charles Davis that you may like to read. From all I've read about the place, it has everything we could hope to find in the Ozarks—beauty, forests, mountains, a long growing season, moderate climate, lots of rainfall, and, probably most important of all, a chance to learn anything we want to learn— dairying, beekeeping, poultry, horticulture, woodworking, etc., etc. They hope someday to set up a community recreation center and folk school there, too. I think that it would be even better for hay-fever victims than the Ozarks. If we should decide in time to give up co-op life, there is plenty of cheap land all about. And I can't help but feel that our folks would fit into that scheme as well or better than any we could devise. Art Wiser is really a swell guy, so is Hank Dyer, who also plans to go there, and the co-op is working local folks right into the picture. Morris Mitchell, from all I've heard of him, is really on the ball—one of the country's outstanding liberal rural leaders. I can't help but think that Macedonia is a really promising and worthwhile setup, that we have something to give to it, and it has lots to give to us. And I think we could probably get started there, build a little home on what we have. Understand that Mary Wiser has written to you about it. But whatever we do, Sweetheart, it must be the thing we both want to do most. Considerable freedom is possible at Macedonia, too. All members work an 8-hour day and have a two-week vacation. At present they are paying 50 cents an hour, and fuel, milk, etc., are, I believe, entirely free.

Am feeling tops, Honey. Hope the railroad strike doesn't hold up our correspondence.

All my love, Darling.

Your husb'ing,

Chuck

◉ ◉ ◉

May 28, 1946

Dearest Betsy,

Like a snake that has just swallowed too big a lunch, I am trying to wrap my system around my fifth force-feeding since May 11. As you know, this process was started on May 24, the 14th day of our fast, and has continued with one feeding each day—1,000 cc's of liquid made up of milk, cream, eggs, orange juice, maltose, sugar, and salt (makes it sound like a breakfast food, doesn't it?)—supposedly figuring up to 1,336 calories. It gave us all an immediate pick-up in energy and I can keep going at something for a few hours now without getting too tired. But I doubt if any of us have begun to regain lost weight and probably won't unless, as we have heard rumored, they should start two feedings a day. So I'm still at a very trim 115 pounds.

Meantime, the process has become easier and less of a psychological hazard for both ourselves and the medical staff. Gradually they are developing greater skill in inserting the tubes down our throats so that it is a little less painful. Really, only one of their tubes is small enough to insert nasally, the others are all too big and inflexible and caused considerable hardship at first. They now feed two of the fellows by holding their heads, forcing a pitcher between their teeth, and pouring it down their throats. The rest of us are still being tube fed.

When I last wrote we had just been transferred to the hospital—a short but sweet interlude that lasted just two days. I think the way we made ourselves at home there, rearranging the furniture for our convenience, and immediately requesting greater freedom than is ordinarily allowed by the hospital's narrow and stringent rules were probably responsible for our return to E2. We are all glad to be "home" again, though we miss the pajamas, bathrobes, and slippers, and it was great fun to take my first tub bath in a year. But most of all I miss the view—what contrasts—on my right: soft, green grass, trees, hills, the river, clouds, a big graceful sweep of white houses, red and green shuttered, kids at play, big black cars, and symbolically over the whole scene, the American flag. On my left: long rows of straight, black windows, the dirty gravel yard, blue-clad figures bustling hither and yon or standing patiently in long lines—ask not for whom the flag waves.

Our first morning in the hospital was greeted by the news that another of our buddies, Hutch, had joined the fast. He had for two weeks been on a self-imposed diet of 1,000 calories per day. I am enclosing a copy of Hutch's letter to the American people explaining his action and suggest you give it any possible publicity. Glenn Hutchinson is single, 31, son of Rev. G.W. Hutchinson, minister of Memorial Methodist Church, Fernandina, Florida. He is a Phi Beta Kappa, with a BA in Journalism from Emory University in Atlanta, Georgia, and an MA in Sociology from the University of North Carolina. Past jobs include three years as director of WPA social research projects, 15 months as a field investigator for the U.S. Civil Service, and 6 months as boys' worker in Philadelphia and Los Angeles. He served 11 months in CPS and has done one year of a three-year sentence. I have already sent similar information on Henry Dyer, who joined the fast on May 18, and Walter Gormly, who has announced his intention of fasting beginning on June 3. This will bring the total number of freedom hunger strikers in Sandstone up to eight.

We are still getting frequent radio and newspaper publicity bits, but I think the emphasis should change now to one of having our friends and relatives use the fast for what moral pressure it is worth on the Department of Justice. Such pressure can do much, I think, to speed our release as soon as conscription expires. It does not seem that Selective Service will be renewed. Pressure on Congressmen may also do much. Some of them are saying some good things now. We are sending about 15 of the more sympathetic ones a group letter explaining the reasons for our fast and including our statement. Follow-ups by our friends would be helpful.

Our bodies, except for the weakness, seem to have made some kind of an adjustment to this peculiar feeding schedule. Hunger pangs do not bother us, but the thought of eating food is one of the most delightful ideas in the world. The most prosaic menus sound wonderful and the thought of raising our own food seems like paradise regained. Igal is collecting recipes—if there are a thousand kinds of food, I'd love to try them all. I think much of our plans for the future and can't decide which idea I like best—the co-op at Macedonia or trying to get started on our own, down in the Ozarks. I'm inclined more towards the former in view of our limited resources and experience. I believe the country in northern Georgia would be just as beautiful and fit for subsistence living, we would have a wider choice of activities, more security through having like-minded people to work with, and would need less to start. I don't want to rush you into a decision, Sweetheart, but I think we'd both do easier time right now if we had something specific to plan for.

Gosh, the last couple of days have been lovely. Our daily hour outdoors plus the sunshine plus my weakness have contributed to making two hours of the most wonderful sunbathing in my life. Up in the hospital I looked through a hardware-dealers journal and did me a little hard time as you can imagine—bicycles, bedrolls, balls and bats, farm machinery, kitchen equipment, hoes, tents, etc.

Warren Stutts, one of our CO friends, left for New York this morning—paroled to a Social Settlement at $50 per month. He felt compromised in going, sees the value of what we are striving for, but plans to get married immediately and you know how love is.

I'd love to hear from all our dear friends. The Warden, G.W. Humphrey, has been quite understanding. Perhaps if folks would write to me through him, I might be permitted to at least read the letters. Anyway, my warmest regards to the network of our kindred spirits.

Sweetheart, I see now the jam you are in. Don't worry about me or this business. An occasional postcard to let me know you're OK, Darling, and I'll understand. I need you much now and I think En lacks understanding, but if that's to be your job, take it easy and try to enjoy it. Wouldn't want you to develop a dislike for country life.

All my love, Sweetie Pie. I'm OK, don't worry about anything. Life will still go along. Nothing can change my love for you.

Chuck

◙ ◙ ◙

June 1, 1946

Flash—The Committee for Amnesty, 5 Berkman St., N.Y., N.Y., has out a good leaflet entitled "Do You Know," containing questions and answers about COs in prison and suggestions for action. Suggest the folks in Omaha order a few thousand (probably cost very little) and pass them out some way or other, e.g., through churches, in letters, etc.

Dearest Betsy,

Please remind me, Honey, never to accept even as a gift, a subsistence farm in this particular part of the country. I'd like to be able to raise something besides icicles! No kidding, no sooner do I get in three hours of sunbathing and rashly conclude that summer may be near at hand, than a 40-degree temperature accompanied by a 40 mile-an-hour wind full of rain takes over, and I mean *takes over.*

Well, Honey, three full weeks have now passed since I have voluntarily eaten food. During that three weeks I have been fed eight times through a rubber tube, a total of some 10,500 calories, about three day's food on an average American diet. Needless to say, this is not sufficient to have greatly benefited our physical well-being. In fact, I feel just about as weak, tired, and worthless now as I did before the force feeding started. So much so, that I told the doctor's assistant today (the doc having been away attending a convention in Chicago all week) that if the government was insistent on keeping me alive, it would have to do a more satisfactory job of it than it has been doing or I would have to change my policy from one of passive non-cooperation to one of open resistance, that I would prefer leaving here in a pine box to leaving as a permanent invalid.

We were up to weigh today—Hamp, Dick, and myself have each put on about two pounds, but this continual tired feeling is too discouraging to be borne much longer. Both Parker and Igal seem to be doing a little bit better on the diet—Parker probably because he has more reserve to draw on, Igal probably because he is used to living on a starvation diet anyway. There is an interesting story in this latter connection. Igal has been a complete vegetarian since he was 8 years old. He is also a collector of limericks—though he claims that even by definition limericks must be "earthy." Well, it seems that Igal was hauled into disciplinary court one day for having a number of such limericks typed off on cards in his possession. I have read most of this collection, thought some of them very good, and greatly doubt if any of them could have very severely shocked the sensibilities of any prison official I have ever met. Be that as it may, he was subjected to disciplinary action. But the payoff came sometime later when Igal asked the Warden if his diet couldn't be supplemented in some way since he found it hard to get along on the regular prison fare without eating meat (he is 6 feet tall and weighs 130 pounds) and the latter replied indignantly that he found it difficult to believe that a person who collected such lewd and lascivious literature could be a sincere vegetarian! Ah well, maybe they have decided to let a couple of us kick off just for the heck of it. Dyer completed two weeks of fasting today without the medical staff saying "boo" about it. In fact, they haven't even so much as asked him how he felt for a week. And Hutch, who was eating only 1,000 calories a day for two weeks, has now been on a complete fast for one week and is in bed nearly all day. Well, misery loves company; I'm glad Walter is joining us Monday.

We had a meeting to discuss the results of our fast the other day and all of us are satisfied. We feel that it is the most effective thing we can do for the course of freedom (our own and others). And none of us now see any reason for calling it off until the Department of "Justice" turns us loose without any strings attached.

Your last letter was a good one, Honey. It reminded me, brought back some of the unity I felt with you after your last visit. Hope you were able to accomplish some of our mutual projects during your last week at home. But if you didn't, don't let it bother you. These are not easy times to decide what to do and why. And being so isolated and circumscribed myself, I know that I can't fully appreciate all your frustrations and distractions. I am still a little surprised though that Enid should seem to fail to understand so completely how much our unity and mutual projects mean to us at this time. Naturally, her family is the most important thing in the world to her, and should be, but to expect it to have the same importance for you is completely unrealistic. Our own family (i.e., each other), our own hopes and plans, our thinking and unity should just as naturally be the most important things in our lives. But I guess we can't too much expect folks to understand problems and situations which they have never had to face for themselves.

I thought the book review very good and heartily agree with your comments. Such a Spartan existence as the Wests' may have a very fine contribution to make toward one's understanding of life as a temporary experiment, but I wouldn't want it as a permanent thing—simplicity, fine, but sub-marginal existence, no thanks. But I was quite surprised at so much understanding and appreciation from a *World-Herald* reporter.

I just today finished *The Holy Earth*. Thought it said some good things but not many that we haven't already thought of. But the old boy does seem to have a very fine attitude toward Mother Earth that I hope we may together grow to appreciate more and more. What's next on the docket, Honey? I'm starting *The Lord Helps Those* tonight—send me three or four titles and a prospective schedule, and I'll try to go along with you on it. I read an interesting book about which I jotted down a few comments (copy enclosed). You might send the comments on to Mammy.

Wouldn't advise legal action on my case because it would be useless. Better cases with complete records and the issues all clearly defined in legal terminology exist and are being acted upon. But any legal basis for my release could be used effectively in a letter to the U.S. Pardon Attorney and Judge Donohoe urging its consideration as a basis for favorable action on my pardon application.

Kept this last few lines open to comment on the letter I got from you tonight and tell you how much I love you. Well, I didn't "get" the letter, but will have to confess I love you anyhow. Don't think I'll be able to write our folks this week, so will you share this letter or pertinent parts thereof? Have fun, Honey, keep your chin up, don't work too hard. I'm OK and expect to remain same.

Your hungry husb'ing,
Chuck

⬤ ⬤ ⬤

June 5, 1946

Dearest Betsy,

Hello, Honey. You haven't asked me to take your name off my list so here I am again. Verily, my Love, your husb'ing has a new lease on life, a new light in his eye, new pep and vitality, in fact, he is a new creature. Sounds like a breakfast food ad, doesn't it? Well, in a way that's just what it is, or at least a strong testimonial to the value of having a breakfast. Monday we were started on a new schedule—two refueling jobs a day of the same stuff and same size as before. And believe me, it makes a difference. Expect I'll get back to the "Small Community" courses again and possibly even a little volleyball. Only trouble with the new schedule so far (though I really shouldn't be looking a gift horse in the tube) is that the feedings have been too close together—10:30 A.M. and 1:30 P.M. Hump wasn't able to keep his second one down and I had some trouble myself—felt as though I had just eaten two Christmas dinners. But this morning we were assured that even this difficulty would be remedied, that our first feeding would take place at 8:30. Gosh, Honey, taking that tube has become as easy as pie, though not as tasty. I still miss eating psychologically, but have found that three or four cups of coffee and a few cigarettes every day come in handy as a crutch.

Am happy, too, that they started feeding Hank and Hutch yesterday. We had just decided that we would have to actively resist our own feeding in order to preserve unity with them. Hank had been without food 17 days and had lost 33 pounds. Hutch had been on a complete fast 10 days preceded by 2 weeks on a self-imposed daily diet of 1,000 calories and was very weak—spent the last three or four days in bed. Gormly started Monday and will probably lose strength rapidly since he is so thin.

Incidentally, I did a little superficial research among the hunger strikers with the following results: average age—30; education— 3½ years of college; IQ (according to tests made by the educational department)—132; time in CPS—9½ months; time served in prison (three of us have done previous sentences)—19½ months; time yet to serve—two years. Two of us are married. There are three Methodists and five other church backgrounds represented. They come from eight different states scattered all over the country—from California to New York, and from Florida to Minnesota.

I sent a long letter to John S. this week telling all about the fast so you needn't write to him (in case you haven't). Which means I can't write to Omaha this week, so will you share this letter with our folks? Mary Ellen wrote the folks expressing an interest in the cause and a willingness to help. Would you send her a card suggesting she contact Dorothy Hampton (John's wife), 611 N. Fairfax, Los Angeles 36, telephone Wyoming 1753? She knows the whole story from A to Z and knows what to do. She must be a regular human dynamo—writes John six jam-packed letters a week, carries on a voluminous correspondence on his behalf, holds down a full-time job as a stock-room clerk, takes care of her own apartment, and takes part in the amnesty campaign. She should be able to show M.E. the ropes. Tell her to call on Saturday mornings. (Slight interruption for breakfast. The doctor's assistant says that vitamins have been added to our diet starting today.)

Finished a very good little book the other day, *The Lord Helps Those* by Bertram Fowler—about the best thing I've read in the "Small Community" course yet. Did I ask you to buy it, Honey? I didn't keep a list of what books I suggested that you buy. It's the story of co-ops in Nova Scotia and the way they have remade the way of life there. Does a darned good job of pointing up the difference between co-ops as a way of life and as a business proposition only. Tells how the folk-school movement works in practice. I think Mammy would enjoy it too, it's well written. Gives some ideas of things we may be able to do some day.

(Another interruption—"yard" this time. Yep, I did it, Honey—played a couple of games of volleyball. My coordination and timing weren't quite up to par, but golly it was wonderful to get a little active exercise again. I'll bet you a buck I get a suntan before you, and a deeper one, too. But don't let that discourage you, my little lily of the valley.)

Art Wiser is back in Macedonia with his wife and baby. He writes to Hank. Thought you might be interested in a couple quotes telling of activities there:

Right now we are excited because of the beginnings of a
co-op store. Had a general meeting Monday night. About 50
neighbors (counting their children) turned up. Really very impressive. Lois Worley acted as chairman. Pretty fair meeting.
Everyone expressed desire for a store (they remember the one
which was here before), and altogether $265 was pledged and
$90 paid on the spot. We elected a Board of Directors—Lois
Worley (later selected chairman), Lucille Roberts, Mary Wiser
(later selected Secretary-Treasurer), Paris Whitworth, two
other local folks you don't know. Well, the Board met two
nights later (Wednesday) and this morning, Thursday, there
were about 15 women down here generally working over and
beautifying a place under the tool shed where the store will
be. In the Board meeting everyone talked and the group had a
strong sense of rapport, which is greatly enriched by working
together. Tomorrow the men put in a floor and put up counters and shelves. Different people have contributed different
things—precious nails, roofing paper (for floor), boards for
floor and counters. Project has contributed some windows
and framed in the part for the store. . . . It's like the stories of
Nova Scotia.

Things in the project move along. This week we must be taking in over $600. Last week we took in $500 odd, but had a
payroll of $425! Some contrast from days I remember when
Evelyn and Lucille had only 19 cents to last through a whole
month, and the only source of income was Morris's salary.

I got a line-up on woodworking equipment and may go
ahead in the next couple of months getting some. Cost about
$1,200, I guess, and of course it would be some time before
developing anything marketable and then marketing it. So for
the time being it will not be an income-making project.

Think I'll write a letter to Morris expressing my interest in the
project there, what we hope to accomplish, would like to learn, may
be able to contribute in skills, cash, etc. Be thinking about it. I'll send
the letter to you to read, add your own comments to, and then if you
see fit, forward to Morris.

Did you talk to Tom about a truck? Maybe I can get permission to write Ray (my uncle) and ask him to keep his eye peeled, too, and write you or Pappy before taking any action. Will send you a carbon if it goes through. I didn't mean to suggest a grist mill of our own would have to be electric. We could fix that up later or grind it by hand. Do we have the essential kitchenware, canning stuff, etc.?

The Warden came through with a little more "liberalization" yesterday—pants and shirts instead of coveralls, and full use of the day room. He denied us more "yard," musical instruments, self-service on clothes, commissary and library, freedom to order our own books, and movies. In response to a letter to Tom Clark requesting information as to whether any means were being considered whereby absolutists might be released unconditionally, we got back a letter most beautifully and nauseatingly misunderstanding the whole problem and I may send you a copy. Honey, do you want me to keep on sending you carbons of this stuff? You so seldom comment that I sometimes wonder if I may only be boring you with it all.

The transfer bus was here over the weekend but is now gone and all of Administrative Segregation is still here together. Personally, I'm glad, though a trip and change would have been exciting.

I've read all about Colorado, thanks, in fact mentioned it in a letter once. Hurrah for the refund. It was about what I thought it would be. Hope we got a good write-up from the reporter's visit. Haven't heard yet. Will enclose a copy of Hank's latest "Small Community" paper if I can get a copy. I thought it was good.

Much love, Darling.
Chuck

P.S. Am also enclosing a copy of our letter. Follow-ups by friends would be helpful.

◙ ◙ ◙

June 13, 1946

Dearest Betsy,

Imagine my surprise and delight last night to receive two letters from my Sweet and Lovely Wife—guess letters from Kennard must take more time en route than those from Omaha. Fact is, you're three letters up on me so I'd better get down to business (I don't count special-purpose letters).

First, since you seem to be concerned about my health, let me assure you that the situation is improving right along. In fact, I felt so much better that Dick and I have been doing the cleanup job this week and enjoying it. And four of we fasters have been playing the four non-fasters in volleyball, and though they have two of the best players, the games have all been close and hard fought. Last Friday I still weighed only 119½, but must have gained more since then. All of us are feeling fine and are in good spirits—except poor old Gormly, of course, who is on the 11th day of his fast and has not yet been force fed, though he is quite weak. Incidentally, they say that there are two eggs per man in each feeding—four eggs a day. Guess we should do pretty well on that, no?

We all enjoyed Adam's letter. He's the darnedest little guy imaginable. Wish you would send him a postcard, Honey, telling him that we were glad to hear from him, that Hank, Hutch, and Walter have joined the "fast for freedom," that our spirits are high and we don't see any reason for calling it off until the injustice is fully rectified, and that we are saving a nice, clean cell for him but hope he won't need it.

I thought your mimeo'd letter was good, Sweetheart, but your plan to hold it for amnesty leaflets a bit naive—that could be a month, you know. Meanwhile, the iron gets cold. This week's *The Christian Century* had a good letter by George Hansen quoting our statement and urging amnesty. The little *World-Herald* story wasn't bad but I think they passed up chances for a good feature story.

Thanks for Buffett's letter, and to Mammy for writing him. It's a good letter until along towards the end where he starts hedging—becoming a politician. I think that continued goading of congressmen will help in our release. Congress can grant us an amnesty by a joint resolution, you know, and many have expressed themselves as being sympathetic. So far we have written over 200 copies of the letter like the carbon I sent you. Of course, such a joint resolution is probably out of the question as long as Selective Service continues in force, which unfortunately now fairly well promises to be a long time. The only argument now seems to be over drafting 18- and 19-year-olds, not over extension. Even Butler voted for a year's extension—the stinker. Wherry has the best record of all Nebraska congressmen or senators. He would be a good guy to get interested in my pardon application and the amnesty campaign.

Despite the conscription clouds, however, there are still a few stars in the sky. The CPS strikes offer a real ray of hope. If CPS should be declared unconstitutional, a pregnant possibility, those of us who have rejected it would stand a good chance for release.

Dyer, in response to a letter to the Attorney General announcing his fast and asking if any plans were underway to get absolutists out of prison, received a reply copy, which is enclosed. We don't know just what to make of it—if anything. Haven't been able to get any more information yet, in fact, the Parole Office here hadn't even heard of it. Gosh, Honey, I hope some of our friends have written Clark; now is the time for pressure. Have you ever written to him?

Yesterday I spent several hours copying letters, etc., from my Selective Service file. Am planning to write a letter to U.S. Probation Officer, Donohoe, and Murphy citing recent legal developments in CPS and requesting favorable consideration of my pardon application.

I'm eager to hear of your response on my SP letter to Morris Mitchell. About a house at Macedonia, they have electricity and have put in inside water systems in all houses so far. These two things make life so much easier and pleasanter that I think they are worth securing even at some cost and sacrifice.

Pretty much agree with your comments on "routine" but don't like that word—reminds me too much of "rut" and "regimentation." But I think you meant "planned" or "orderly" living—the difference in my mind being that in the latter, the routine doesn't become too severe or an end in itself, but rather a means to fuller living, still allowing opportunities for spontaneity and change.

Copy of *Science, Liberty, and Peace* came last night and I finished same this morning. I thought it a good clear statement of the situation, though probably nothing that both of us have not thought of before. But it's good to have En like Huxley supporting our judgment of values. No? Also read recently a "Small Community" book about the Hopis. Knowing some of these people intimately made it more meaningful to me. Their way of life and whole cultural pattern is extremely different from ours and most interesting, in fact, loaded with implications regarding culture if we are to change from a competitive to a cooperative society. I've finally written another "Small Community" paper. It's not much but will send copy to you when it comes back from Arthur E.

I think you will find those government agricultural bulletins a gold mine. Would you send another postcard to: Agricultural Experiment Station, South Dakota State College, Brookings, S.D., requesting copies of Bulletins 336, 298, and 277 (revised)? These are bulletins on rammed earth construction. No need to send them on to me as I've read them, but would like to have them for future use. Also, order Bulletin No. 41 from Kansas State College of Agriculture and Applied Science, Manhattan, Kansas, on the same thing.

Will try to get a letter off to folks in Omaha, one or the other, this week and may write to Frank and Marie—though I am beginning to doubt how far I can bring them along. Frank seems to be settling pretty deep into the smug intellectual rut of a Christian preacher. But maybe it's only the difficulty of maintaining understanding by correspondence—seems like I've experienced that problem before.

Back to houses again. At Macedonia they build chiefly frame houses, I think, because lumber is so cheap, but Art and Mary plan a house of native stone walls, I believe. I've designed another small, inexpensive house plan that I'll send along soon—not as a suggested plan but more as a game, something to think about and play with.

Am enclosing copy of a note from Bennett in answer to my letter protesting Adam's loss of "good time" some three months ago. It's a masterpiece of misunderstanding and evasion—either intentional or not. It really brought forth a howl from the boys when I read it to them.

The amnesty campaign seems to be making some progress. The Union for Democratic Action, including many big shots, sent at our suggestion a strong letter to Truman requesting our release.

G'bye, Honey. I love you an awful lot. Have fun.
Chuck

◙ ◙ ◙

June 17, 1946

Dearest Betsy,

My goodness, Honey, I certainly hit the jackpot last week—six letters, four of them from my Sweetheart. You know, Betsy, I can say I appreciate your problems and understand when you don't write, etc., and intellectually, mentally, I do. But the heart and brain follow separate paths of reason and sometimes the heart fails to understand things that the mind sees clearly. Which may explain seeming contradictions that pop up from time to time. Do you have the same trouble? Anyway, I enjoyed all the letters—they seem to help maintain our spirit of unity.

Yes, Darling, it's almost a year since we said goodbye out at 3315. In retrospect, the past year seems as short to me as the four months we lived together—since we seem to measure past time by the amount of living—action, change, excitement, etc., that takes place. Wish the next year ahead looked as short as the one just passed. However, I am not too pessimistic about the future and release possibilities even though continuation of conscription is a lead-pipe cinch. But Andresen was finally released unconditionally after being on a hunger strike for about seven months, though he had a three-year sentence (or more)—wasn't even eligible for parole yet. Then, too, the CPS rebellion may help, and there may even be something to Tom Clark's letter mentioning a point system for release of COs. So keep your fingers crossed and your pen as busy as you have time for. Incidentally, Honey, would you send a postcard to Louise Rounds? Tell her I often get to wondering about some of the old gang—where they are and what they are doing. In particular, I've been wondering about Scoff, Forest, Trav and Flo, Jerry, Dolve, Ella and Erna, Lucille, George Roach, Doug Corey, John, and Dick Dinning. Of course, she may not know about some, but bet she could give me a line on most of them.

I'm feeling fine, Honey, in fact, quite a bit better than during the past few days when I seemed to have a slight case of intestinal flu (which is making the rounds), and my stomach was rather upset for three days. This morning we fasters declined the tube in order to maintain unity with Gormly, who is now on his 15th day without food. Looked for a while like they were going to call in more help and force it down us, but apparently they decided not to. Weighed 118½ this morning, which looks like a pound less but is really a pound gain since I didn't have that two pounds of "eggnog" in me this time. All of us are in fine fettle and good spirits. Hope you are the same.

It has rained lots lately and the air has been extremely damp— condensing on our cold toilet bowls and making a little puddle beneath. It rained us out of "yard" this morning, but fortunately let off long enough yesterday for a double-header ball game with a team from St. Paul. FE1 won both games handily, thank you. These boys have a team that (in popular vernacular) just won't quit. And we in Administrative Segregation have the best seats in the house.

I've been greatly enjoying the evening and morning symphony of late—the frogs, crickets, birds, etc. Have been getting up with the sun to read. The chukars start the day off at the first flush of dawn with clucking and strutting. I like getting up early and going to bed early—spending as much of the day as possible by natural light. Maybe we can keep a couple of roosters to take the place of the chukars on our own place, huh? The purple martins have been visiting the yard before the boys get up—also some little bird with a very nice song—haven't identified it yet.

They finally asked me to return the library's copy of Thoreau so I got real busy reading *Walden*. Gosh, I like it, Honey, it's my Bible. We just have to have a copy of that Modern Library edition. It's just packed with good stuff. That first chapter is practically a whole philosophy of life. (I know you've read it, Honey, but I still can't help commenting.) I like it better every time I read it. It should help keep us on an even keel regarding materialism, etc.

You mentioned how my hair curls when it gets long. You should see it now. We haven't had haircuts since late April and then I only had mine trimmed. Quite a bush. It's OK for a change but not nearly so handy as a "butch."

I certainly don't think we'd be wise to spend $500 for a vehicle, do you? In fact, I don't think we can afford to spend much over $200 for one, considering how much cash we have and how many more important things we need, or will need. A bus isn't a necessity for us, I'd say, but a nice thing if we can get it on our own conditions. Before you buy a bunch of new stuff by mail, I'd suggest that you try a few secondhand places in Omaha when you have a chance. There may not be any good secondhand stuff in circulation now and the price may be high, but we wouldn't know that until we tried. And sometimes one can pick up much better stuff that way for almost nothing, make a couple of minor repairs and have a real piece of goods.

Subsistence livers should learn to be bargain seekers, I think—it's practical. Also, since every dollar spent is a "vote cast for some kind of system" (to quote my friend Walter Uphoff), I think we should try to patronize co-ops when possible, then the better type of businesses second. Sears, for example, has a much better labor policy than Wards. Incidentally, did you ever check to see if we have a patronage refund coming at Farmer's Union? I'm sure we have.

Had two teeth filled the other day. The dentist said not to chew on it too soon. Bet I'm the most obedient patient he ever had.

Our fast is still getting a little publicity. P.V. had a short article. Gen. Hauser had long letters in *The Christian Century* and *The Progressive,* also long and detailed report in *The Grapevine.* Am glad you wrote to him and Hassler. Haven't yet received June *Fellowship.*

Hank said he'd be interested in Borsodi's comments on his paper. No, he has not read Hugo Fach's stuff.

Got another letter from Art Wiser; they are finding many problems to work out at Macedonia. Another co-op group at Bass Lake, Minnesota, are talking about going to Macedonia en masse. Sounds like it might get a little congested, which, to my way of thinking, would make it less attractive. But it could be anything by the time I get out. Final decisions on such things, as I said in a letter to M.M., just aren't possible at this time. Did you get the letter to Mitchell yet? If so, any reactions?

Wrote my folks last week and told them to get on the ball. May write Mammy this week.

Our little pansy just had a lovely little blossom, reminding me that there is beauty in life. You are the most beautiful thing in my life, Darling. I love you more than I can say.

Frank and Marie should be in Omaha soon. I wrote to them last week.

Have fun, Sweetheart.

All my love,

Chuck

P.S. Regards to the Wardells, and folks in Omaha, should you see them.

◙ ◙ ◙

June 21, 1946

Dearest Betsy,

As I sit down to write this letter, not much comes to mind that I want to say, but I have another letter to spend on this week's quota, am one up on all my other correspondents, and besides, there's no one I'd rather have another little visit with, though only by correspondence, than my Sweet, Good-lookin' Ol' Lady. Suppose you noticed that my last letter was somewhat delayed—trouble is that the allowed government $.03 wasn't enough to carry so many enclosures. (Personally, speaking as one who has spent over $8,000 in postage as a professional mail boy, I think their scales weigh too heavy.) Hope this one does better. It should since there are only five pages, all on onion skin. And guess what? Yeah, ain't that a b---h! Recipes! Guess that shows the direction my fancy runs these days. If you don't want 'em, just throw 'em away. Incidentally, I have another six pages from the same book. Maybe it's only that these recipes are written simply enough for men that made them appeal to me, or was it this hunger strike? The very thought of masticating some good old chow certainly does have a glamour that it never had before. The other day I ate an orange which I had won from one of the other boys. Golly, it was positively wonderful. Bet the Gods on Olympus never enjoyed their ambrosia and nectar half so much. Since last writing you, the new tubes have come in and we are all getting two refuelings a day.

Well, today is the first day of summer (purely a theoretical hypothesis in these parts) but anyway, the sun is trying to cooperate in celebration of the day. Gosh, Honey, we surely could have used some of that 108 you all had last weekend. Since last Saturday it has been cold and rainy here—and I do mean COLD and RAINY. Don't know the amount of precipitation, but the thermometer was down in the 40s, too much for my blood. It made Georgia or Arkansas seem mighty attractive.

Sounds like you are getting a very fine and extremely liberal education as regards the childbearing process, including, I suppose, a demonstration of the new Christian Science technique of painless delivery. But I'd better be careful, seeing as how you always take my joking too seriously. Honestly, I imagine there is a lot to the idea. Fear of anything undoubtedly increases the pain connected therewith, even for sound physiological reasons. Remember our poem—"Even pain is oftener friend than enemy, and the fear of it is more poignant than the pain of it." On the other hand, you know how I instinctively react to anything that purports to know all the answers, that goes off the deep end, so to speak. I still doubt that there is any human who knows all the answers about anything—and I sometimes wonder about God.

So Jim Robinson is going up to Christianize the heathens. Well, nothing like opening up new markets for refrigerators. Hope he has read Steffanson's credo in "I Believe" so his mind will be open to learning something about genuine mutual aid and goodwill. Haven't yet heard about the letter Carlberg was going to write. Sounds like you got in a good "witness" to the gang.

Flash! The man just two minutes ago came up with Carlberg's letter, allowed me to read it and then took it away. She said, "Yes, Chuck, I'm still a G-Woman. I think government is here to stay." I greatly fear that she doesn't even suspect the half of it. She told about all the discussion of decentralism. Said something about that you seemed to know all the answers and that it turned out to be a very good topic for discussion.

Our little pansy, now under my care exclusively, is doing very well, thanks. It has very deep purple flowers with a wonderfully sweet odor. Hope I can be nursing something more than one lovely little pansy next summer.

The latest rumor on Clark's "point system" comes from one of the COs out in population who talked to the Warden about it recently. He quotes the letter as saying only two men in this joint are eligible and they have both rejected it. Wow, the requirements must be gigantic. CPS time is said to count, which brings my total time done to 47 months, and Hank's even higher, and apparently we aren't even eligible. We've got it figured out as follows: total points required, those earned plus those the inmate will yet earn in the remainder of the full sentence. Then he may apply for parole to CPS or police duty abroad.

I don't expect you to keep up with my reading schedule, Honey, but if you would just tell me what books you have and assign the order in which you plan to read them, then I could read them even if we didn't stick together on the schedule. Too bad you haven't enough time to pick up a little practice and a few pointers from En on your piano playing. But maybe you will have more time later in July, or maybe you aren't interested.

My latest creative effort is an attempt at a shepherd's pipe, made out of paper smeared with paste and wound around a stick to make the shell. It hasn't dried yet so have no idea if it will work. Also don't remember how the holes should be spaced or the sound opening.

Hope you have sent the letter on to Morris Mitchell by this time as he plans to leave Macedonia July 1. Another letter from Art tells of more interesting developments. Seems like some of the local folks have been drinking a little too much homemade corn squeezings—possibly even squoze out right there on community property. Morris put his foot down in a rather undemocratic fashion—threatened to call in the law. It seems to have had the desired results, temporarily at least. Also, some have quit for higher wages elsewhere but are still living on community premises. The co-op store is coming along fine and doing a thriving business—$10 worth daily. They are expecting to have a Brethren work camp there this summer to raise and process food for shipment abroad. Art is trying to work out articles of incorporation and a more satisfactory method of compensation, distribution of produce, etc. It's all so nebulous that I won't mention any of the details now.

Read an ad of an 80-acre farm mostly woodland and pasture, 20 acres in cultivation, fully equipped with cows, machinery, fruit trees, two small houses, etc., for $2,700. Bet Cecil and family would be willing to go in on something like that if we should lose interest in Macedonia. Well, I've squandered away my quota.

Love and kisses, Darling. You're still my favorite wife.
Chuck

P.S. Wrote to Mammy today also.

■ ◙ ◙

June 28, 1946 [No. 1]

Dearest Betsy,

Hello, my Dear Wife. Perhaps, just for variety, I should start this letter off with a little inspirational poem.

> *The year's at the spring,* [Check: Browning's poem, "The
> Year's at the Spring"]
> (You know how Minnesota is—winter and July, which makes
> this still spring.)

> *And the day's at the morn;*
> *Morning's at seven;*
> (Well, I wouldn't call a man a liar for half an hour, but it's
> really only 6:30.)

> *The hillside's dew-pearled;*
> (That's putting it rather mildly, My Dear. In fact, we're having
> one helluva rainstorm with some hail and sharp thunder. If
> this isn't the darnedest climate. I'll bet it has rained at least
> every other day this month.)

> *The lark's on the wing;*
> (He'd better get off of it darned quick if he has any sense—
> enough to get in out of the rain, that is.)

The snail's on the thorn;
(Probably got stuck there by a butcherbird.)

God's in His heaven—
(Hmm, well, could be, but sometimes I wonder. Yet it's pretty
obvious that he doesn't spend much time on earth. Besides,
he's probably heard about atom bombs and is holed up for
safety.)

All's right with the world.
(Good Lord, now isn't that a nice honest way to start the day
off? If "all's right" now, I'd certainly hate to see things get in
a bad way. No, Honey, poetry just doesn't seem to be what it
used to be.)

Gee whiz, here it is Friday already and I'm just now writing
my first letter for the week. How come? I dunno. Certainly, it isn't
because I have been too busy this week. Looking back over it, I can
think of hardly a thing I've accomplished—let's see—read about a
book and a half—a life of St. Francis (not so hot), about 200 pages
in gardening encyclopedia (I really get a kick out of reading all
about fruits and vegetables, how to raise them, etc.) and 100 pages
in anthropology book that came with our "Small Community"
course—very good. Oh, yes, and a miscellaneous assortment of
magazines, papers, etc.—June *Fellowship* (noticed they had my
letter in), *Time,* etc.

Made one shepherd's pipe, which doesn't work very well, by rolling and pasting paper around a brush handle to make the shell. Also
made a coin purse out of an old softball cover. A very busy week,
no? Do you, by any chance, happen to have complete instructions on
making shepherd's pipes? If so, would you send them to me? Don't
go to any trouble about it, however, as I'm not that interested.

Dick Zumwinkle sent in a letter to the Warden today stating
that he was willing to resume eating voluntarily again, that with the
extension of Selective Service he didn't feel that continued fasting
would be effective in securing amnesty for COs. To a certain extent I
can agree with him. Despite the fact that there has been and still is an

effective campaign and considerable pressure on the administration to grant amnesty to COs in prison, I am not optimistic of amnesty being granted as long as Selective Service continues in force. I agree, too, that perhaps the major purpose of our fast has been achieved i.e., we have done a fairly good job of acquainting the public with the fact that COs are still in prison in America because of their religious beliefs. That we and our outside supporters have done a good job is shown, I think, by the fact that nearly every religious convention meeting lately has passed a resolution urging amnesty. The very fact that the Department of Justice has announced this point system for release of COs reveals that the pressure has been felt—even though this point system turns out to be only another way of stalling. And the Selective Service has been extended. I do not at all doubt that our action has had some effect, though we can never measure it, and will continue to have some effect in opposing the war-conscription-totalitarian forces. However, even if amnesty is not granted for many years yet, pressure can still secure for absolutist COs an unconditional release, short of amnesty—individual commutations, for instance.

None of the rest of us agree with Dick or at present see any end to the fast short of our release from prison. We feel that pressure will continue to grow as time goes on, and we do not wish to abandon the fast until its possibilities seem to be exhausted. Of course, we recognize that the price may seem to become too great, as it apparently became for Dick, but at present it has not reached that point. Of course, some of us are in perfect condition, we have some trouble with bowel movements, headaches, etc., and are all quite a bit underweight, but we still feel we are in pretty good shape—and perhaps our chances for release would be better if we weren't.

Personally, if I ever do decide to quit fasting, I am sure I will never be content to merely sit back on my fanny and do time and nothing else. You know, Honey, my life has been conscripted by the government for four years now—17 months in CPS, one month in jail, 13 months at Tucson, five months on CR from Tucson, and 12 months at Sandstone—total 48 months. Frankly, I just don't intend to do much more of it. What further action I might take I have not yet decided but am considering a couple, neither of which is entirely in keeping with my philosophy of life, but which I might feel were justified by conditions. One possibility would be to deliberately hurt my health—regurgitate my food, let my muscles deteriorate, not bother with bowel movements, etc. Another possibility would be to deliberately make myself so costly to the government that they might wish to get rid of me. In other words, adopt a program of outright destruction, which, in the long run, would probably be just as hard on my health since they would probably lock me up in a strip cell of some kind. If I should make either decision, however, there would probably be at least one or two (maybe more) others who would go along with me on it.

As I say, this idea of destroying prison property may be rather alien to my personality, but on the other hand, so is it alien to my conscience to let the government use my body to enforce its growing totalitarianism if there is anything further I can do to oppose it. And when I think of all the government has destroyed of my time and freedom and creative living—for instance, the spring just gone by was completely destroyed as far as my enjoyment of it goes—I am not sure my conscience would balk at the destruction of inanimate objects used for immoral, undemocratic purposes. (To be continued.)

If you wish to comment on either of these ideas, feel free to do so. I am willing to give this so-called democratic process at least another month's trial, however, so if you know anyone who hasn't written to Tom Clark or our senators suggesting my release, you'd better have them write soon. I imagine you must become discouraged at times and think such letters are useless, but I assure you that they aren't. In fact, I'd suggest that you write one letter to me and one to Clark each week. Your letters to me help me lots, but letters to Clark might do more good.

Love,
Chuck

■ ■ ■

June 28, 1946 [No. 2]

Hello, Honey, it's me again,

Obviously, I should have started these letters long ago. Now it's near the week's deadline and I may not get it all thought out and written down. Maybe I should elaborate on the suggestion in letter 1, that you share your letter writing to me with Tom Clark. Please know that I greatly appreciate hearing from you. Letters help lots in "walking this lonesome valley" (which sometimes gets quite lonesome). But right now I'm more interested in getting out of the valley. Of course, you should change the emphasis with each letter. There are many different points you could stress:

> Our family life is broken—after all, even Truman has a wife, and the fact that I should be supporting you, not the charity of relations (not that I doubt you are earning your board and room at En's).

> Our future plans to farm, the fact that such work would be a real contribution to humanity whereas prison is pure waste, etc.

> That imprisonment for conscience denies a basic freedom guaranteed by American traditions and the Constitution.

> The fact that amnesty has been granted in past wars and to thousands all over the world since this war's close.

> The fact that the public supports amnesty is shown by church-conference resolutions, big names on Amnesty Committee, etc. (Do you have the dope on any of this, e.g., church-conference resolutions?)

> The fact that I have already done four years—tell how.

> The fact that CPS, which I refused, violates the Constitution and Draft Act in many ways, etc., etc.

I have permission to receive from home my Webster's dictionary and my copy of *The Prophet*. The Warden says to have them come addressed to me in his care. Would you please do?

About the tax-refund check, do with it as you see fit. It makes no difference to me. But reminds me of something that has been on my conscience for a long time. I sometimes wonder how justified we are in so carefully hoarding up our little shekels when thousands of our fellow men, women, and children are starving to death. Especially since it is all for some uncertain future use while at present we are well-fed, clothed, and housed. How well are we living up to our ideals and philosophy in this respect? Is there any difference *in the spirit* that prompts us to lock up our savings in this way and that which prompts huge capitalists to exploit the people? I am not going to make any specific suggestions. I am not opposed to saving, in fact, I think it's a good idea, but I also believe that sharing with others in much greater need is also a good idea. What you do, if anything, will be OK with me. I only wanted you to know how I feel about this matter.

Hank got a letter from Morris Mitchell last night but he didn't mention our letter. Have you sent it to him? Not that you should unless you see fit, but you have not said whether or not you ever sent it. As I said once before, he is leaving Macedonia July 1. He may be here for a visit. What questions should I ask him?

A letter from Mom Monday night says you had just been there and had a good tan—congrats. Honey, I didn't think it possible. Suppose she told you all about Pop's taking a three-month leave of absence and the fact that they are thinking about trying to locate a little farm. Maybe we could get them interested in looking over the part of the country we have been thinking about—i.e., around Fayetteville or those parts.

Had a letter from Frank written at Clear Lake, Iowa. They'll be in Omaha July 1–15, then on to Phoenix. He was in a much more understanding mood this time. Thanks for sending on Harry's, Bob's, and M.E.'s letters. Send my best regards and congrats to Harry. Igal R. corresponds with Barte, a New York sculptor, who corresponds with Harry's brother, Gene, now in the Marines. Gene knows Igal also. He says our fast was carried in the Italian edition of

Stars and Stripes. If I had Bob's address I might put him on my list. He is a good guy and Paul hasn't written to me, or me him, for six months or more.

Wonder how much M.D. had to pay all those good lookin' CPS guys to pose with her. She says she hopes to go to Davis—where the heck and what the heck is that? Sounds like a darned girls' school to me. I thought Carlberg's letters to Truman darned good. Should you write to her, please tell her so and thank her for me.

We've had some more information on the point system. Vivien wrote Igal and then the Warden talked to Hampton and Bailey, who are supposed to be eligible, so now we are really confused. Seems it is a form of 8641 parole but extremely liberal as to conditions. "Nominal" conditions, he said—whatever that is. Anyone over 38, anyone who has done three years of time, anyone over 26 with three natural children (guess that means those conceived by mental telepathy, etc., don't count). If there are any other classes eligible, I don't know. Maybe this would be a good theme for a letter to Tom Clark—telling him that you are my dependent wife and telling how much time I have served, telling how long I've been fasting (49 days today), etc., and if Dad or Mammy would write on the same theme, we might get some action, who knows? Of course, they should make it clear that I will accept no conditions, and why I shouldn't.

You ask who the Boyds and Welches are—they are families living the "Small Community" way of life out in Tracy, California. Have done much to change the attitudes of neighbors and town folks, have had friends' work camps (that's how M.E. knows them), have built up co-ops, etc. Good people.

Thanks for the rammed-earth enclosure. Blocks are not as easy or practical, in my opinion, as a solid wall, but his method of covering the wall sounded very interesting and easy if dependable. Am glad you sent for further information about it.

Whoever heard of a rat coming into a beautiful gal's bedroom for plaster and wall paper? And if that's all he wanted, why do you call him a rat? Sounds fishy to me.

Undoubtedly, I've forgotten to mention some things I should write about, Sweetie Pie, but if so, will get them next week. One thing I don't want to forget, in fact, can't forget, is how much I love you and how nice I think you are. I'm feeling fine, can even notice improvement on the volleyball court. Don't work too hard or worry.

All my love and kisses,
Chuck

◩ ◩ ◩

July 3, 1946 (one more day to Independence day—good joke, no?)

Dearest Betsy,

It's me again, still doing business at the same place. Thought I'd drop you a note to let you know I appreciate your patronage.

So, Robert Donald Warhill has finally put in an appearance. Poor little sonofagun, did anyone tell him what he may be in for— either he must be very brave or something of a sucker—in fact, I greatly suspect he is the latter, especially. I suppose he was trying to delay his arrival until after this atomic bomb experiment. Well, now that the bomb has gone off and the world hasn't, he should have a darned good chance to live to the ripe old age of 18 or 19. Please give the little codger my most affectionate greetings; and to his parents, congratulations.

Regarding the Christian Science birth process, you may be interested in the story Hank Dyer told me about his sister. She is apparently a great big, husky gal with a zest for living. After her first baby came she was sort of disappointed—it was too easy—she just passed out and when she came to, there it was. So on the second one she told the doc she'd like to try it without the ether. He said OK but arranged to have it handy in case she changed her mind. She did— though I very much doubt she was afraid; in fact, she was interested and eager to find out what it was all about. And according to what she told Hank, it was really something, hardly comparable to having a tooth pulled.

Before I forget it, Honey, that truck deal you mentioned sounded excellent to me. For gosh sakes, tell Pappy to snap it up if he gets half a chance. Don't know where we can store a truck, but it wouldn't do it any good to stand out in the weather, and a little driving would be good for it, too. But we'll worry about little things like that when we get one.

Am including a bunch of carbon copies of letters which you might like to read: 1) A letter from Tom Clark to Representative Clare B. Luce regarding our imprisonment; 2) Our answer; 3) A letter from Vivien; and 4) A letter from Eleanor. For the last time—do any of you get the *Amnesty Bulletin*? Or should I copy and send on interesting items? I've asked every correspondent in Omaha if anyone there gets it, but never an answer. In fact, so many of the questions I ask or suggestions I make are ignored that I wonder if folks can't read my writing, or just don't bother to notice what I say, or if they just forget, or if I should enumerate and list requests separately, or what. Not that I mind or blame folks for not following all my suggestions—I know you are all busy with problems and responsibilities of your own—but when I ask a question or make a request I'd appreciate hearing whether or not anything is going to be done about it. Then, if one correspondent doesn't have the time or interest or something, I would know about it and if I think the thing is important, could make other arrangements.

They've hired a bunch of new guards here, about six or nine, and it is very odd, in fact almost ludicrous the way some of them act. I don't know whether some of the other guards have been filling them up with a lot of lies or what. Though we may stand right in front of them and say, "Good morning," or ask some question, they won't bat an eye or say a word. My theory at first was that they were deaf mutes, but I have since seen them talking to other people. The other day at volleyball, the ball rolled toward one of these new guys and as he and all of us stood watching, it rolled up and hit his foot. But he maintained his stern countenance and didn't twitch a muscle. As the ball stopped after hitting his foot, I thanked him quite cordially—no response. It was very amusing and many of the boys couldn't resist the impulse to laugh. Golly, Honey, why anyone would sell his soul, his personality, his manhood for a few paltry dollars is a hard thing to understand. These poor guys are constantly being required to perform some of the most disgusting and childish jobs. Today, for instance, a gang of them went through the dorms snooping through everyone's personal property—"shakedown," as it's called. I don't know just what dangerous weapons they pick up, but God knows the world would surely blow up or something if they weren't so careful. How would you enjoy the job of reading another man's letters to his wife?

The parole judge was here Monday and Tuesday and the boys out in population had their hair neatly combed and their mouths held just so. Needless to say he didn't bother to interview anyone from E2. Four of us were eligible to appear for a hearing but had made no application. Well, at least our present situation in E2 will make it easier for COs to get parole if they will take it—just as at Santa Barbara there was no detached service of any kind until a bunch of us went over the hill, and then all kinds of detached service opened up.

The mail just came and I hit the jackpot—one postcard from Bill and three letters including one from my Sweetie, one from Morris M., and one from Mom. Bill is on his way to K.U. to take his exams for an MA—he wants to start teaching in a junior college somewhere this fall. He comments on the advantages of the Midwest vs. California and finds much to like in each. Mom mentions seeing you in Omaha and hearing Frank preach. She also says Bob, Jane's husband, wants a divorce. I am not too surprised, though I had heard nothing about things developing in that direction. Bob had never grown up, never kicked around enough to get the love for adventure and change out of his system. But Jane wants to just settle down and make a home and she is a hard-handed, unyielding person. If she would have been willing to go camping and roughing it with Bob for a few years, all might have been well. Mom apparently sees it all as Bob's fault, mentions that he wants to "smoke, drink, and be wicked"—apparently can't see that such things are only a poor substitute for a desire to be independent and self-reliant. Though I haven't been invited to do so, I may express my opinion in my next letter home.

Will send Morris M.'s letter very shortly as this one is already carrying all possible weight. Will also send Arthur Morgan's comments on our latest "Small Community" papers. Your letter doesn't seem to require much comment except, as always, I'm glad to get them. Apparently Frank doesn't like criticism of his church or some of their compromises and weaknesses.

Am OK, weather beautiful. We fasters have slightly upset stomachs. Probably something they put in our "formula." Have started reading *War and Peace*. It should hold me a while.

Lots of love, Darling—
Chuck

◙ ◙ ◙

July 5, 1946 (Now we have independence.)

My Darling Wife Betsy,

Well, all us boys here at the institute spent a nice, quiet, safe, and sane holiday night here on the reservation—sort of intramural, so to speak—no excesses, no firecrackers, no overeating (just the regular hosing for me), no sunburn, no auto accidents, not even a ball game. The "good boys" out in population, i.e., those who say "Mr." to the screws and enjoy the "work privilege," had an extra movie and lemonade in the evening, neither of which we were invited to share; but I don't begrudge the poor suckers, they certainly earn anything they get.

The day's only excitement was a rumor from one of the cons who said he had seen an article in the *Minneapolis Star-Journal* in which Clark is said to be conferring with other government officials regarding pardoning all COs over 28. Don't know if there is anything to it. I'll believe it when the other six fasters (all of whom are over 28) tell me goodbye, but the rumor has since been verified by other cons and by the doctor's assistant who tubes us. However, I'm not excited about it, especially since it wouldn't even apply to me for another eight months, if then. In the second place, it still fails to correct the basic injustice of imprisoning men because of their loyalty to conscience, still fails to recognize the principle of religious freedom. Needless to say, I'll go right on fasting as long as I'm under control by the Department of Justice. After all, if it is wrong to imprison 29-, 30-, 35-year-olds for their religious beliefs, why is it right to imprison 28- or 25- or even 18-year-olds, to say nothing of those who have never been officially classified as COs? I am enclosing Morris's letter. Don't believe it needs any special comments.

When I spoke of an orchard he apparently thought I meant a big commercial proposition for making money, whereas I had chiefly in mind a small one for subsistence purposes. Am also including a couple pages about Macedonia that Hank copied out of one of our "Small Community" books. Am also enclosing Arthur Morgan's comments on our last batch of "Small Community" papers. He doesn't have much to say about mine, but thought you might be interested in his comments on Hank's paper since you have read it. Though I don't always agree with Morgan's ideas I think he must be a remarkably fine person.

I wrote to the folks today giving my impression of Jane's and Bob's troubles and some uninvited advice. Maybe I shouldn't be sticking my pug nose in, but I hate to see anyone's marriage going on the rocks, especially when I think a little intelligence and unselfishness could solve most of the problems. I suggested they talk the situation over with Mammy; maybe she can help them out a little.

Gosh, Honey, we have so little really nice weather that when a day like today comes along I can't help remarking about it. Really is lovely, and though most of us have been about half sick lately—stomach trouble, diarrhea, etc.—we all felt better today and even had a couple good games of volleyball during "yard." I even got up a little sweat. Don't know whether the stomach trouble came from something they have done to our formula or something that is just going around. Some of the other boys haven't felt so good, too. Even the doc has been sick. But today he was back on the job and at our request came over for a visit. We showed him the letter Tom Clark sent Mrs. Luce. He was quite burned up about the falsehoods and derogatory innuendos, especially the remark that two of the men were "drinking their formula." He said he personally appreciated the fact that they hadn't had to employ strong-arm methods, that having your head forced back and stuff poured down your throat was as much force feeding as any other method. (Incidentally, this pitcher feeding was the medical staff's idea from the start. Now they have found that tube feeding actually takes less time, and since they have enough tubes, are now tube feeding all of us—though Parker and Hutch have a great deal of trouble with their gag reflex, throw up frequently, and Parker's throat bleeds sometimes.) Doc said he was going to check this matter with the Warden to see just where the Attorney General's falsehood came from and expressed the wish that we'd write Clark before taking any steps that would make his job more difficult. Doc also pointed out that Clark's efforts to smear us were undoubtedly a defense mechanism to justify his own position.

Got a letter from Mammy last night telling about the peace caravan expected to arrive on the Fourth, and also about the school band's discussion on ROTC. Am glad she got in a couple of good licks on militarism. I'll be interested to know how the peace caravan makes out—if they can get any weeds to sprout in the cold climate of Omaha's conservatism.

My intentions have greatly exceeded my achievements lately. Seven books are stacked up in my cell awaiting attention—two or three of them in various stages of perusal, namely *Principles of Feeding Farm Animals*, *Study of Man*, and *War and Peace*. I may have to hurry or else refuse to leave prison if this pardon business develops too rapidly—a very pregnant possibility, no doubt.

I'm running low on stuff to say. Could quote a couple poems, but these enclosures ought to give you enough to read. Looks like you'd better introduce some subjects a little more intellectually stimulating into our correspondence if you want me to write two full pages. Am also including a balance sheet of Macedonia as of March 1. Balance sheets don't have much appeal for me, but maybe they do for you.

Every time I weigh I am surprised to find myself still about 120 because each time I expect that I must have put on some weight. Which shows that at least I feel up to par physically even though I might not be able to do much hard labor or a good day's work.

I love you much, Honey. Can still faintly remember how lovely you are—your gorgeous hair, lips, etc. Have fun. The man is here for the mail.

Lots of love, in fact, all I have.
Chuck

P.S. It looks like one of those new guards is going to have to learn the hard way—the one that couldn't talk for so long. Now he insists on barking at us as though we were a bunch of trained seals. And since we are still laboring under the delusion that we are somewhat human, we may not respond too well to such commands in the future. This guy must be trying to work up to a captain's job.

▣ ▣ ▣

July 10, 1946

Dearest Betsy,

Hello, Darling. Yesterday the boys were admiring the pictures of some shapely females in the *Chicago Sun* and for some reason or other it reminded me of you. But rest assured, Honey, I have never been so "true," so "chaste," even in my thinking, as I have been since we started this fast. Now I know what these mystics mean when they say that fasting purifies. There just doesn't seem to be enough vitamins, calories, or something to keep up both one's body and sexual urges. Doc may say we are getting 2,600 calories a day but I greatly doubt it. Several of us went up to weigh yesterday and none of us have gained any weight to speak of. In fact, Park and Hutch were at the same weight as when forced feeding first started. I weighed 121 (a one pound gain) but had just been fed my two pounds of "guck" (Parker's word) and hadn't had a b.m. for four days. The medical staff has a new addition—a young kid in his early 20s, just out of the Navy. I guess he is an OK guy, but being rather nervous and embarrassed he jabs away with that tube as though he were trying to stuff it up a rat hole—which had a rather unpleasant effect on our throats for a while. He is doing better now. Since he is a local boy, I suppose he'll stick around longer than the fellow who preceded him. This latter fellow was from New York City. I guess Sandstone didn't seem quite like home to him, so after two days he left. We also heard that he didn't like sitting around on his b--t all day in the approved government fashion.

Was permitted to read En's letter Monday, so I guess the baby is official now. The government probably already has his name down in its Little Black Book of future heroes. Which reminds me of the June issue of *Peace Action* (1013 18th St. NW, Washington, D.C.; price $.50 per year). It has a very good analysis of the conscription situation—how, in spite of almost complete public opposition, the Army and big business were able to push it through and why they wanted it so badly—for power politics (now called "foreign policy"), imperialism, and a means of controlling labor. It also reveals some of the outright lies that were used by Army officials and the newspapers to put it across. Maybe folks get tired of hearing me harp on the same old tune, some may even think I have a persecution complex, but I am thoroughly convinced that this conscription situation is one of the most sinister omens of the totalitarian path we are pursuing. By gradual degrees we are drifting farther and farther down the road to fascism. Every day I am more firmly convinced that our fast is a most valid and appropriate protest against the trend of our times. I wish there was something even more effective we could do, some way we could wake up our stupid, sheep-like fellow citizens to their peril, but I can't think of anything. So whether we are able to secure our freedom by this fast or not, at least I think I shall always be happy that I have had a part in it.

Incidentally, four of us complete our second month of fasting today. In that two months, I have voluntarily eaten one orange, one sack of peanuts, a few crackers, and on three or four occasions (in an effort to bring about a normal bowel movement) a few spoonfuls of roughage—salad or spinach greens. And a couple of the fasters eat commissary stuff occasionally for the obvious psychological benefits. But for two weeks now I haven't eaten a bite of anything, chiefly because of the pharisaical attitude of fellows who are not on the fast. I guess they want long-faced martyrs sprouting wings. I'm not sprouting any wings, but I am willing to make this one concession to the Pharisees (i.e., not a long face but no snacking)—though I think their attitude is stupid. As long as it is necessary that the government force feed us to keep our bodies alive, I think our purpose is being accomplished.

There is certainly strength in numbers. A con quit work a few weeks ago, but instead of putting him up here with us they stuck him in solitary confinement up in the hole. Solitary confinement is pretty hard on some people and apparently this guy blew his top and tried to commit suicide. So now they have him in a "strip cell" up in the hospital as a mental case. The prison system certainly has a delicate technique—drive a person to insanity and then, since he is insane, any type of treatment can be justified as a medical necessity, especially if the person has no friends on the outside to take up for him.

A visiting ball team from a nearby town came here for a game last night. Some of the boys began calling up for Dyer to come to the window. Darned if the visiting team's third baseman wasn't a discharged CO who had known Hank in CPS—small world, no?

Morris Mitchell plans to be here for a visit on July 28 and I may get to talk to him. It would help me know what to talk about, if in the meantime you gave the matter of Macedonia a little more thinking and then shared the product of the process with me. Don't misunderstand me. I'm not trying to sell you on Macedonia, in fact, I'm not sure just how sold on it I am myself. And as I told Morris in my letter, it would probably be best that we not make up our minds finally until I am out of prison, but if you should have any new thoughts on the subject, do pass them along before July 28.

Everything is going rather quietly. We've had no red-hot rumors lately except that *Time* might do an article on COs in prison and the Sandstone hunger strikers. The Amnesty Committee followed up our letter to congressmen with a darned good letter of their own and a covering note by A.J.

I'm now reading a biology book. The sunrises have been lovely the last few days. 4 A.M. is a wonderful time of day. This morning I got up to enjoy the dawn and then went back to sleep.

G'bye, Sweetheart. Hope you are finding life satisfying and stimulating—more so than prison.

All my love,
Chuck

◻ ◻ ◻

July 12, 1946

My Dear Wife,

Hi there, Country Gal. How y'all getting 'long wid yo work? I really don't have a whole letter full of stuff to write about or I'd have started a little sooner. As it is, this being Friday afternoon and the week's deadline, I'll probably stop when the mail pick up is made. But I do want to share with you a copy of Vivien's latest letter to Igal. It encouraged me a little bit and might do as much for you—though with your present life being so full and active maybe you don't need encouragement as much as I do. Anyway, it seems that something may be cooking back East. Not all of her letter is important or significant, of course, but I was too lazy to edit it. The sentence on the second page, which I underlined, certainly hurt my feelings. Here we are just going along minding our own consciences and trying to do the right thing—and then to learn that Tom regards us as a terrific bother . . . Well, it just shows to go that no matter how hard you try you just can't please everybody. I sent copies of Viv's letter in a letter to Mammy this morning, so you needn't relay this one.

According to the latest *Reporter,* the NSB has out a directory—names, addresses, etc.—of all the men who have been in CPS. I want to have a copy of this, so will you please sign the enclosed letter, buy a money order for 50 cents, and send it in? This directory should come in very handy in any traveling we might do—in fact, it might almost be considered a nationwide meal ticket.

Here's a hard luck story for you. An inmate, Acre, an old man, rather badly crippled and, as a guard described it, sort of wired together, was scheduled to leave prison Thursday morning. While getting all cleaned up for the occasion Wednesday night, he fell down in the shower and was so badly hurt that he had to be taken over to the hospital. The report is that he may be hospitalized for several weeks before he will be able to leave.

I read rather carefully the latest issue of *The Interpreter* and also *The Key,* which you sent, but I am still rather disappointed with it. Some time ago I thought this attitude may have been caused by the personal misunderstanding we had at that time. But now, after reading it with the greatest detachment and objectivity, I think not. I would be more favorably impressed with the first of *The Interpreter*'s two-fold program—i.e., its personal action—than I am with its adult-education program. I am not interested in presenting a detailed critique and you probably wouldn't want to read one. In general, my chief objection still stands—seems to me that Mil, after pointing out that other over-simplifications are wrong, commits the same error herself. "The conviction that what was wrong with both (city and country life) was centralization and that the cure for the over centralization of modern life called for decentralization. . . . " Also, it seems to me she defines words to suit her own purposes and then judges others on the basis of her own arbitrary definitions—e.g., "progress," "economics," "normal living," etc. The JWs do the same thing.

You know I agree that we need decentralization—all kinds—but I certainly don't think it is a panacea, "the answer." Also, isn't it just as much an economic problem as it is a social problem? I think Mil overlooks the fact that our institutions arise from our philosophy (i.e., our sense of values). She seems to assume an agreement in life philosophy, which actually doesn't exist, and then propounds her ideas on the basis of that false assumption. Ah well, you probably don't even see what I'm driving at—certainly it isn't very well expressed. Maybe I could summarize my attitude by saying that when anyone tells me that he knows what's wrong with life and also what the answer is—well, I just don't have time enough to talk with such a person.

You have made a couple of remarks which would seem to indicate that you were opposed to OPA regulations. If you should have time to jot down your ideas on price controls, why you are for it or against it, and under what circumstances, I'd be interested.

Oh, here's the man. Didn't get the letter finished but am enclosing an order blank.

Lots of love, Honey,
Chuck

◙ ◙ ◙

July 18, 1946

Dearest Betsy,

Hello, my Darling Wife. Yes, intellectually I well remember that that's what you are even though emotionally the word has lost much of its meaning. No fault of yours, Sweetheart—emotions just can't remember very well. Some courses can be carried on by correspondence and some can't—marriage, unfortunately, being among the latter.

It's raining today, raining hard. I'm glad; the weather has been awfully muggy lately. Maybe that has contributed to the unmitigated boredom I have been experiencing the last few days—unable to settle down to anything. Or more than likely it's just a normal psychological curve. Some folks can settle down permanently to intellectual pursuits and find it perfectly satisfying, but not me. For best results I have to hit a balance somewhere between thinking and action, and lately I've craved action, had no interest in intellectual stuff.

Honey, you've had a husband in stir long enough now so that you should be getting wise to how these places operate. Just because I ask for information on shepherd's pipes doesn't mean you can send me a book on the subject. As previously stated, I have the Warden's full permission to receive my dictionary and *The Prophet,* but you make no mention of sending these.

I really can't even imagine how you must appear with your gorgeous locks cut short. Your brave assurance that it looks better doesn't convince me no how. In fact, I imagine that it looks like . . . well, that you only look half as beautiful, but I'm glad you did it. For two reasons: In the first place, it sounds like such an eminently practical idea. I've found that one inch of hair is even more comfortable than two or three (please take my word for it, though). Secondly, it's a sort of declaration of independence, an assertion that you intend to dress as you darned please—which is exactly as it should be and expresses my sentiments to a T. But if you really look 15 years younger, we'd better stay separated until you look a little older. Believe me, Honey, I'm getting rehabilitated—I wouldn't want to hold down a prison bunk for just any old reason a-tall.

The New York Times Sunday, July 14, edition had an excellent letter more than a column long by the Amnesty Committee. I am enclosing a carbon copy. Please pass it along to my and your folks. I think that such letters will do much to encourage their own efforts. A letter from Mom Monday included carbons of two letters Pop wrote (to Department of Labor and Butler). His own letter was well written and he enclosed copies of the U.D.A. letter.

Any fruitful discussion of means to oppose my imprisonment and its causes must be made in the light of what ends are desired. As long as one feels that the most important end is to propagandize the public against war and conscription, then no doubt a program of obstruction and destruction toward prison would be a mistake. But if one should feel that the issues involved are no longer of public interest or concern and will not affect public opinion one way or another, then isn't it possible that one's most effective leverage could be brought against the prison system itself? Certainly the major reason why COs fared better in this war than in the last was not because of what the public thought (that this government doesn't give a damn for public opinion is shown by their action on both the draft and OPA) but rather because COs gave the Army such a headache in the last war. I think it is wrong, absolutely wrong, to put people in prison because of their conscientious beliefs, and I think such a program should be opposed. I don't have any delusions that anything I can say or do could so soften the heart of our oppressors that they would open the prison gates. And there is not much chance of getting to the ones who determine the policies with reasoning or idealism. They don't seem to understand that kind of talk. But so far I am inclined to believe that the public is still quite concerned in this issue, that war, conscription, and related phenomena are in the balance.

Consequently, for the present at least, I rather think that the most beneficial long-range effects can be secured through a more passive program aimed at public opinion. Don't think for a minute that I will ever adopt any course of action that I do not feel is right. The destruction of property is, in itself, neither wrong or right. Chopping down trees or eating are both destruction of property. The moral aspects of the matter are determined by the effects of such destruction. None of the foregoing is given as dictum but rather to stimulate further thinking of both of us.

I still feel fine but still have a little trouble with elimination. Wasn't it Lin Yutang who said that happiness is pretty much a matter of a good bowel movement? All of the boys are being tube fed now, which is better since it can't possibly be misunderstood even by the most critical. Golly, nearly 70 days we've been on this thing now.

After a period of thinking "Oh, h--l, what's the use?" I am again trying to compose a letter to Donohoe urging action on my pardon application in a tone which will not automatically preclude a favorable response. Maybe I'll succeed one of these days, and send you a copy.

Pass a little bit of my love around, Honey, but keep most of it for yourself.

Chuck

◙ ◙ ◙

August 4 and 5, 1946

Dearest Betsy,

Honey, I hope you are not too downhearted about our visit. I knew it was going to be rather hard and hadn't anticipated it very much. But I am not a good liar. I couldn't have possibly concealed my true feelings if I had tried—and I didn't want to try. Though the truth may hurt at times, I think it is the most precious ingredient in human affairs, it and love. I could never deceive you and I hope that goes both ways. And I hope you don't blame yourself too much for my apathy and discouragement. Remember that there are lots of factors involved: The fact that when one is in prison it becomes almost an obsession. One's horizon is restricted to prison walls in more ways than one. All the other things in life fade gradually out of sight.

I had perhaps allowed myself to become too optimistic about the chances of getting out. Wishful thinking. Maybe by an act of will I can yet settle back peacefully to "doing time." We all have our ups and downs. It's natural. Probably there is nothing you could have done to prevent my discouragement.

Prison, with its limitations and restrictions, isn't the easiest way of life in the world, so I hope you'll forgive me if I slip up once in a while. You see, there is no emotional outlet here, no activity, no change, no one to love you or admire you or encourage you. So it is a great psychological prop if you can feel that there is someone who wants to, and can, share every problem, every hope, everything. Of course, I have no *right* to ask you to do this. But when I went away to prison my life was so wrapped up in yours that I think I had come to take such unity for granted. Whether we can or should even try to maintain such a relationship under these conditions, I don't know.

What do you think? Maybe this is something more than you bargained for in marrying a prison-bound CO. If we are going to try to maintain the spiritual unity of marriage, I think we must work at it just as hard and as consciously and as *imaginatively* as if we were together—or more so. Please let me know how you feel about this. To me it seems to make all the difference between being wife and husband and just being acquaintances.

But on the other hand, I have the feeling that somehow I have failed to be truly democratic, that I have gone too far to try to make you fit your life into my pattern. I feel as I mentioned to you that probably I have made entirely too many suggestions to you about what you should do, think, etc. Consequently, our relationship is not one of true sharing and mutuality. It seems to me that in your attitude toward me you are pretty much on the defensive. Many things you said would indicate as much. This is certainly not as it should be and not as I would wish it to be. True love and true marriage are not possible without *complete* mutual respect and *confidence.* Yet this situation is probably my own fault. Am I correct in this impression, Honey? If so, why should you be on the defensive? What is it I do that causes this? It was for this reason I said that maybe I have been making too many suggestions. I would many times prefer that you wrote on a little postcard because you really and truly wanted to and thought it would be a good idea than that you should write 10,000 letters just because I wanted you to and suggested it. It's the difference between having a servant and having a wife. I'd much prefer the latter.

In fact, there may be many things I do, Sweetheart, that affect our relationship adversely—faults I may not even be aware of. In which case I hope you will point these things out to me frankly, but gently. I wouldn't want to find out 40 years from now that all along I had been doing something that offended you.

Though you may have not felt that the visit was entirely successful, I am nevertheless glad you came. At least it served to remind me of your appearance and something of your personality, and the fact that you are my wife—all things that had pretty much slipped my memory. And incidentally, you did look lovely. This isn't just my impression, but that of the other boys as well. I like your shoes also. I think your visit will give us another chance, too, to rebuild something of our unity, if you think we should try to do so. Also, your visit here put me in a more constructive frame of mind. Life doesn't seem quite the farce that it did.

Probably the amnesty campaign is getting along as well as we have any right to expect. I'm sure that an amnesty eventually is a cinch. It is only a matter of time. Unfortunately, it's hard time to do—like the last 200 yards when I used to run the half-mile. Am enclosing the copy of a story in the Saturday *New York Times*. Such pressure as this can't be resisted forever.

This morning I cut off my whiskers. They have been something of a nuisance lately but I wanted you to see them. Maybe I should have cut them off before you came. I actually think I look better with them but all the boys say I look anywhere from five to ten years younger shaved. So probably they only added to your feelings of doubt and strangeness. All the boys were disappointed that you didn't have anything more to say about my beard.

I forgot to tell you how much I appreciated the colored picture you sent recently. It is very beautiful. Thanks, too, for sending *The Prophet* and the dictionary. I've received both. Also forgot to tell you that Bill Stafford wrote recently. He has just finished writing a book about his CO experiences as his Masters Degree project. I hope he gets it published—it's probably very cleverly written. Did I tell you that Taylor's wife may send you a copy of the booklet that Parker, Dyer, and I worked out?

Suppose that someone came up suddenly, grabbed you and started beating you. Do you think you would have a right to try to dissuade the person, or to move yourself out of reach, or to ask for help? Isn't this similar to the relationship between myself and the government? I was minding my own business and doing construc-tive work when, in violation even of their own stated principles, they came along and threw me in jail, deprived me of freedom, family, etc. Do I have a right to protest such treatment and urge that it be stopped? Does this explain satisfactorily En's accusation that I am trying to coerce others to think as I think or do as I do?

I am enclosing six pages of copies of various letters, newspaper stories, etc., that you may find of interest. Give my regards to all the folks and tell them I am OK, in fact, on the up and up. What is it like to be not riding around on trains?

All my love, Honey, and keep our chins up.
Chuck

◙ ◙ ◙

August 13, 1946

Dearest Betsy,

Good morning, Sweetheart. It's a nice, bright morning here in Sandstone and warmer than yesterday—49 degrees this morning, 40 degrees yesterday. It'll be a good day to enjoy the yard "privilege," which was restored to us yesterday. Though I had felt it was essentially more honest to refuse to stay in our little restricted area and had felt right about leaving it, I respected the restrictions yesterday and played volleyball with the other boys. Hampton, however, refused to stay in the volleyball court and went walking about the compound, whereupon they conducted him inside. I expect he will do the same thing every time they let him out. I'll probably stay within the area unless I have a strong urge to leave it. As far as I can see, there is no fair or logical reason why our "yard" activities should be confined to such a small area. It deprives us of playing horseshoes, basketball, softball, in fact, everything but volleyball. So, about the time I decide to play horseshoes instead, I'll probably be up here walking the hall with Hamp.

We had a little excitement Sunday. Those of us who went to church were frequently not fed since the feeding is at 9 A.M. and church isn't over until 9:15. And one hospital attendant refuses to wait—in fact, has even walked out of E2 as the boys returning from church walked in. Well, that's OK with us. Feeding us was their idea and is their business, not ours. But we do feel that all of us should be treated impartially and we want to preserve a group unity—no one having advantages over the others. So, last Sunday when they came up to feed and four of us were in church, Igal R. asked if they intended to stay and feed the others. On being told "No," he replied that in such case he would also like to be skipped. But the medical attendant said his orders were to feed us and, by God, he was going to do it. So, with the help of two guards, they dragged Igal out of the shower, held him wet and naked on the cement floor, finally forced his mouth open (after trying unsuccessfully to push the too large tube down his nose), forced the tube down his throat (cutting his lip rather badly in the process), and poured in the "soup." Naturally, we were all pretty much upset and concerned about such a performance.

We have all along been fairly cooperative since our action was not directed at the public-health service and we had no desire to make their job more difficult. This time (for the first time) they decided to come back at 11 A.M. and feed the rest of us. When they came back we talked the situation over with Clark (the hospital attendant). From what was said I was convinced that the schedule had been adjusted and that another similar incident would not occur again, and allowed them to feed me. One of the boys said he wouldn't be fed until he talked the matter over with the doc. They respected his wishes and didn't try to force feed him. Yesterday the doc came up. He was very friendly, said he greatly regretted the incident, that it was a case of misunderstanding and temperamentalness, and wouldn't happen again, that hereafter the Sunday morning feeding would be at 8 A.M. So now we are to have both spiritual and physical food. Though to call that stuff we get from these preachers "spiritual food" requires a terrific stretch of the imagination.

Hutch discontinued his fast Sunday. In the statement he issued explaining his act, he said, in part:

> While my action, together with the hunger strikes of other COs, has not secured the release of men imprisoned because of their loyalty to religious convictions, it has nevertheless succeeded in bringing, forcefully and dramatically, to the attention of the public a basically unjust situation. These hunger strikes and other types of protests and publicity have resulted in a widespread demand for Presidential amnesty. Newspapers, religious journals, church groups, labor organizations, liberal political parties, prominent writers and artists, members of Congress, and others have joined in this demand. Because actions such as mine have served as a stimulus to awaken many American citizens to the fascist reality which is being perpetuated under the name of American idealism, I feel that they have been successful and worthwhile protests.
>
> Those who feel compelled by their own consciences to continue this form of opposition to their imprisonment have my utmost respect and admiration. However, due to my own desire to recover and maintain my normal health, together with the feeling that I have made an effective protest in line with my original intentions, I have decided to resume my normal eating habits.

Dick Zumwinkle had a letter from his brother, who had visited the Rev. Nelson in Minneapolis. Rev. Nelson was among the delegation of preachers that called on Clark and wrung the promise from him to consider amnesty for COs. You may be interested in some of his remarks. "Things are done in Washington by pressure and influence." The Attorney General's reply referred to amnesty for all CO prisoners over the age of 29. His reply was a personal one, not official. Rev. Nelson says the trouble lies in slow, inefficient, uncooperative administration. The only mention made of fasters, Clark said, "I want to get rid of hunger strikers." Apparently he, like everyone else in the government, is sick and tired of the g-------d hunger strikers. Nelson thinks the Attorney General's attitude is a reasonably good one. He is convinced that if Clark had his way, the release of men over 29 would be going at a much faster rate. The two chief stumbling blocks appear to be Patterson and Bennett (with emphasis on the latter in Rev. Nelson's opinion). (I can understand Patterson being against it and greatly suspect the opposition of the military is what is really holding things up. But I can't see how Bennett's opinion would make any difference as he is inferior in rank to Clark. —CW)

Wally Nelson (the preacher's brother, a hunger striking CO in Danbury) has not yet been released. Wally demanded these conditions: That he would have to sign no papers, that he would have to make no reports once freed, and that his friend Tom Parks (Negro, age about 30) would be released at the same time. Bennett refused only the latter demand, on the grounds that Parks was a nasty character and that his objection to war was not a religious one. Nelson says that strings have been pulled and he is reasonably sure Wally Nelson and Tom Parks will be released within 10 days. Although Wally will sign no papers, Rev. Nelson has agreed to supervise Wally's activities, thus easing the legal conscience of those in Washington.

Will continue in another letter. Guess my spirits must be higher—my pen's working again.

Lots of love,
Chuck

◙ ◙ ◙

August 13 and 14, 1946

Hi Honey,

It's me again. It is encouraging to know that Clark wants to get rid of hunger strikers. As long as we are a thorn in his flesh, the fast is a success. In this connection I might mention that I can understand how Mammy would find it hard to open people's understanding by telling about the fast. I don't think it has any value in that way. It is not intended as an argument but as a protest—a dramatic incident to arouse to action people who already see and are concerned about the threat to civil liberties and personal freedom involved—and as such I think it is effective. It is a lever with which to pry on the administration, a peg on which to hang the case for amnesty. It is a pressure technique pure and simple, designed to dramatize and publicize an injustice, not to explain it. Its chief value lies in the amount of pressure it brings to bear on the President and Attorney General, who probably don't have an entirely clear conscience in the matter.

Just how long I shall continue fasting I have not yet definitely decided. Right now my intentions still incline towards those I announced during our visit—i.e., to continue at least until the 1st of January. But in this and other confidential matters I trust you will be discreet in your references, remembering that I am not the only one who reads your letters, and that the prison system is eager to protect itself in any way possible.

Your letter came last night and I was very happy about the tone of it. I think probably we are getting back in "the groove" again. It is good to know that you are no longer on the defensive and I hope you can stay that way forever. Please know that above all else, at all times and in all situations, I want most of all that you fulfill the nature of your own true self, that you express and develop and live your own personality. That is a responsibility that transcends all others—our responsibility to life itself, or God, or whatever you want to call it. Human personality is to my way of thinking the most fundamental and most sacred of all human values, and it was chiefly to preserve and protect that value that I have refused to obey the Selective Service Act. In this connection, Honey, I think both you and

Mammy err in your interpretation of things I have said recently. I do not want anybody to treat suggestions I make regarding the release of COs as though they were orders. They are intended as suggestions and nothing more. Nor do I want my requests regarded as demands. If your actions contributed to my recent discouragement, I think it was chiefly because I feared, perhaps erroneously, that you didn't understand or didn't care to understand my position. I am concerned not necessarily that you agree, but that you understand not only what I believe but what you believe. As said before, I do not want a servant who looks to me for instructions, but a wife who, if she is going to share some aspect of my life, does so on the basis of equality, a partnership in which she is mutually concerned. And who, if she does not wish to share some aspect of my life, will do me the honor of thinking the thing through thoroughly and then telling me *why* she doesn't wish to be a part of that aspect. Since our lives are so closely connected I think we have a responsibility to let each other know what we think and why we think that way. And this requires habitual self awareness and self analysis, a constant reevaluation of our motives, drives, intentions, etc. Does all this make sense to you? Do you see what I'm driving at?

A friend and fellow CO, Art Lavae, has been in the hole for about a week—he is refusing to eat as long as he is in the hole. Art was one of the boys who went on a sympathy strike when Parker and I were sent to the hole for refusing to haul in the officers' coke last fall. It would appear that the administration has been riding him ever since. Have kept him on the worst crews, put him in the hole for not working fast enough, etc. This time he had refused to haul sacks of cement because his back was bothering him. When they sentenced him to the hole this time, Lavae reports that the Associate Warden told him, "You probably want to go to E2. Well, you aren't going there," or words to that effect. It looks like a case of discrimination because of a personal grudge. Trouble is that Lavae is not a very aggressive fellow or a very good talker so they probably figure they can get by with whatever they want to.

I have some comments on your past two letters . . . I am filling out and sending out to you today the proper forms to transfer $110 from my account to your possession.

I greatly approve of your letter to the Warden, but as far as I know nothing has come of it. My stomach has been behaving quite admirably for a couple of weeks now, though four of the other fasters apparently had a slight touch of intestinal flu that was making the rounds. Hank had to spend a couple of days in the hospital. My weight as of yesterday: 121 pounds.

I know exactly what you mean about the way Jane and Laura raise their kids. Every time I hear Laura yapping at her kids over some insignificant little thing or punishing them for something they can't understand (and Cecil is probably worse than Laura), it hurts me inside just as I'm sure it does the kids.

Morris M. is going to be in Lake Forest until the end of September, says Hank, so if you should write to him before that date, please be advised accordingly.

I am glad you wrote to that guy in Oklahoma about his covering for rammed earth houses. The bulletins from South Dakota that I have read didn't seem to have a very satisfactory answer to the problem. Even Gormly, who plans to build a little rammed earth "Chateau Thoreau" for himself some day, copied those paragraphs from your letter.

A letter from Mom yesterday mentioned a Mr. Longnecker whose job is "to get people out of prison who don't belong there." Betsy, I've been in this jail business a long time now and have never heard of anyone whose job it is to get people out of prison. In fact, I very much doubt if there is any such job. If so, who supports it? Unfortunately, folks who want to get someone out of prison will often grasp at any straw and as a result sometimes get taken for a ride. One of the boys who left here in the spring went to the wife of one of the fellows here. Told her he had just been with her husband and that they had worked out a plan to get him out of prison, that he could swing it if he had $200. She scraped up $100 right then and said she'd try to have another hundred for him the next day, but the man who was going to get her husband out of jail never came back. So, beware! Even if Mr. Longnecker is on the level, I very much doubt that he can do anything you couldn't do. You surely know by this time that getting a person out of a federal prison is not a matter of some legal trickery or knowing some little local official.

The Warden has said we'll get the typewriter back soon.

Give my love to everyone, Honey.

I love you and miss you very much and am feeling very good again. You're my favorite Wifey.

XXX Chuck

▣ ▣ ▣

August 19, 1946

Dearest Betsy,

Hello, Sweetheart. How's my "little woman," my "better half" (literally so by weight comparisons)? How is that nice C.V.? Besides, is it her fault that you're such a wizened little shrimp? No! OK, then. Honey, I really oughta be sending this letter to Mammy, she certainly deserves a couple. But the only really personal thing I have to say to you is that I love you. And Mammy probably already suspects as much, so maybe you'll share this letter with her.

But I certainly haven't been wasting any love on the Bureau of Prisons lately. They "bum-rapped" me—took away three weeks of "yard" without any good reason and without even bothering to state the no-good reason. Finally, after writing a letter to the Warden (copy enclosed), I received a copy of the charge against me, as follows:

> Officer Stull brought above inmate to the hospital and *told him to wait until called* for by an officer. As soon as treatment was completed he left without notice. I found him visiting in the yard with inmate Lavae in segregation. I told him to come with me and report to Mr. Doughman. He said arrogantly, "You are no custodial officer." He said he would report to Mr. Doughman but *instead went off to the west side to play volleyball* with the other inmates in E2.

My own statement describing the incident is likewise enclosed. All of the charges against me are false, except the one that I was talking to Lavae up in the hole. Specifically, neither Stull nor anyone else told me to wait in the hospital until called for.

I was no more arrogant in my conversation with Troolin than I am in my regular speech. If failure to kowtow, bow and scrape, and say "yes, sir" and "no, sir" is arrogant, than I am guilty and have been ever since I came to Sandstone. Troolin is only a kid (about 23), fresh out of the Navy. Apparently his position has gone to his head slightly and he is looking for insults.

The charge that I didn't report to Doughman is likewise a lie. Doughman happened to be supervising segregation, and so joining the group in volleyball was exactly what I was supposed to do. But apparently Troolin thinks I was supposed to go up and salute the man or something. As for talking to Lavae, I am in no way ashamed of that. I think it is a crime to lock men up in solitary confinement. But for that matter, whom I talk to or when or where is no business of Troolin's since he is not a custodial officer and an employee of the Public Health Service.

When Troolin came up to feed us and I asked him about these false charges, he began to change his story—said that Stull told him to have me wait. Regarding the arrogance, he said I gave him a lot of "cheap chatter" and that *I'd never get away with that in the Navy.* About my not reporting to Doughman, he didn't know what to say. Apparently, he was somewhat confused. Some of the other fellows have written in verifying my story and plan to refuse "yard" or leave the area unless the sentence is rescinded.

The incident made me pretty disgusted at first, but it is so in character with the whole nature and philosophy of prisons; such arbitrary and unreasonable authoritarianism is not hard to understand. Probably society, which condones such institutions, is as much to blame as the local administrators. To put some men in complete and absolute control over the lives and liberties of others corrupts both parties. No one is fit to occupy such a position. Authority, and its maintenance, becomes an end in itself to which reason and justice must at times be sacrificed. "The king and queen can do no wrong," you know.

The weaknesses of prison grow out of the philosophy of prisons in which a few men have unlimited authority and the rest have no rights. (Even going over to the hospital is, according to the Associate Warden, a privilege.) So I cannot agree with those who say that prisons will never be the same because of the COs. Prisons will always be the same until the whole basic philosophy changes. The few superficial liberalizations gained can be and probably will be just as quickly and easily revoked. I have seen the instructions to officers expressly prohibiting them from striking or laying hands on an inmate except in self defense, to prevent an escape, etc. But because of the master-slave nature of prisons, I am quite convinced that sporadic beatings cannot be prevented. One of the COs (now released) whose cell adjoined those in the hole said he heard a rather simple-minded colored boy being beaten about a week ago.

The boy himself says a guard named Klanche beat him. He has since been up in the hospital. The captain officially denies that Nichols was beaten, so maybe, like Hampton, he just "fell and hurt himself." Such sporadic acts of violence (if they occur—I have never seen one) should of course be kept at a minimum but, in my opinion, they are not nearly so harmful as the constant psychological violence, the violence to personality inherent in the very nature of prison.

Four of the COs out in population sent a letter to the President recently announcing their intention to quit work on September 3. I thought it a good letter (though their figures may be a little outdated) and am enclosing a copy. So apparently we'll have an increase in membership in the SRAS soon. Maybe the *World-Herald* would be interested.

There was quite a long story, well written, in the 8/17/46 *Minneapolis Star-Journal* about the letter of 300 leading ministers recommending Presidential amnesty for COs. Four Minneapolis signers were pictured, including the minister of the First Congregational Church, Phillip E. Gregory. You will perhaps read the letter in the *Amnesty Bulletin* so there is no use of my quoting it. Such letters are very heartening as they add considerably to the pressure on Truman. And such pressure can't be resisted forever.

I am greatly pleased because of your interview with Buffet. Whether he personally does anything or not, his advice as to how our government operates is invaluable. I have been trying to say the same things, but don't believe I put it across very well. In light of what he said, I think you can better understand the value of the fast. It is a means by which we can remind people that COs are still in prison and bring adverse criticism to bear on Truman. Incidentally, four of us recently passed the 100th day of our hunger strike. Hank and I celebrated the occasion by dividing a candy bar—it tasted wonderful. One hundred days without voluntarily eating a meal. It's not exactly fun, Honey, but it may be worth it. We are hoping they will use turkey eggs in the goop on Thanksgiving so it will be a regular Thanksgiving dinner.

I waved at Pappy at about 8:30 yesterday, but doubt if he saw me since I didn't hear the whistle.

Bye and lots of love,
Chuck

◎ ◎ ◎

August 20, 1946

Hi di, Gal,

It's yo triflin' husbun again. Golly, but this has been a beautiful day, Betsy. Clean little clouds and a soft blue sky. And by some strange freak of circumstances I was permitted to enjoy the hour of "yard" today. But don't jump at any false conclusions. The Associate Warden did not relent. A strange and stern officer was in charge today. He didn't know one of us from the other so let us all outside and then came around looking for Worley and Hampton. Well, it didn't take him long to find Hampton. He was way over on the other side of the yard. And then the most whimsical thing happened. He took Hutch away and locked him inside instead of me. Wasn't that whimsical? So, there I am outside sunbathing and playing volleyball and poor old Hutch looking forlornly out of the window. But I don't suppose it really makes much difference—just so someone is paying for the dastardly crime I didn't commit. Strange indeed are the ways of justice.

But such a whimsical thing probably won't happen again. The man came up this afternoon with a rotund lieutenant who went around so casually, oh ever so casually, addressing each of us by name and making a little small talk. Of course, none of us knew what was going on, but I could feel the man's eyes boring holes in Worley, so there wouldn't be another case of mistaken identity. Today (it's now the next day) if they refuse me "yard," several of the other boys also plan to stay in. Then we plan to lay our mattresses out on the floor and have a gym class instead. Since the doc is on the disciplinary court, it would seem like they would try to find some other way of punishing us than taking away our badly needed little period of sunshine.

By the time I have paid for my crime (Sept. 4), summer in these parts will be almost over and I will have spent 1½ months of it without setting foot outside. It seems strange to think that summer is already on the way out. As far as my own experience goes, summer never came. None of those little things has happened to make summer a distinct and meaningful part of the year: no new leaves and flowers, no fresh fruit and vegetables, no glasses of cold lemonade on a hot day, no napping on the grass, no picnics or hikes in the woods, no flies and mosquitoes to swat, no sweat running down my face and smarting in my eyes. I just haven't experienced this summer.

I am much pleased at the new approach, the new attitude Mammy expressed toward the amnesty campaign. Out of misunderstanding, it seems, comes understanding. I have not at all wanted to be running a campaign for my release. To do so would put me in the position of asking others to do things they may not understand, agree with, or are the value of a sort of imposing on their personal loyalty to me, which I didn't wish to do. Now I can feel free to make suggestions since I can be sure that they will be treated as such.

All of the boys enthusiastically approved of Mammy's and your letter to Loutland. Trouble with most of our friends is that when some official gives 'em the old run-around, completely ignoring the principles involved and confusing the issue with talk of parole, they think their letter has been answered. The Department of Justice has been handing out that parole line for so long that they are probably starting to believe themselves that there is something to it. They seem to have two stock answers, one telling why parole is the answer, and the other telling why those who applied for parole are not eligible.

It's too bad that you don't think much of the suggestion I made to picket the White House. I've been talking it over with the other boys and think the idea has possibilities. My idea would be to get four to six gals, preferably *wives* of imprisoned COs, preferably *good-looking gals*. Admittedly, I can only think of one such, but there should be a half-dozen whom the Amnesty Committee could get lined up. Hank says he is quite sure they could bunk, do their cooking, etc., in the basement of the Brethren Church in Washington. Of course, it should be done, if at all, before the weather becomes too cold. To picket during the whole month of October would be an excellent demonstration, should get considerable publicity, and might jar some action out of old Harry, or at least help.

My goodness, I really can't imagine Mom and Pop taking off for California. Maybe it marks the beginning of a reorientation, a redirection of their aims and interests. But the news about Mary Ellen really tops it off. I've seen so little of her in the past ten years that she still seems like a little girl to me, can't seem to imagine her being engaged, least of all to a CPS walk-out. Guess family pride is a thing of the past now, no? I haven't M.E.'s address but perhaps you would send my most affectionate regards to her and Mal. And if it's the same Mal Campbell that Hank Dyer knew in CPS, he wants to send his best wishes also.

I'm glad you sent the song, Sweetheart. I've sung it before but pretty much forgotten how it went. You mention baking bread in a pressure cooker, but didn't say whose cooker. Mom mentioned having recently bought one. Was it hers, or does Mammy also have one?

Well, we just had "yard" and sure enough John and I got no farther than the door, so all but two of the other boys also refused to go out. Hutch and I made a mat of mattresses and I pinned him three times in about five minutes. He's about 25 pounds heavier but doesn't know the first thing about wrestling. It doesn't take much of this sort of activity to tire me out nowadays.

The New York Times carried the full text of the preachers' letter to Truman—good letter. We are waiting eagerly to learn what transpired at the Amnesty Committee meeting, which was to have been held last week.

I'm running low on "cheap chatter" so I'll conclude with a quote (page 43) from Arthur Morgan's *The Long Road*. I think it has a bearing on some of the questions we have been discussing recently as to ends, means, etc.: "Thought is an ethical act which is good when judged by its total consequences—which is good for the future as

well as for the present, for society as a whole as well as for ourselves." Maybe it doesn't help much, but at least it shows that we
must constantly weigh and evaluate our acts in view of the expected
results. There is no shortcut, no panacea, no authority but our own
intelligence. Guess I've contributed my share to this week's applesauce.

All my love, Darling
Chuck

P.S. All copies of the booklet have been sent out. Was printed at
Taylor's personal expense. No more available.

◼ ◼ ◼

August 28, 1946

My Darling Wifey,

Hello, Sweetie Pie. I really haven't anything much to write
about, Honey, but it's a nice, bright, sunshiny morning and a good
time to put it in the record that I like you an awful lot and think
about you sometimes. Besides, I'm enclosing enough stuff to keep
you out of mischief for a while, I betcha (as if it were necessary! tsk,
tsk!). Probably the most important enclosure is a copy of a letter
from Tom Clark to A.J. Muste. It is the fairest and most honest letter
I have yet seen coming from his department. Am also enclosing five
copies of a letter which I sent to him yesterday on the basis of his
remarks. Thought perhaps you might want to send a copy to Buffett,
Butler, or somebody. Igal probably works harder at propagandiz-
ing for amnesty than the rest of us here. The other enclosures are:
1) A letter from Dorothy Thompson in reply to one of his, and 2) A
sample of the kind of letters he has been sending out—this one to a
labor leader.

After a long dry spell on the amnesty front there have lately
been some signs which would seem to indicate that the Attorney
General may have finally decided to do something about the problem after all. About a dozen JWs, all of them under the 26-year age
limit, have recently been approved for parole, in a couple of cases,

I am told, over the protest of their local boards. One of the four COs
who had announced his intention to quit work on September 3 has
also been notified that he will be paroled; from what we hear, they
didn't even ask his wishes in the matter, indicated that he was going
out on parole whether he wanted to or not. Then last night one of
the boys got a note from the Warden stating, "For your information,
there is under consideration a revised point system which should
be announced within the next month to six weeks. The details and
mechanics of this revised system are yet to be announced. As soon as
I receive them, you will be advised. Since this revision is being prepared in the Attorney General's office, I believe it is the plan to which
the editorial refers." (The editorial referred to is one printed in *The
Washington Post* urging revision of the government's undemocratic
treatment of COs.) Of course, all of this goes no farther than parole,
but the remark that they are giving special consideration to the problem of those who will not apply for parole may contain some basis
for hope. At least I think it is worth following up.

Wish you could know how much we all appreciated hearing
from Adam. We could even read his Polish accent between the lines.
Perhaps you could find time to send him a note summarizing the situation here and enclosing a copy of the letter which the four boys sent
announcing their intention to quit work. He is certainly an uncompromising little cuss—so much so, in fact, that they may not wish
very much to see him back in prison.

Haven't you heard from any of my other old friends? No, I'm
sure you would have mentioned it if you had. I often wonder what
they are all doing now, how they are getting along, etc. Through
Hampton's wife I heard that an old CPS and Tucson buddy, Forest
Stratton, was engaged to be married soon. But no news from Jerry,
Scaff, Travis, Emma, Gordy, Don Larson, etc.

Am glad you sent some money for relief in Germany. Like everything else one can do, it is a pitifully futile gesture in view of the
terrific mess the world is in, but it is probably better, as the wise man
says, to "light a single candle than to curse the darkness." As to sending money to the Amnesty Committee, you may do as you see fit. I'm
sure it would be put to good use, but my own feeling is that those
who can contribute nothing more should give money, but that the
most valuable contribution is of one's own time and efforts. Or, as

The Prophet says, "You give but little when you give of your possessions. It is when you give of yourself that you truly give."

The FCI softball team won a little poetic justice last night.
Earlier in the season they were beaten by the very worst of all possible opponents to lose to, the local Sandstone team. Last night in a
five-inning game, one of the COs whammed out a homer for a 1–0
victory.

Dr. King, a big shot in the Public Health Service, was here yesterday but he didn't go through E2. I wonder why. I wonder what
he would have thought of the practice of depriving men on a liquid
diet of their only opportunity to get a little bit of sunshine, especially
on false charges. Incidentally, none of us ever did rate a reply from
either the Warden or the Associate Warden regarding our letters of
protest. Ah well, such is prison.

Would rather like to attend the FOR conference in Chicago next
month. I hardly feel that I am or care to be a part of that or any
other organization anymore, but I would no doubt run into a lot of
old friends.

They're coming around with the tube so I'll close now. Lots and
lots of love to you, My Darling, and please say hello for me to Phyl,
Mammy, and Pappy, and any of the Worley clan remaining in those
parts. Maybe I'll get a letter from my Honey tonight, I hope.

Lots of kisses,
Chuck

◼ ◼ ◼

August 30, 1946

Dearest Wifey,

I really haven't a darned thing to write about, Honey, and hadn't
planned to do so (until 30 minutes before this week's deadline), and
then it occurred to me that this law somebody had passed about
reaping what we sow and all that sort of thing. And then it occurred
to me that there's probably a darned good reason why I haven't gotten a single letter yet this week. So I'll work hard at saying nothing
until the boys come up with the "guck" and the man carries away
the mail.

The FOR members up here in E2 got together at the last minute to draw up a statement to send to the FOR conference in Evanston. We should have known better by this time. It generally takes at least a week to write any kind of statement that is acceptable to any two of us. Well, this case was no exception. The result was that we finally sent in a letter that didn't satisfy any of us. In fact, I was so dissatisfied that I sat down and wrote up another one and then didn't have guts enough to present it to the group because we had all finally agreed on this other one. So I'll send it on to my poor, long-suffering wife and let her throw it away instead of doing it myself.

The Christian Century that came last night had another editorial urging amnesty and also a petition to be signed and sent in. But the best CO article I've read for some time was Milton Mayer's piece in *The Progressive,* September 2, written in his own inimitable style. Also in the September 2 *Progressive* was an answer by Beston to Mrs. Coleman's column on city vs. country life. His answer is cleverly written and ever so much more tolerant than the letter Aunt Mil had published commenting on the same column. I think that I'll never again waste time reading a newspaper, but instead get the news from some liberal little weekly, such as *The Progressive.* It does a pretty good job at it. In my last letter I mentioned the editorial on COs, which was published in *The Washington Post.* Finally typed off a few copies and am enclosing some in case you should wish to send them on to anyone.

The four boys who announced their intention to quit work on September 3 are already getting results on their letter. At least one of them was suddenly approved for immediate parole. They even remitted his $500 fine, we are told, since that was one of the reasons he had refused parole previously. And the other three fellows were all given better jobs. Whether or not they will allow themselves to be bought off in this way yet remains to be seen.

They are planning a sort of field day for September 2. We in E2 haven't been invited to participate so maybe we'll have to put on a little whist tournament of our own. There is going to be a ball game, bean-guessing contest, horseshoe tournament, broad jump, football kick, etc. Also, a gunnysack race—the event I won in the big track meet we had at Tucson when I was Recreational Director there.

We are hoping that A.J. Muste will be able to visit us when he comes west for the conference. We would like to get a first-hand account from him as to the progress on the amnesty campaign. Maybe after talking to him I can come to some definite decision as to how long to continue on the hunger strike. Right now my inclination is to continue on until some provision is made for those of us who can't conscientiously accept parole.

Yesterday was Paul's birthday. I should have written him a letter of congratulations—intended to, in fact. And then I remembered that I had never had his address changed so couldn't do it this week. Maybe you, as my Sweet Little Wife, will convey my brotherly greetings to him.

Has anyone heard from Mom and Pop? I haven't, nor have they sent me any California address.

Well, Sweetheart, here are the hospital boys with the eggnog and rubber tubes. Lots and lots of love, Betsy. I'm hoping that maybe I'll get home for Christmas—I hope, I hope.

Give my love to all the folks. I'm feeling fine and hope you are, too, that your tooth came out OK, if it had to come out. Several big kisses to make up for this sorry letter.

Chuck

◾ ◾ ◾

September 4, 1946

Dearest Betsy,

Hello, Honey. What's going on down that-a-way? Must be either so much that there is little time for writing, or so little that there is not much to write about. Certainly the reports I get from Omaha wouldn't seem to account for a full 24-hour day. Say, maybe that's the answer. I've noticed that the days seem to be getting much shorter lately, whether from natural causes or government interference I wouldn't be knowing, but I wouldn't be too surprised to find that it is the latter.

With several associates I am still doing business in the same old place—working for freedom of conscience. It's a slow, hard job and

I sometimes wonder if we're getting anywhere, or if we ever will . . .

> . . . God knows 'twere better to be deep
> Pillowed in silk and scented down,
> Where love throbs out in blissful sleep,
> Pulse nigh to pulse, and breath to breath,
> Where hushed awakenings are dear . . .

. . . and all that sort of thing. Ah well, such is life. Maybe I can get a furlough some time and spend a few days behind the lines before my hair all falls out.

Relationships with our employers continue to run the gamut from whimsical fantasy to nausea. Lately, they have seemed to border more on the latter. For several nights now we have heard the guards snooping around through our apartment during the wee hours, but yesterday a whole contingent of them went through E2 like Sherman's March to the Sea, and when they were gone we had as little productive equipment left as the Russian saviors-of-civilization likewise overlooked on their way back home. Specifically, the hot plate and the automatic pop-up toaster, which one of the boys had constructed with his bare hands out of miscellaneous materials picked up hither and yon, were gone, along with such lesser items as library books, medical supplies, razor-blade holders, writing boards, etc., ad infinitum. It will be more of a challenge and perhaps somewhat more detrimental to our physical environment to replace certain of these items since the available raw materials are running short.

The worst smudge smeared on the face of fair democracy for some time, locally, of course, appeared yesterday when the disciplinary "court" decided to put the three COs who refused to work up in the hole to "think it over." You will recall from the copy of their letter, which I sent to you, that their refusal was made just as much on the basis of principle as my own. In fact, I should think that they actually have a better case since all of them have performed their slave labor for a long time now and have tried to secure relief via the established parole procedure, inadequate as it may be, and all have been denied. (Incidentally, Joe Kentie, one of the four original signers, has since been approved for parole and didn't go through with his intention to quit work.) This treatment denies not only the democratic principle that a person should be permitted to follow the dictates of his own conscience, but violates even the expressed policy of the Bureau of Prisons to treat each prisoner on an impartial basis.

Those of us in E2 are certainly receiving preferred treatment over the boys who have been stuck up in solitary confinement without blankets, on a restricted diet (theoretically no longer being employed in the prison system), without books or other type of employment or amusement, and without opportunity for exercise. Since we feel that we cannot conscientiously be a part of such an arbitrary and discriminatory practice, we are considering various ways of protest, and of expressing our solidarity with these men who have taken the same position, in respect to their unjust imprisonment, as ourselves. I think that beginning tomorrow those of us on the hunger strike will refuse to be fed as one of the effective protests available. Whether this will resolve into a daily wrestling match or only a matter of getting slimmer remains to be seen. I think it would be quite appropriate for you to register a protest with James V. over this most recent denial of conscience on the part of the authorities here.

In your last letter (August 27 & 29) you mentioned enclosing something from the Department of Justice. Did you forget to enclose the item or did the censors forget to send it on to me? If it is the latter, I hope that you will make enquiries with the Warden as to what could have happened to the material. Incidentally, in my last several letters I have been including numerous enclosures but you make no mention of having received any of them. Are these things coming through as they should?

You ask for my comments regarding the Pinecrest Hall deal, but what am I supposed to say? I'm sure that Mammy would find it an opportunity to make a real and lasting contribution to the lives of a bunch of young girls who certainly deserve a break. I can see how it would be a more satisfying job than the superficial contacts provided by her present employment. And if you want to stick around as a head cook and bottle washer, well, if that's what you really want to do, then do it. What else did you expect me to say?

Had a letter from Mom yesterday. She sounds happy. Hank

knows Mal and has told me something about him. Would seem to be a fine guy.

Love and kisses,
Chuck

◙ ◙ ◙

September 8, 1946

Dear Mrs. C.V. Worley, My Wife,

Does that salutation make sense to you, Honey? I declare, it doesn't to me. Theoretically, we've now been married for 19 months, actually for about five months. Ain't that a bloody . . . you know what! I just can't remember what it means to have a wife, my heart has forgotten. Though mentally I can still remember that at one time, when I was a somewhat more free person living under more natural conditions, that concept was very meaningful and satisfying to me. Maybe we'll have to (or get to) fall in love all over again. Well, it was a wonderful experience the first time and with that much practice it should be even more so the second time. I'm anticipating that day more eagerly than you can ever imagine, Sweetheart.

But in the meantime, there are a few little local matters that need attention. The most significant item at this time, from my perspective at least, is the fact that the Sandstone hunger strikers have gone on a hunger strike. (Things don't have to make sense in this world of ours, you know.) What actually happened is that those of us who take our meals through a rubber tube called in the doc the other day, explained that we had no argument with the medical staff, but that about the only protest still available to us was to resist the tube feeding to the best of our ability to do so. Doc said that to force feed us against our active opposition would probably be pretty rough on us, that he would respect our protest, using coercion only as a last resort, that he didn't want to be a party to our demise. I'm glad he turned thumbs down on the rough stuff. I'm hardly in shape for a wrestling match with a couple of these big, husky cops. As you probably know already, this protest is being made because the authorities have seen fit to punish the three COs who, on September 3, refused to work any longer for the system which unjustly imprisons them. (Flash—One of the original four signers, Joe Kentie, left on parole this afternoon.)

A copy of my letter to Bennett about this situation is enclosed, in case you are interested. Though this is only our third day without sustenance, we are all pretty much pooped already since we didn't have much reserve to fall back on this time. That old rubber hose sure makes a difference in how a guy feels. I had been considering the idea of quitting the fast on September 11, when it will have gone on four months, but the local situation makes that out of the question now.

Our "fast within a fast" ain't the only battle cooking here right now. Thursday, when I was allowed to go out for "yard" after a three-week denial, several of us walked over to talk to our buddies in the hole, to assure them of our support and solidarity. For this dastardly crime we are to be denied "yard" for another two weeks. It is my understanding that this provision, for at least one hour of outdoor exercise, is made by the medical authorities in order to protect the inmates' health. Of all the men in the joint, probably none of them stands to benefit so much from this little bit of fresh air and sunshine as those of us on the liquid diet. I wonder what Dr. M.R. King of the U.S. Public Health Service in Washington, D.C., would say if he knew that we had been denied our "yard" for eight consecutive weeks—especially for such petty, flimsy reasons?

Another little incident that you may find interesting took place Friday afternoon when I was taking a nap. I am enclosing Hutch's own report of the affair as given in the enclosed copy of his letter to the Attorney General. Such experiences as we have been having lately only serve to make me more convinced that freedom for the individual is worth fighting for—in an intelligent way, of course. I'm afraid life wouldn't be a very tempting prospect to me if it had to be on the same arbitrary, authoritarian, totalitarian basis as we have it in prison.

There is not much to report in the way of amnesty news. In fact, since the latest *Bulletin* hasn't yet been received here, you may know more about the situation than I do. Igal had a letter from Blumberg, chairman of the American Labor Party of New York State, assuring him that they were sympathetic with our cause and would probably pass a resolution on our behalf at their convention this fall. The ALP isn't a very powerful group, but this action would seem to indicate a favorable attitude on the part of labor leaders. We have heard that two letters urging amnesty have been sent to Truman recently, one by a large group of writers and another by a group of artists. A letter from Hampton's wife in Hollywood says that a friend of hers heard Donald Nelson, formerly chairman of the WPB, called Truman on the phone and said that he had been to visit the Glendora CPS Camp, that the whole program was a disgrace and should be closed down entirely. From a selfish point of view I'm glad that the government is carrying through on its prosecution of the CPS strikers. This will tend to identify them with those of us in prison who have refused CPS, will swing the strong strikers' defense committee into the amnesty campaign, and may even secure a Supreme Court ruling in our favor. Whatever helps CPS helps us.

The *World-Herald* story on COs came with your last letter. It is so full of mistakes that I hope someone will advise the editor as to the true situation. The most insidious aspects of the story are: 1) The implication that no "sincere" or "genuine" COs were sent to prison, and 2) That those in CPS are receiving fair and just treatment as compared with the Armed Forces. I am returning the clipping herewith.

I thought your answers to "What would have happened if we'd have all been COs?" pretty good. I wouldn't have answered it much differently myself. It seems to me, however, that you do not have the courage of your convictions. If this is true, it is probably because you don't read enough on the subject and, consequently, don't have enough *facts* to back up your points. Even having the facts, however, doesn't mean that you are going to be able to "convince" anybody of anything. The very question shows the most profound misunderstanding as to the true causes of war. And it is probably not easy to reason with anyone who can seriously entertain the absurd idea that either Japan or Germany could or would even try to conquer a country much bigger and stronger than themselves, many thousands of miles away and with big oceans on both sides. No doubt it is much more just that our enemies should occupy their countries and indoctrinate their children than vice versa. The way things are shaping up after the big war for freedom certainly impresses me that this is a darned poor time for pacifists to be on the *defensive.*

You have mentioned articles about us in the July *Fellowship* and *The Grapevine*. Since we've seen none of these items, perhaps you would clip them out and send them in your next letter.

I'm afraid that the Venture Club meeting, as you describe it at least, would have given me a stomachache and headache, too.

I don't seem to be up to my reading other than fiction of late. Am now on Upton Sinclair's *The Jungle*.

It has been cold and rainy the past few days. Went down to 26 degrees a few days ago.

Read in the paper about a big storm in Omaha with the Little Papio on the rampage.

In the past two weeks I've sent out six letters and received three; pretty good average, no? Give my affectionate regards to all the friends and folks. To you I send all the love I can muster.

Your lonely and hungry hubby,
Chuck

◙ ◙ ◙

September 9, 1946

Hello, Sweetie Pie,

It has been dreary and rainy and chilly all day, but for some reason, I've felt somewhat perked up over yesterday—probably because I had to spend a goodly portion of the day in bed in order to keep warm—the heat was on for only two brief periods. Maybe it's also due to your good letter, which came last night. It's pretty easy to feel discouraged and let down under such circumstances as these, so a letter like that does lots more psychological good than you can ever imagine. I'm glad you sent out the copies of my letter to Clark and thought your covering note was excellent—well-worded and to the point. Also, your letter gives me many things to discuss, which is good.

Cranston Briggs is an absolute fundamentalist and probably not overly intelligent, but at the same time he is one of the most sincerely

Christian fellows I have ever known. He is very humble and self-effacing and just naturally loves everybody. I really feel quite honored and complimented to hear from him. Will try to set down here with a postcard's worth of reply.

Dear Cranston,

I was very pleasantly surprised to hear from you, especially in view of my present circumstances, and I rejoice in all your good fortune—being out of camp, married, and having a job that you like. Congratulations, my friend, though it is nothing more than a fellow like you deserves.

As you may remember, I had to serve one 18-month prison sentence in Tucson, Arizona, because I left Santa Barbara. Shortly thereafter, I was again ordered to report to CPS, refused, and in June, 1945, I was given another three-year sentence at Sandstone, Minnesota. But that ten months between prisons wasn't wasted, in fact, it was the most profitable period of my life for I, too, found a wife, a very lovely wife, through whom I am sending you this note. We have been married 19 months now and have lived together only four, but we hope to make up in the quality of our marriage for all that we are now missing in quantity.

I'm still not much of a Christian, I guess, Cranston. Spiritual things don't mean much to me, though I shall always try to keep my mind and soul open to new insight. But I am mightily concerned about human welfare and feel that freedom of conscience is something that we must try to preserve. As long as we are free to follow the way of life that we believe to be most true and worthwhile, then we may hope to grow in grace and understanding. Conscription and imprisonment of COs denies freedom of conscience. That is chiefly why I am in prison and why I have refused to apply for parole. There is a very good committee working for our release, however, and many outstanding citizens have petitioned the President on our behalf, so perhaps before too long I may be able to go home again. For more than 100 days now six COs here, myself included, have been on a hunger strike in protest to our unjust imprisonment. We are being fed by the medical staff by liquids poured down our throats through a rubber tube.

Betty and I hope to join a cooperative group in northern Georgia when I am released. Maybe being that far east will enable us to visit you and your good wife some time. I hope so. I would like nothing better.

Brotherly regards and best wishes,
Chuck

Our three fellow COs are still up in the hole, and so we are still refusing the tube feeding. They are denied blankets except from 10:30 P.M. to 5:30 A.M., have only coveralls for clothing, and though today has been quite cold, they had no heat in their radiators throughout the day. Furthermore, though the prison rules require that even men in punishment status be given full meals at least every third day, these boys have been on a restricted diet every day for a week.

I am not sure that your letter will get to Morris because he is probably still at conferences, but I don't think it makes any difference. If you don't get a reply, just write ahead to Macedonia and tell them you are coming. You have already been invited and I am sure they will be able to take care of you. I think your idea of possibly staying there and making your own way until I get out is an excellent one, and I think it could be done. Such a plan would at least make it possible for you to see if that is the way of life you are interested in at this time, and would also give us something of a head start if we should decide to stay for a few years. In trying to think of questions we should consider, I find four that seem important:

- Could we secure satisfactory living accommodations?
- Would the work be satisfying and give us a chance to learn the things we want to know?
- Could we save a little money so as to be able to go off on our own hook someday?
- Would the people contribute to our enjoyment and understanding of life?

The news about Jane and Bob is too bad, but it is well to find out how the situation stands while they are still young and can make adjustments. The telephone call and losing the job, and all, sounds fishy to me—as though it were a put-up job. But even if that is so, it probably really doesn't make any difference.

Had a good brotherly letter from Frank last night.

Goodnight, My Darling. I'm going to take a good hot shower and sign off. Keep plugging and so will I.

All the love I've got,

Chuck

◉ ◉ ◉

September 12, 1946

Dearest Betsy,

This is yo' somewhat chastened husbin replying to your letter of 9/9. Honey, I'm deeply sorry to hear about your weeping "bitter and angry tears." If you were just disgusted with me that wouldn't be so bad—I even get disgusted with myself sometimes. But a person can be disgusted and still understand the situation. But anger doesn't indicate understanding. In this case especially, Honey, because I'm afraid you were reading lots of things between the lines that I never wrote there. If it will help any to try to explain things, I'll try. First, as to my remark that your letters didn't account for a 24-hour day, you apparently took this as an implied criticism as to how you spend your time. If so, you missed the point entirely.

You see, Betsy, a person in prison is extremely restricted in his experiences and contacts. We have no children here, no women, no trees, birds, stars, kitchens, streetcars, music, sidewalks, dogs, etc. So the things that make up normal life fade gradually out of mind. (If I can't even remember the sweetest thing in my life, how can I remember these little things?) Your life, by comparison, is full of adventure and excitement—train rides, discussions about pacifism, etc. Sharing our thoughts and adventures can do much, I think, to maintain our unity. Maybe I don't do any better in sharing my life with you. But you see, Sweetheart, it is exactly because I do have a loving interest in what my wife does that I made that comment. About my references to Pinecrest, I likewise plead not guilty. When you wrote to me about it, you may remember, you mentioned that Mammy was considering the job, then went on to say that if she got it you might go along to help cook, etc., and then said you would like to get my reaction. The way it was written I naturally assumed that you wanted my reaction to your working there, not to the whole idea. I would have been interested in discussing the latter but would have thought it rather presumptuous to do so without an invitation—after all, Mammy and Pappy probably know what they want to do a lot better than we kids. And as to discussing your working there, I didn't feel free to say very much because you had said very little about why you were thinking about it, and I didn't want to assume the paternalistic role of advising you. I want to think with you about such things, but not at you.

So if my comments seemed too brusque, please forgive me. It is difficult, Sweetheart, to be separated for so long with no more common experiences and background, especially under such trying circumstances. All we can do is try to be understanding and tolerant and keep our faith in each other. I say this for myself as much as for you. And if things I say make you bitter or angry, please feel that way toward me rather than toward yourself, as I think I can defend myself a lot better than you can. Guess I'm just naturally thicker skinned or else hardened by experience—or maybe just more egoistic.

Our three fellow COs are still up in the hole. Fortunately, the captain says that their conditions have been improved, that the cold treatment was not intentional and would be remedied, that they now have soap, toothbrushes, etc. But the fact remains that they are still in solitary confinement.

The hunger strikers, all but Gormly, who allows one feeding a day, are now starting their second week without food. Funny thing is that I actually feel stronger and better now than I did the first three days. Maybe food is just a habit after all, or maybe my motor has switched over to a reserve tank that I thought was empty. Schweigert and Kasner are having a little difficulty explaining their actions to their folks—of course, they haven't really had much of a chance since they can't write letters now. I've sent you so much stuff about it that you probably understand as well as anyone why men would go into segregation, the rightness of it, and that it is not a tough go, but actually has some advantages. Would you try writing to Miss Connie Schweigert, Rt. 1, Lehr, North Dakota, and to Mr. R. Kasner, Picture Butte, Alberta, Canada, explaining the situation? You may also assure them that I talked to the boys last night, that they were all in good health and good spirits. We are all hoping that this coercive action on the part of the administration will not be continued much longer. Thanks lots for writing to Bennett about the matter. Such letters do more good than you think, even though you may get the old run-around as you did from the Attorney General regarding your letter on political prisons.

The fast-within-a-fast has not prevented our long-contemplated Norwegian whist tournament from finally getting underway. There is much interest. Last night Hank and I won our first round over Parker and Taylor, 2–1. There are candy bars in store for the winners and if I'm one of them, I think I will feel free to eat the bars, hunger strike or no hunger strike.

I finished a great big book on dairy cattle husbandry yesterday. Wish I could remember all that I read. Also finished *The Jungle*. It's enough to take one's mind off his own little troubles.

Be assured that I love you much, Darling, and will try to be more careful in my comments to prevent misunderstanding. It's cold here. I'm wearing winter undies now.

I love you much, Betsy.
Chuck

◙ ◙ ◙

September 16, 1946

My Darling Wife,

Hello, Sweetheart. Your good letter of September 12 came up this afternoon—a most unusual time—probably indicating that because of the enclosures it had to go through other than the regular channels. Though I think the feelings expressed in your previous letter arose from misunderstandings largely, I am not sorry that you wrote as you did—in fact I am glad. We should never pretend to each other that our heads are always in the clouds—it wouldn't be honest, nor would it contribute to our loving understanding. I hope and believe that it will become increasingly easy and natural for us to share our feelings openly and objectively. Such growth should contribute to the meaningfulness of our marriage.

After a long spell of stagnancy in E2, something of a small bombshell burst today. Hank Dyer left for Washington, D.C., where his aged mother is seriously ill. To prevent the large personal expense this visit would cost Hank, the Bureau is transferring him to the Federal reformatory at Petersburg, Va., and arranging for the Washington stopover en route. The whole thing happened today, necessitating some rapid last-minute decisions, including a decision on Hank's part to discontinue the fast. They immediately sent up a meal for him— the first regular one in five months. Even so, I fear he will find it a tough trip as he was awfully weak and thin, so much so, in fact, that he had fainted briefly a couple of times last Saturday. We are hoping, however, not without some reason, that his prison days may be over. It was stated that he would have a chance to talk to Bennett, and it may be that he will be released on parole since his good-time release date is only three months away—such things have happened before. If this should happen you may see him soon at Macedonia.

I'll certainly miss the guy. He is really a swell fellow, one of the finest I have ever met, and had become my closest associate in E2. I'm hoping a release comes out of it since he could explain our situation here to you very well. I've also instructed him to give you a big kiss for me should he see you first.

The Associate Warden is going along to Washington, so perhaps some solution may be coming through on the present work-strike impasse—i.e., the boys in the hole. Yes, they are still there and we are still going hungry and getting skinnier—a situation no one seems to be much concerned about—at least the doc hasn't even bothered to see if we are still breathing.

I actually don't feel too badly, Honey. In fact, this stretch has been easier than that first 14-day fast, probably because we were not so much enslaved to the eating habit this time. Friends were due to see Bennett about the matter today. Can you imagine a person looking forward with longing to having a rubber hose shoved down his throat?

Well, the Warden told Hank that the new point system was to become effective on October 1 and that several of us, myself included, would be eligible, that he would have us down for interviews soon. Unfortunately, it is still parole, still leaves uncorrected the wrong done in denying freedom of conscience. Consequently, I am not inclined to think favorably toward it—not now at least. According to a letter from one close to the situation in Washington, the Attorney General is feeling the amnesty pressure considerably and there may be a 50-50 chance for some type of amnesty before the year's end. Unless something is done soon, I'm expecting the amnesty howl to reach quite a crescendo toward Christmas time.

From all the projects mentioned in your letter it sounds as though your own private campaign is really in high gear. I don't think there is a Chinaman's chance of getting anything on COs in *Reader's Digest,* in fact, it is one of the least promising mags I can think of, but if Jane is willing to give it a try I'm 100 percent for her. *Newsweek* had a good article on COs, but mostly about those in CPS. Incidentally, the latest issue of *The New Yorker* is reputed to have had a very fine article on the atom bomb situation, the whole issue is devoted to the article. Why don't you try to buy a copy and tell me the gist of what it says? No, Honey, I have never read *Heavenly Discourse* or *No More Peace,* but both sound very enjoyable, something to look forward to.

You should see my haircut, Betsy (or should you?). It's about half an inch long—but feels good as my scalp has been bothering a bit of late.

Bailey and Dick won the whist tourney. Hank and I finished next to last. Ah well, luck at cards, unlucky at love, etc. *The Fellowship* write-up was quite good. Thanks for sending it and *The Grapevine.* (My goodness, this is a mixed up letter. Forgive me, Honey. But others are waiting for the typewriter. Besides, so much happening today (comparatively) leaves my poor old brain a little befuddled.)

A letter from John S. said he received our letter to the conference and read it to the whole group. Also said several persons were planning to mail their registration cards to the President on October 16 in protest of the continuation of conscription. If you can find mine among my stuff, would you mail it in for me?

Wish I could travel with you to Macedonia. Give my love to Mammy and Pappy and also my folks. I hope the Pinecrest Hall deal goes through, especially if Mammy has her heart set on it.

Your lonely, loving hubby misses you, Honey.

Chuck

◉ ◉ ◉

September 19, 1946

Dearest Betsy,

Hello, Sugar, it's your old man again, still going strong and maybe even a little bit stronger. Just think, Honey, this may be the last time I'll ever write to you at 3315 N. 58th Street. And even this letter may not get there in time. But if you wait until the 20th, I suspect you'll wait until the weekend travel rush is over.

It's almost impossible to imagine the little yellow house passing out of our lives, especially out of your life in which not one year of memory is not somehow attached to it, where you played, grew up, finally got wooed and even engaged. Many of my happiest memories center there; I recall, for example, a New Year's morning, 8 degrees below zero, when I hitchhiked out to 3315, embraced a very lovely girl, and then sat down to a luscious hot dinner. Oh, ecstasy! And the beautiful backyard, the cardinal in the rose bush, the turtledove's nest, the croquet course, and those wonderful outdoor suppers with fresh asparagus from the garden, and the family love and kindness. Oh, ecstasy! Well, the little yellow house isn't out of the picture yet, and won't be as long as Mammy and Pappy are there.

How I'd love to be going with you on the train to Georgia. Couldn't we have fun together, loving, laughing, adventuring, meeting new friends, watching the night come and go? Why don't you write up a little journal on your trip for your old stay-at-home hubby?

You may see my good buddy Hank in a few days. A guard told us last night that Hank was released on parole upon reaching

Washington. I don't know how he would know this, but I had expected some such thing to happen. Hank had planned to go to Macedonia upon his release so, depending on what happens to his mother, you may see him soon. I've instructed him to give my love and a big kiss to My Darling Wife, if he got a chance, so don't be surprised if he does.

We are still on our "fast within a fast"—15th day. We are all in much better condition than we had anticipated. In fact, it has been easier this time than the first time, and we have all felt better and stronger. Maybe that liquid diet, though not enough to build up our weight, was actually better from the standpoint of minerals and vitamins than the regular diet. Of course, we have not been quite as strict with ourselves this time as we were before when we wouldn't even drink coffee if it had milk in it. An occasional cracker or a little bit of juice off of one of the vegetable dishes sent over for the other boys makes it lots easier.

Hampton was sick Tuesday but is OK now. Doc came up yesterday, but found us all in good shape so our protest is still continuing. In the meantime, the situation seems to be looking up somewhat. The three boys are still in the hole without books, exercise, church, and other so-called "privileges," but they now have towels, soap, blankets, etc., we are told, and beginning at noon today they have the full diet, marching over to the dining hall with the quarantine boys. This arrangement was made known to them yesterday when they were called into "court." In "court" they were told that they would never be sent up to E2 because they were not COs (which is not true). When they asked why Taylor, who doesn't even claim to be a CO, was put in E2, they were told that this had been a mistake. The boys were also threatened with being transferred, each to a different institution—which threat I believe to be pure B.S.

The support our protest is getting from our families and friends (including my own Dear Wife—bless her heart) is most encouraging. It seems like things are really cooking in Washington. The Julius Eichel "Friends and Families of Imprisoned COs" group is even threatening to stage a sit-down strike in Tom Clark's office. In fact, Hampton's wife writes that they wired her to see if she could participate in such an action and offered to pay all her expenses. I thought the *World-Herald* article was just dandy, Honey. You did a fine job. Incidentally, it appears like you must have provided most of the news for the latest *Amnesty Bulletin.* It tells about Buffett's sermon and also mentions Pop's and your interview. Well, something should happen soon, but until we are convinced that our three fellow COs are not being given discriminatory punitive treatment, we will probably continue to refuse the tube feeding.

Guess I forgot to tell you, Betsy, that Dr. King of the U.S. Public Health Service is in charge of the medical service in all federal prisons.

I've been studying up on orcharding again and have recently plotted an orchard of about an acre with 9 peach trees, 6 apricots, 6 pears, 6 cherries, 9 plums, and 12 apples. Guess I'll do the same for a small fruit plot—grapes, raspberries, dewberries, currants, gooseberries, etc. Such planning may not mean much, but it's kinda fun. Have also got a floor plan for a small house. Will enclose a copy for your criticism. With Taylor's help, I think I can draw up the complete plan—sills, joists, beams, roof, foundation, etc., so that if we should decide to build at Macedonia, or somewhere, I'll be able to go ahead on my own. My idea for the enclosed plan includes cement floors and frame walls, electricity, running water, etc. Kind of cook stove, etc., would depend somewhat on local conditions. A fireplace is almost as cheap as a good heating stove and would be much more fun, don't you think? Good, built-in closets could handle all of our meager possessions I think, and a combination bed/studio couch would be very practical.

Miscellaneous items: I owe Mammy an apology for not writing to her but will promise to do better when you are gone. I think she understands. Do you ever spend any time thinking of names for all the kids we're going to have? I do, but have more ideas for girls names than for boys. Among some I like are Nancy, Ellen, Jean, and Carol. Am happy to have had a part in the nice dream you mentioned recently.

Mil had a pretty good article in *The Christian Century* recently. Some very fine people have gone to Ames. I'm confident that Phyl will have a wonderful experience and lots of fun. Got the clipping about Bill Durand—thanks. Would like to be sitting beside you now with a dish of applesauce, piece of chocolate cake, and a glass of cold milk. Guess that shows how a person's thinking runs when he's fasting, huh?

Bye, Sweetheart. Give my love to all the folks, and have fun. I love you much. You're a Sweet Gal.

Chuck

P.S. Am not too sure of your new address.
P.P.S. Be sure to read Wallace's letter to Truman in Wednesday's papers (9/18/46).

◉ ◉ ◉

September 23, 1946

My beloved Betsy,

Hello, Honeybunch. I was nearly bowled over when your three letters arrived all in one envelope Saturday night—a three-letter day is a red-letter day for me. We were all overjoyed to hear from Hank, to know that he is out. It is unfortunate that such joy should have to be brought about by the loss of his mother. All the fellows wished to express their sincere sympathy to Hank and his family. I trust that you sent some appropriate expression of our feelings as you said you would.

Meantime, things have been happening here. First of all, we are still refusing to be tube fed, but the situation is "looking up" somewhat. The three COs in the hole now have blankets, sanitary facilities, three square meals a day in the dining hall, and according to an interview which Igal had with the Warden today, they are to be given all their personal belongings, "yard," library, and full correspondence "privileges" beginning today. To my knowledge no provision has yet been made for church, commissary, or visits, and, most serious of all, they are still locked up in their cells all day. This is probably the toughest aspect of the situation to these three boys because they are all young and quite active by nature. However, even this matter may be straightened out soon, as Igal reports that the Warden is considering transferring them over to C2, our old headquarters, with their cells unlocked all day as ours are. If this provision is made I think I shall be willing to again submit to the tube feeding, trusting that the other inequalities will gradually be eliminated.

That old tube seems pretty inviting. We've been without food 19 days now, and though it has been psychologically easier this time, we are all getting weaker, though we are still up and around. Gormly had a chance to step on a scale today—the results: 110 pounds (and he is 5 foot 10½ inches tall)—but I believe he is the thinnest of us all. Doc was up and checked up on our condition today, but apparently decided that compulsory feeding wasn't necessary yet. But don't worry about us, Honey, I'm sure we'll be OK.

The Warden says we misquoted his remarks about these boys— he didn't say they were not COs but only that they have not been so classified, that if they were to be classified IVE, they would probably be released on the new point system, or else placed in E2 with us. Igal is writing to A.J. today about their classifications since Tom Clark had asked him to help correct their records on who in prison is and isn't a CO. Both Schweigert and Lavae come from pacifist churches and should have no trouble getting recognized as COs. Kasner has no CO background but has paid plenty for his ideas, including his wife's leaving him.

Our "fast within a fast" has certainly stirred up a hornets' nest, considerably more so than any of us expected. Hellzapoppin in Washington. Got the two *World-Herald* clippings and will appreciate getting any others that might appear. The same AP picture and story were in several other papers. Incidentally, this week's *Progressive* has two good articles on COs—Milton Mayer pleads the cause of the imprisoned COs in his own inimitable style, and the other Mayer tells why he'll be a CO in the next war.

Betsy, I think we ought to have a year's subscription to *The Progressive*. I'm enclosing an order blank, which entitles one to a free book or two additional months' subscriptions. Among the books offered are: 1) The Beard's *Basic History of the U.S.*, 2) *The Story of Mankind*, 3) *The Writings of Thomas Jefferson*, and 4) *Looking Backward*. Why don't you order it and either one of the books (I'd prefer the first one) or the two subscriptions—maybe for our folks if none of them get it.

Hutch, Gormly, and I also had interviews with the Warden today about this new point system which is supposed to become effective on Oct. 1. (In segregation all of us are eligible except Zumwinkle, who hasn't done 18 months yet, and Taylor, who does not have an IVE classification, a requirement which reeks with injustice.) I'll not try to reconstruct our whole discussion. In brief, I told the Warden that I would like nothing more than to leave prison. I felt that parole was inadequate since it fails to correct the injustice of imprisoning men for loyalty to conscience. To leave it seems that one must have some kind of parole plan and a parole advisor who will make some kind of reports as to his whereabouts and activities. I told the Warden that I could not conscientiously cooperate with making any such arrangements and that if released I intended to live as a free man entirely, do exactly as I pleased, and would recognize no restrictions of any kind. The Warden already knew, however, that you and I were considering going to Macedonia. Morris Mitchell had already told him when he visited here that he would be willing to make any required reports on Hank and me, and he said he would write to Morris about the matter.

More thought may give me more insight, but right now I look at the matter this way—and will you please pass the following on to Morris right away so he'll know just how I stand:

> If he wishes to put this pinch of incense on the altar of Selective Service, that is his concern; that I personally wouldn't wish to advise him one way or another. But though I want to leave prison very much, I personally cannot accept in any way the government's right to supervise or control my life. That if released I intend to do what I think is right, go where I see fit, refusing to make any commitments or promises to the government or anyone else. That my relationship to Morris will be to me only that which arises from our friendship, mutual interests, and possibly our living and working together, no more, no less. If released soon, my plan tentatively would be to first return to my wife and family in Omaha and then make a leisurely trip to Macedonia, visiting friends, places of interest, etc., en route, to see if that is where we wish to settle down at this time. At present, I am inclined to feel that we

would want to live there for a few years, but of course a final
decision in this matter would be feasible only after visiting
and thinking it through with Betsy.

If you wish to add your comments, Honey, please do so. I want
to be sure that you understand and if possible appreciate my position. If I were absolutely consistent with what I think is right in the
matter, I would ask Morris and everyone else to refuse to have any
part of any parole plan. But I have interests and loyalties other
than just fighting conscription—you, the folks, my own physical and
psychological well-being, small community life, etc. So, if they take
me to the front gate and tell me to go, I'll go. Let them call it what
they will—to me it will be unconditional release and I shall
act on that basis even though doing so may result in being returned
to prison.

It has been miserably cold and rainy lately—seems to me like
it should be snowing rather than raining. Adding to the discomfort
is the fact that they are apparently trying to save on coal so have
the heat on only for brief intervals during the day. (The weather felt
much more balmy in the Warden's office yesterday.)

I think Hank would like to know of recent developments here,
in the hole, my attitude toward parole, etc. Presumably you have his
address. I understand he is working for Fred Libby at the NCPW
office in Washington.

Love to all the folks, and something more than can be expressed
in words to my Golden-Haired Sweetheart.

Chuck

P.S. Hold onto your hat, Honey, and we'll see what happens.
P.P.S. Please send me Cos's and Ray's address in your next letter.

◙ ◙ ◙

September 27 and 28, 1946

Dearest Betsy, My Darling,

Hello, Baby. Your last letter would seem to indicate that you
were sitting in a very uncomfortable, if not positively embarrassing,

position—smack dab on top of a fence. So if you haven't already stepped off on the Macedonia side, maybe this letter will help to relieve the situation somewhat. Frankly, Honey, I'd advise you, if it's not too late, to stick around Omaha for a while. Of course, it is impossible for me to give you any halfway reasonable guess as to what is going to happen. Even God doesn't know what our omniscient and infallible President is going to do. We both know how adept our highly principled forces of justice are at stalling, evasion, etc. Nor do I want to get either yours or my own hopes built up unduly. But the truth is that the CO pressure program is getting hotter than a pistol. The sit-down strike at the Department of Justice is threatening to become a regular he-man demonstration. Word received by Hampton tonight states that two of our friends in California have left, post-haste, to join the action. And you know as well as I that if guys are going from California, there'll be others doing likewise from points nearer the battle front. Apparently our tube refusal provided the spark needed to set off the tinder box. Even funds are said to be coming in to support the sit-downers, which is something.

Now for local developments. Yesterday (it is now Friday), Lavae and Kasner were transferred to Terre Haute, reputed to be a pretty tough joint, and Schweigert returned to his old job as G2 orderly. (The Warden was confident that he would be paroled under the point plan.) The latest reason given for refusing to put these boys in E2 with us is that the officials didn't want them to come under the Hampton influence—a flimsy excuse if I ever heard one. In fact, this whole episode has provided one of the sorriest, most malodorous exhibits of prison fascism I have yet witnessed, and that's saying a lot—arbitrary, unjust, and entirely unnecessary. Unsatisfactory as this "solution" is, however, we now feel (i.e., all but Hampton) that the situation is out of our hands, that nothing is to be gained by further protest on our part. We do feel strongly, though, that our friends on the outside should follow through on the case of the boys transferred and see to it that they receive fair and just treatment. Kasner said just before leaving that they intended to continue on a non-cooperative basis. Should it be desired to contact their families, their addresses are as follows: Mr. A. Lavae (father), 3013 W. Cermak Rd., Chicago 33, Illinois; and Kasner's brother: Emil Kasner, R. 1, Arpin,

Wisconsin. Igal plans to write A.J. about the matter, but it would be appreciated if you would promptly send this information on to Hank (if you have his address) so he can share it and other local news with the Washington folks—also tell Hank we're hoping for a letter soon with full details of his situation.

Now about the fast. We have now been 23 days without food except for an occasional bite taken chiefly for the psychological value. Gormly, of course, has been permitting one feeding per day. My "snacking," I figure, has probably amounted to about 3,500 calories during this entire period, and the other boys (except Gormly, who hasn't eaten one bite since June 3) have probably taken about the same. This has probably helped maintain our physical condition somewhat, but it has helped psychologically even more, doing much to take the sting out of fasting. Igal, Gormly, and I are now willing to submit to force feeding without active resistance, but Parker and Hampton have determined to resist feeding from now on out.

Parker explained his decision, saying he feels it lends a sense of urgency to the amnesty campaign, thus strengthening the position of our friends' demonstrations and protests. A policy of non-resistance seems to be an easy victim to misinterpretation. For instance, many newspaper accounts attributed to the Warden (though he denies originating such remarks) stated that our hunger strike stopped when force feeding began—which doesn't give an accurate picture of the situation. He feels it is a valid next step toward further non-cooperation with our imprisonment. Hamp's reasoning is pretty much the same, plus the fact that he feels that the shabby treatment given our three fellow work-striking COs by the prison system justifies further protest.

We have all pretty much decided that if we ever have to make such a protest again, we'll go without liquids, too, in order to bring matters to a head more quickly. I don't think any of us realized we could go so long without food. This whole experience has been very good in that it has served to help me overcome the slavish attitude toward eating—has given me a new degree of freedom.

The possibility of being released soon has me all agog, Honey, and I've been working up a most delightful little daydream as follows: If you haven't gone to Macedonia yet, and if I should get out while the weather is still fair (early October, say), and if you could enter into the plan wholeheartedly, I would like nothing more than to get us each a bedroll, raincoat, some good warm clothes, and hitch-hike to Macedonia, taking all the time we wanted and making a real trip of it with stops planned wherever we have friends or kindred spirits—up through Iowa, southern Wisconsin, Milwaukee, Chicago, Brookville, Philly, New York, Washington, and south to Georgia, hitting all the places of interest and good friends, staying as long in any place as we wanted to—a week at Mil's, a week in New York, etc. After the confinement of prison, such a trip would be heavenly to me, provided you could enter into the spirit of it without any reservations. On the other hand—the agitation for amnesty has grown to such a pitch that I've half a mind to tell the Warden that I will refuse to leave prison on anything short of a full pardon, that I can't accept anyone else's accepting S.S. responsibility for me. If I should do so, they might kick me out anyway—I wouldn't be surprised—in which case I might feel impelled to see if funds and accommodations couldn't be provided to enable both of us to join the demonstrations in Washington.

Enclosed is a very good and comprehensive letter by Taylor urging equal treatment for all S.S. violators. I think it would be very appropriate for concerned friends to write or wire Clark expressing agreement with the contents of Taylor's letter. Guess I'll have to get a letter to Mammy so as to rate another from her.

Was happy about your good report on the folks' trip. Give them, Jane, Paul, and everyone my loving regards. Same to Mammy, Pappy, Phyl, etc. The enclosed poem is dedicated to—guess who! Hope you like it.

All my love, Darling.

—*Chuck*

P.S. Congratulations on the mighty fine little news release!
P.P.S. Please send me Hank's address.

◙ ◙ ◙

October 1, 1946

Dearest Betsy,

Hello, Mine Dahlink. We just came in from "yard," Honey.
Gosh, it was wunnerful—deep blue sky, warm sunshine. It was
down to about 20 degrees last night but warmed up rapidly
enough so I could take off my shirt, roll up my pants, and go about
with my bare ribs and shin bones sticking out—well, almost bare
anyway. It's kinda rough to have to do days like these inside—ah,
well, it can't last forever—even our great and mighty government
can't stop the passage of time. Why, whadda ya know—here it
is October 1 already—just one year ago today Administrative
Segregation was inaugurated at Sandstone, and Parker and I joined
our buddies up in C2. There've been some changes made since
those days. What do we have to show for the past year, Betsy? Not
much, I'm afraid—maybe just a little teeny something on the altar
of freedom—I hope, and a little self respect.

As noted in my letter of last Friday, tube feeding for Igal and
myself was resumed on that day. At first we were given just one
feeding per day to break us in gradually, I guess, but yesterday the
former twice-daily schedule was resumed. Believe me, Betsy, that
"guck" makes a terrific difference in the way one feels. So much
so, in fact, that I've taken up swishing the mop this week. Not
saying I don't feel like resting when the job is done, but at least
I'm picking up fast.

Parker and Hamp still haven't been "forced," and so have
been without food for 27 days. They both look pretty gaunt
but are still up and around. If anything, John is in a little better
shape than Mal, who never spares his body any, but has been on
cleanup, played volleyball, and in general "throws himself around
like handbills," as our old friend Ike would say. I made Parker
say uncle in a game of volleyball singles Saturday. Not that I was
exactly flashy, in fact, it was my first game in a couple of months,
but the trouble was that Parker would sometimes see two or three
balls coming at him and the net kept shifting around. Finally, Mal
thought he must be getting a bit dizzy and we stopped. Doc was up
to check the boys' condition yesterday and to comment on a letter

Parker wrote calling Bennett's hand on a long line of bunk he has
been putting out about how these boys are getting examined by
a doctor twice each day, how they are kept in an A1 hospital, etc.
Doc said he had confidence in his own methods and wished Bennett
wouldn't put out such a line.

Yesterday at "yard" Schweigert, the recent work striker still at
Sandstone, came up to us all excited. He had just been notified by
the Parole Office that he was to leave the next morning on parole,
and sure enough he did. Apparently, it was under this new 18-month
point-system deal. We were all greatly elated about it, but many of
the boys out in population are growling plenty and apparently beginning to wonder if they are on the right track after all. Only a few
days ago the September Parole Board's reports came back with very
discouraging results. As far as I now know, only one CO, Daniels,
made it, with most of the others "continued to Washington." Fellows with a German name or accent seemed to get an especially cold
shoulder—Kratz, Dummer, Heine, etc.

Your scrawny hubby was really the center of attention when
Hank's letter came. (You were a dear to send it on so promptly.) It
was sure swell to hear from the guy and get the straight goods on his
release. It stirred up some excitement and explained some recent mysteries—how Parker came to have a "sponsor," for instance. I've put in
to have Hank on my list, but in the meantime you might send him a
copy of this letter so he'll know the score here.

The E2 lineup on this new deal is somewhat as follows: Gormly,
Hutch, Parker, and I are all in about the same boat—probably
wouldn't object too much if someone else wants to stooge for S.S.
and sponsor our release. But we will sign nothing, agree to no obligations or restrictions. Gormly feels it would be more honest to make
his own reports and has agreed to do so. Zumwinkle and Taylor
would be willing to accept a similar deal but are not eligible, Dick
not having done 18 months, and Taylor not having an IVE. Igal and
John will actively dissuade anybody from sponsoring their release.
The enclosed letter from Igal to Clark explains his position. I reckon
they'd have to tote him out, a la Axford. But believe me, Honey, my
conscience is far from clear in this matter.

By accepting such a deal I would be accepting preferred special

treatment over other S.S. prisoners, a "privilege" won by pacifist
agitation on the outside. And then I think of some of the other fellows here—fellows whose imprisonment represents even a worse
insult to justice than my own and whose release is so much more
urgent than mine—Taylor, e.g., who has three little kids and whose
wife is not well; or Kratz, a quiet, humble fellow with a rheumatic
heart condition aggravated by being in jail, and with a wife and three
little kids on relief. And these aren't isolated cases, either. To leave
boys like them behind and relieve the Department of what pressure
my presence here is worth seems pretty darned selfish. Besides, it is
absolutely wrong to tolerate the continuation of the farce of government presuming to judge conscience. Yes, Betsy, these are soul-
searching times. There is really only one just solution and that is an
all-out amnesty; but short of that, all S.S. cases are deserving of equal
treatment. Of course, the Department is playing that old "divide and
conquer" game.

I think it will be easy (and fun) for us to build a house that'll
satisfy us both, Betsy, since our ideas seem to run along similar
lines. Taylor has had quite a bit of experience in house building and
designing. He made some good suggestions for revising the plan I
sent you and has agreed to help me draw up complete plans so that,
inexperienced as I am, I could go ahead and do the job myself. Right
now we're waiting for the Warden's reply to my request for drawing
materials. You're going to have a hard time talking me out of cement
floors, though, Honey. I think they are cheaper, cleaner, more attractive (dyed, not painted), more durable, not necessarily colder, and
as far as wearing your legs off—well, I've walked many and many
a mile up and down this corridor in my bare feet and they feel just
fine. I'm not so sure I think much of your bed idea either, but we can
"fight" that out later—no?

A whole bunch of new officers—"the Jesse Cops," Dick calls
them—are starting work here as of yesterday. They are supposed to
be plenty wised up, having passed exams that sifted out a few stink-
ers—Beckman and big Stephan, for example, and a few good guys
like Edstrom. The latter came up to say goodbye to E2, and wish
us luck. Funny thing—they either like us fine or hate the very air
we breathe.

All my love, Darling, but don't get your hopes built up too high.
Regards to all.
But, gee Ma, I wanna go home.
Chuck

P.S. All the boys send regards to Hank, and from the fact that K. Taylor can't find him at home, we assume he is "circulating rapidly."

◼ ◼ ◼

October 7, 1946

Dearest Betsy,

Hello, Darling. I hope you haven't "blowed your top" yet waiting for me to come home—on account of 'cause your top has certain aesthetic qualities, which I value, and to be going around without it would be simply intolerable—yes, intolerable. And besides, you might catch cold. Sounds as though you have a case of "shortitis" every bit as bad as Hutchinson. He has it bad. And boy, do the guys razz him about it. Every time the phone rings downstairs it's somebody calling to have Hutch brought over to the clothing room to get fitted out. And Bailey has worked out a regular skit about how, when Hutch went down to talk to the Warden about this deal, he gave the Warden a long line about how he couldn't conscientiously cooperate, etc., etc. And then the Warden (Bailey, that it) says, "But you don't have to do anything. All you have to do is let me write to your father to arrange for a sponsor." And Hutch (Bailey) says, ". . . don't write, . . . (pause), . . . WIRE."

Poor old Hutch . . . our perennial scapegoat. He gets ragged no matter what he does. He's talking about trying to make a cattle-boat trip to Europe when released and comes in for some kidding, not always lily-white, on that.

Of course, it would be strictly wonderful to getting out of this joint, and I feel most flattered and happy to know that my Dear Wife wants me home so badly. But, Darling, I greatly fear you're in for nothing but "hard time" if you're going to sit by and hold your breath anticipating the government to act, "for when that hour and

day shall be knoweth no man; no, not even the angels" (free trans-
lation of the King James Bible—Matthew 24:36). When I get out,
I'll get out—not before, and you may be pretty certain it won't be
sooner than the end of this month, if at all. So you might just as well
start breathing and eating your meals again. And there is no use in
jumping for the telephone anytime it sings because, in all honesty,
Honey, I can't think of any reason why I should be calling you up on
the phone when I am being propelled personally in that direction as
fast as circumstances permit.

Meantime, Betsy, I hope you won't forget that it is that last-minute spurt that wins races. This is no time to relax the pressure. As of
today, four of us have fasted for 150 days—an excellent excuse for
telegrams and for letters to Clark, with carbon copy to the *World-
Herald.* (Incidentally, you're treading on extremely thin ice when you
speak of our being force fed as "eating again, figuratively speaking."
Just such figurative speaking quoted in the newspapers has led to no
little misunderstanding betwixt the Warden and ourselves.)

Have been feeling tops lately—better than at any time since
May 11—more pep and energy. Maybe this is also due to "shortitis,"
or maybe it's because I am getting psychologically adjusted to the
idea of going without meals, or maybe because I have lately been
permitting myself the pleasure of a little commissary and an occasional bite of something leftover from the other boys' meals—more
likely it's all three.

On Wednesday, the 28th day of fasting for Park and Hamp,
the entire medical staff came over and gently but firmly ended that
situation by feeding each of them 500 cc's of "guck." They are now
back on full rations, as are all of the hunger strikers, Park put up
enough resistance to the feeding so that it was necessary to put the
tube down his nose, causing it to bleed, but since then his and John's
resistance has been a mere token of the real thing—pretty much the
same as the rest of us. (Hank has not yet been approved, nor was
I permitted to receive the letter he sent me. You might drop him a
postcard stating that we are all being "hosed" again and anything
else of interest contained herein.)

I'm afraid Morris is a little confused on this 8641 release
business—a perfectly understandable situation. The Warden and

Tom Clark *are not competing with separate plans* in an effort to get
me out of prison. The stuff Morris sent Humphrey, and the "surety"
letter, are part and parcel of the same deal. The latter is necessitated
by the fact that I will not cooperate in any way with accepting the
status of a criminal, so if any reports are to go in on me, somebody
else will have to make them. It doesn't have to be Morris, in fact,
anybody could agree to serve as "sponsor" and send the required
letter to Bennett. A more complete understanding of how it works
can be obtained from the enclosed copy of a letter from Fred Sibly
to Allen Hunter (explaining the situation so he could go "surety" for
John). (You will notice the kind of line the government puts out—
they practically have three of us out already.) I didn't want Morris
or anyone else to think I would lose my respect for him should he
decide to sponsor my release. I personally couldn't render that degree
of cooperation with S.S., but I am not so intolerant as to insist that
others accept my standards. There is a right path for every person
and it isn't the same for any two. I greatly appreciate Morris's telegram on our "fast within a fast."

I'm very happy to learn that you liked my hitchhiking idea. If
it won't add to your severe "shortitis" you could be planning an
itinerary of stops to which I could later make any additions I thought
essential—right now, I'd want to include Milwaukee, Chicago,
Brookville, New York City, and Washington, D.C. Essential to the
fulfillment of such a plan and of our, or at least my, philosophy of
life is the possession of good sleeping bags. Pop knows the owner of
the Army and Navy Store and could probably get us a good deal on
some Army surplus-property bags. So, if you want to ask his help in
such a purchase, you have my blessing, but be sure to insist on good
ones—they should be lightweight (down-filled) and covered with
waterproof silk. (No, I wouldn't want one double-sized bag—
it wouldn't be as practical—twin beds, no go; twin bags, Amen!)
But we certainly wouldn't want to tote any of those big, cumber-
some, blanket-filled things across the country—not on my back
at least. I assume you were joking when you suggested we stay in
Omaha for a while first. If you think you could possibly pry me out
of that town before I get stocked up on vittles and some of that fine
family fellowship—well, you'd just better think again. Incidentally,

just what is the score at 3315 right now? If Mammy has already
started to work at the Hall, my private correspondence must have
slipped up—I've had no official report to that extent. Guess I'll plan
to write Mammy this week and see if I can get back on her correspondence list. I hope, if she has started there, that they aren't
keeping the house open on your (and my) account—that would be
expecting a little too much, I fear.

Don't go to any work in collecting my poems, Honey, because I
have lately been typing them up in booklet form with the thought of
sending copies to a few friends when I get out. You could be making
covers for 30 copies if you wish—same size paper as this sheet, but
printed sideways and folded down the middle.

The amnesty press still looks good—preachers marching to
Washington on October 16, more good editorials, etc. Be sure to
send in my registration card to Truman on October 16, in case I'm
not there, and you'd better tear it in four pieces first so they'll understand my intentions and still be able to read the name.

You mention a Dorothy Thompson broadcast—what was it
about—amnesty, Pekingese puppies, contraceptives, or what?

Here's the man, Honey. Must close quickly.

Much love, etc.

Chuck

◙ ◙ ◙

October 11, 1946

Dearest Betsy,

Hello, Sweetheart. Last night, during some unknown hour as
I lay awake thinking, there were a couple of snatches from *Alice
in Wonderland* that kept flitting through my mind: one from "The
Walrus and the Carpenter" in which ". . . The eldest oyster winked
his eye and shook his heavy head—meaning to say he did not choose
to leave the oyster bed," and the other from "The Lobster Quadrille,"
". . . The snail replied too far, too far, and gave a look askance. Said
he thanked the whiting kindly but he would not join the dance.
Would not, could not, would not, could not, would not join the

dance. Would not, could not, would not, could not, could not join the dance." And those lines seemed to summarize, somehow, a conclusion I had been gradually reaching. But perhaps at this point of the story it would be well for you to take a chair.

You see, Honey, yesterday afternoon at about 2 the officer came up for Gormly, said he had a "visit" and that Worley was next on the list. When he came back for me he said Gormly's "visit" had been with the Associate Warden and had wound up with Walter's going over to be fitted out for clothes (meaning he was going home).

When I got to Mr. Madigan's office, he said that neither the Warden nor Parole Officer were in their offices that day, but that he had read my letters of that morning to the Warden (copy enclosed) and that I had nothing to fear, that I was not being asked to collaborate with parole in any way, nor did I have to sign anything or commit myself to anything. But they would like to have me read a certain printed form so they could protect themselves by saying I had read it. Now then, did I plan to go to Omaha, Macedonia, both or what?

I explained that I rather planned to go to Omaha when released, and then hitchhike to Macedonia, but that I didn't intend to leave under the plans they had made for me because I felt that it entailed further compromise and commitments than I was willing to make, that I would probably not object to leaving on the same basis as Dyer or Bishop had, but that I could go no farther than that. He said this was really the same deal, that I had seen the Parole Advisor and Employer forms and that I didn't even have to read the paper referred to above (parole conditions, I suppose), that they could sign it for me anyway. I still demurred and said I wanted to know for sure the conditions of my release, and he promised to try to take the matter up with the Warden, but in the meantime I should go get measured up for clothes—which I agreed to do—and did—work clothes.

The first flush of excitement over the prospect of leaving the next day was pretty near intoxicating for a while. I could anticipate most vividly the glorious feeling of being free again, of going home, of eating, of traveling, but most of all, of being with you again. But gradually the drug wore off. Reason and emotion again assumed their proper proportions and adjustment. In the still of the night I realized that my earlier determination to refuse anything more involved than the "surety" letter plan was the right thing for me to do. I could get away from prison any way, but would still have to live with myself.

So, when they came up for Walter's commissary book this morning my mind was made up and I declined to turn mine in. And when they came up for Walter a few minutes later, I stayed behind. But about ten minutes later, two officers came to my cell and said I was going out also. I explained that I didn't wish to go, but they had their orders. One of them picked up my things (which I had packed up when still undecided about going) and the other took my arm and led me gently but firmly down to the discharging room. I again went through my song and dance but was told that when you gotta go, you just gotta go.

I said, "Oh, yeah," and asked to see the Warden. Whether he was there or not, I don't know. Anyway, he didn't come to see me. Instead, the Associate Warden came in and asked what the trouble was. I told him I had thought the matter through thoroughly and had decided not to leave under the present arrangements. He asked how I knew what the arrangement was, said that I had seen no parole forms, that he had asked me no questions, that I had read nothing and been asked to sign nothing. I replied that I knew Parole Advisor and Employer forms had been sent in, that I therefore had good reasons for guessing that I was being released on that basis, and in any case would not be willing to go until I knew exactly what the basis of my release was. He said it was too late to stop things now, that they had a railroad ticket for me so I'd have to go. Then he left. Well, I stood around for about 15 minutes parrying the remarks of three or four officers who were eager to help me see the light, and who kept telling me to change my clothes—sort of giving the impression that if I didn't, they would. Finally, the discharge officer got on the phone and asked, "What shall we do with this guy?" And the answer apparently came back—take him back upstairs. So here I am back in E2.

I hope you are not too discouraged or disappointed, Honey. Personally, I feel very good about my decision. I don't think you'd really want me to do anything I didn't feel right about. Please know, Darling, that I want to be with you again just as badly as you want me to be, and that this decision to remain, though difficult, was the one which was for me most true. Since I am still willing to go out on the "surety" deal, I may even be leaving anyway.

Meantime, I'll write to Morris and ask him if he will withdraw the Parole Advisor and Employer forms he sent here. Am sorry I didn't understand the situation sooner so I could have asked him to do so in my letter of yesterday or the day before. This may seem like a foolish consistency, but it is still one I wish to maintain. And just to make sure he gets the word, will you send him (and John Swomley, also) a copy of this letter? (John wanted to hear, through you, what was happening at Sandstone, and since I want to be sure and get a letter to Mammy next week—couldn't send one this week as promised because Hank has just been approved and I want to get the news to him—I won't be able to send one to John directly.) Incidentally, Mammy's good letter was received most gratefully last night.

So now there are only eight of us in Administrative Segregation since Walter got out on the same deal I refused. Maybe you can meet him some time as he plans to spend some time in Milwaukee, Chicago, and may eventually wind up in NW Arkansas or thereabouts.

As regards Hank's letter to you, you may want to know that the four Sandstone hunger strikers (myself included) are determined to continue fasting to the very end—bitter or what have you.

Am enclosing a copy of a *Minneapolis Star-Journal* editorial which Mammy, if she has the time and the necessary information, is cordially invited to write her friend Seymore about.

Goodbye, Sweetheart. I love you like all get-out. Please don't do "hard time" waiting for me. Just keep busy planning and preparing for our life together. You are a Sweet and Adorable Creature.

XX Chuck

Afterword

Well, that's the last of my "Letters from Prison," but the story goes on. When I went to leave prison, I was handed some papers that, as I had expected, told where I was supposed to go, what I was supposed to do, etc. So when I got down to Minneapolis, where I had to change trains, I crossed my name off of the packet, wrote "Tom Clark, Attorney General," on it, and tossed the whole batch into a mail box. And that was that.

When I got home to my dear wife, we talked it over and decided to go down to the cooperative experiment some of my old CPS friends had started in Georgia (and where we had been assigned).

So we went. We'd had enough of communal living, though, having somebody report on us, etc., so we went up to Washington, D.C., and went to work for the National Council Against Conscription.

One interesting little event occurred when we were in D.C.— the Congress had a hearing about what should be done about the COs who were still in prison. One of the leaders of one of the peace groups who had a little time gave me a couple of minutes, but they didn't seem interested in what any CO had to say. However, when the Attorney General walked past me, he shook my hand and said, "I guess I saved your life, didn't I?" I said, "Thanks a lot."

About this time we discovered that Betsy was pregnant, so we went back to Omaha so we could be near some help if any was needed. Eventually we ended up with six fine children. We also finally found where we wanted to live, in the foothills of western Colorado. I found I could make an honest living doing plumbing and heating, and trying to protect the beautiful environment.

It has been a good life, but the main problems remain—there is too much power in the hands of a few very rich people and mammoth corporations. Unless this can be changed, more and more people will be spending their lives in poverty and in prison until the whole big mess finally collapses. At least that's my opinion.

Chuck Worley
Colorado, June 2010

Acknowledgments

I want to thank John Ellison and Lesley Link. Without their vision
and hard work, this book would not have happened. And I give
special thanks to Brenda Bafus-Williams, who patiently read and
typed all of my many letters into electronic form.

C. V. W.

▫ ▫ ▫

This book began when Kim Stafford introduced me to Chuck and
Betsy Worley a few years ago. What started out as plan to interview
Chuck turned into an ongoing conversation with Kim about the
history of conscientious objection. Kim has generously offered advice
and encouragement from the beginning of my work with The CO
Project and throughout the long editorial process of this book. I'm
deeply grateful for all his help, and for his insightful Foreword. The
Stafford family connection to the Worley family began with CPS and
continues strong today.

I'm deeply grateful to Chuck and Betsy Worley for their early
faith in The CO Project and for our fledgling peace press (part of
Speak4Peace.com), and especially for trusting these amazing personal
documents to our editorial care. The Worleys followed this project
from the beginning from their home in Colorado, offering encouragement and many helpful suggestions, as well as patiently answering
what must have seemed like a never-ending list of questions.

Many people volunteered their time and expertise to help us
make this collection of letters and poems into a book, and I am in-
debted to them all. Kevin Williams and Brenda Bafus-Williams
supplied us with electronic files from the original letters; their belief
in the historical value of Chuck's prison memories, and that this
material should be collected into a book for future generations,
never wavered over the years. Most of the prison poems were drawn
from a first-edition copy of *Ruminations of a Certified Groundhog,*

generously given to The CO Project by Alan and Marilyn Kieffaber of Indiana. Perry Lawson acted as personal assistant to Chuck and relayed valuable input to us in the final stages of the book's production. Bonnie Olvera expertly transcribed my 2006 interview with Chuck. Helga Aguayo and Kathy Mishima spent many hours carefully putting the poems and other writings into electronic form. The cover photograph was generously supplied by London-based journalist and photographer Barney Britton. Henry "Hank" Worley kindly searched his family's photos to provide the 1940s photos of his parents. Robin Long, Agustín Aguayo, Helga Aguayo, Gerry Condon, and James Branum all lent their enthusiastic support for getting the word out about this book by writing cover quotes.

Deep thanks to my friend Gary Snyder for his encouragement, and to my friend Mark McCulley for Montana. Thanks also go to Tracy Faulconer and Katrine (Katie) Barber, who shared resources and information from their studies of conscientious objection.

For their belief in The CO Project and for so graciously sharing their wisdom and experiences with me, heartfelt thanks go to Ercell Lynn, Harold Bock, Louise Bock, Les Abbenhouse, Gloria Abbenhouse, Miriam Cable, Clayton James, J.R. Burkholder, Henry Blocher, Mary Blocher, Joe Gunterman, Emmy Gunterman, Galen Beery, Larry Gara, Lawrence Templin, Eleanor Ring Davis, Chuck Cooley, Charles E. Davis, Francis Barr, and Ernie Barr.

For his incisive thinking and ongoing dialogue, I owe much to my friend James McDaniel.

Out of Bounds was designed and produced by my multitalented wife, Lesley Link, co-publisher of Speak4Peace.com, and master editor and book person. Without her faith in me as a writer and editor, her editorial expertise and project management magic, and her tireless support of The CO Project, this book would never have been published.

The CO Project has benefited much from the support and friendship of so many. If I've inadvertently overlooked anyone, please forgive.

J.E.

www.ingramcontent.com/pod-product-compliance
Lightning Source LLC
Chambersburg PA
CBHW032043050726
47590CB00001B/111